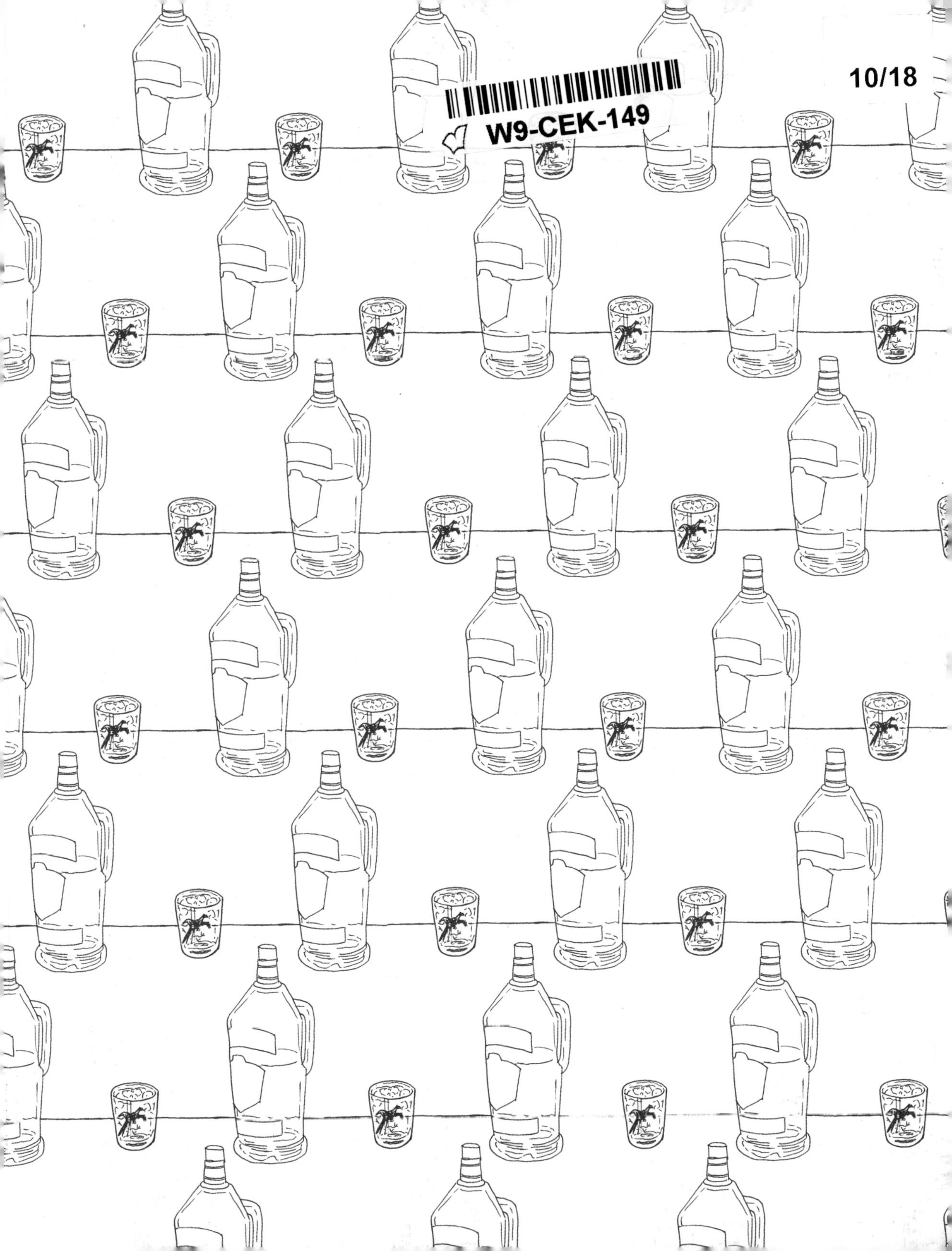

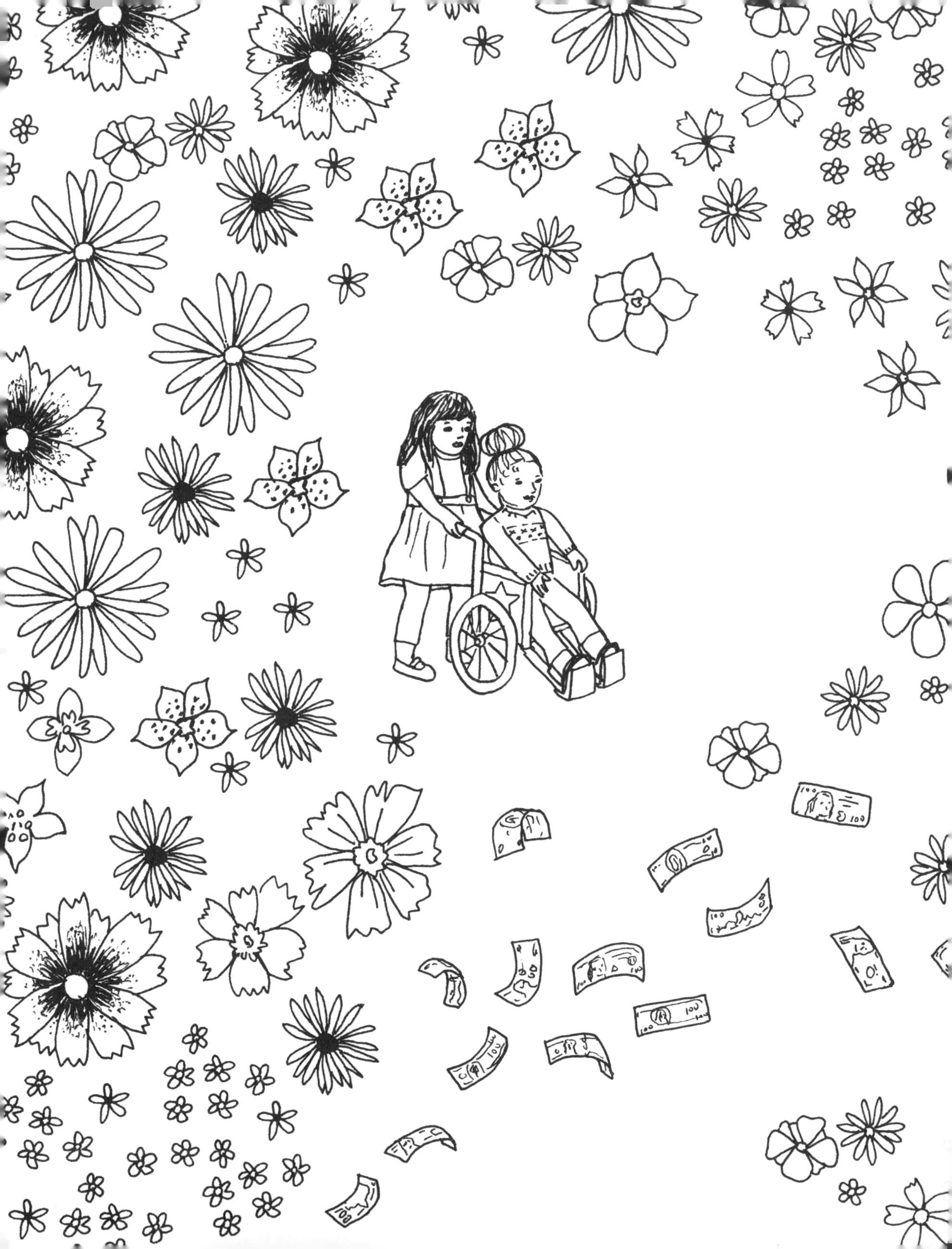

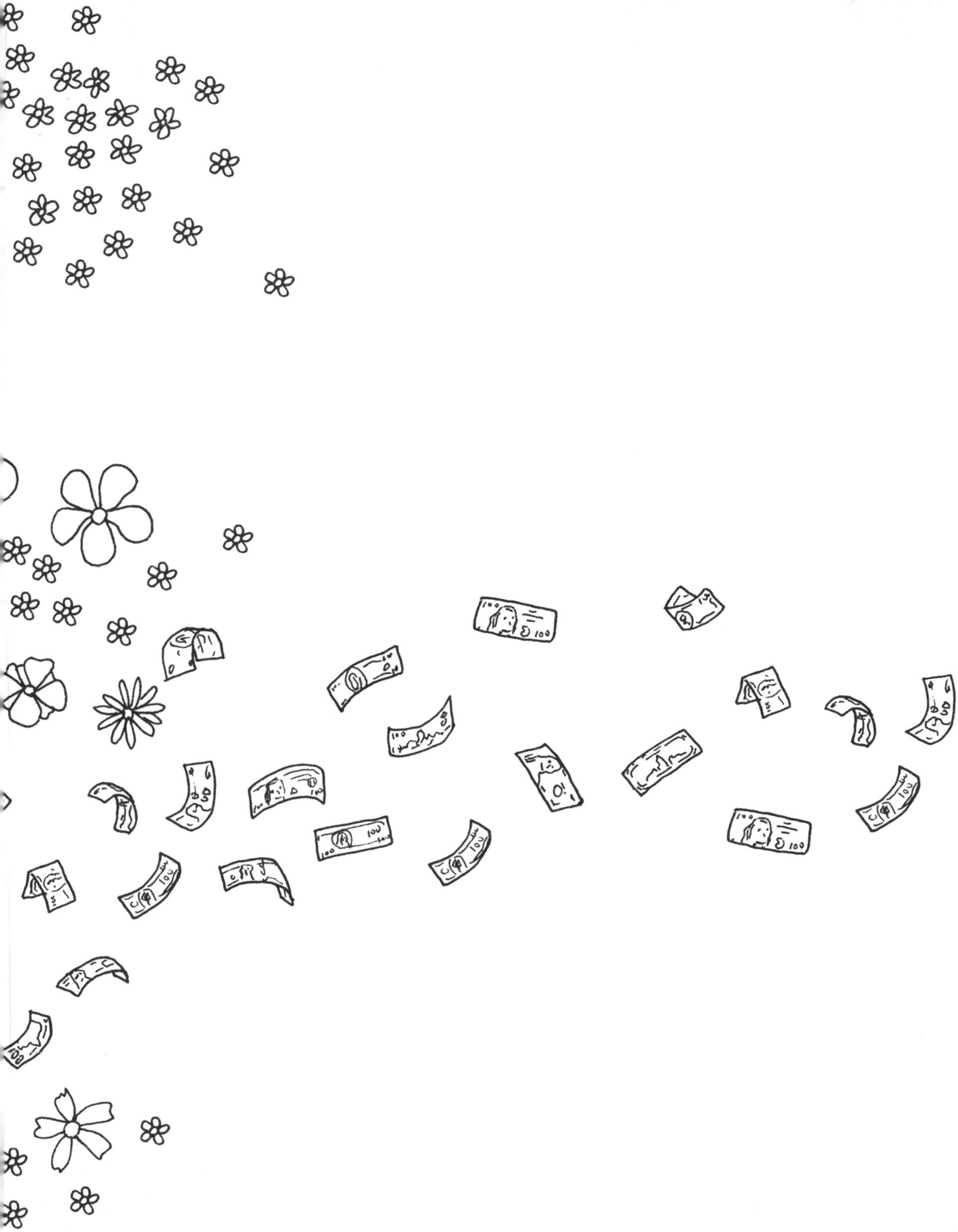

dedicated to Kate, Jim, Lee, and Loki

Published by Koyama Press
koyamapress.com

First edition: September 2018

ISBN: 978-1-927668-58-0

Printed in China

Chlorine Gardens

Keiler Roberts

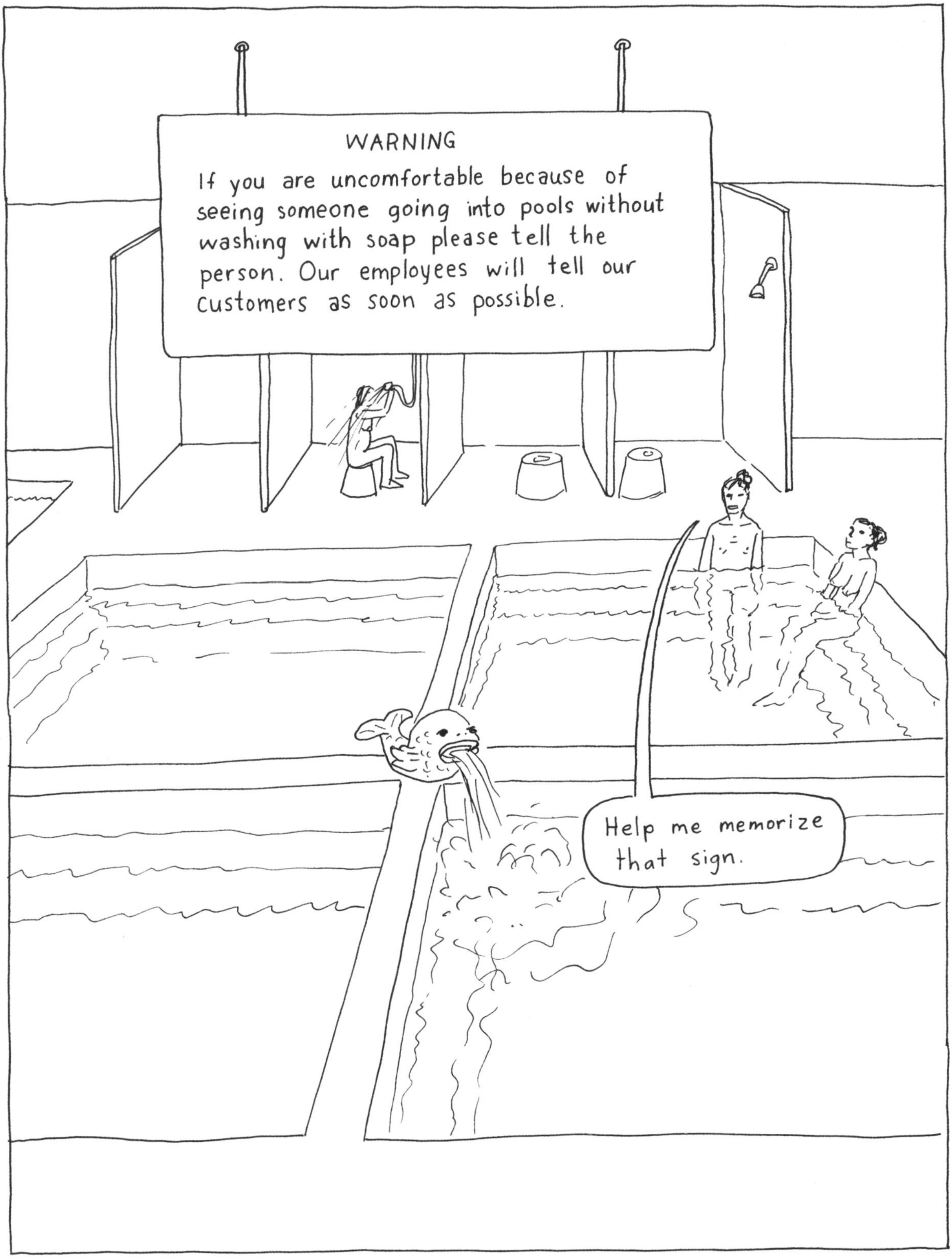
WARNING
If you are uncomfortable because of seeing someone going into pools without washing with soap please tell the person. Our employees will tell our customers as soon as possible.
Help me memorize that sign.

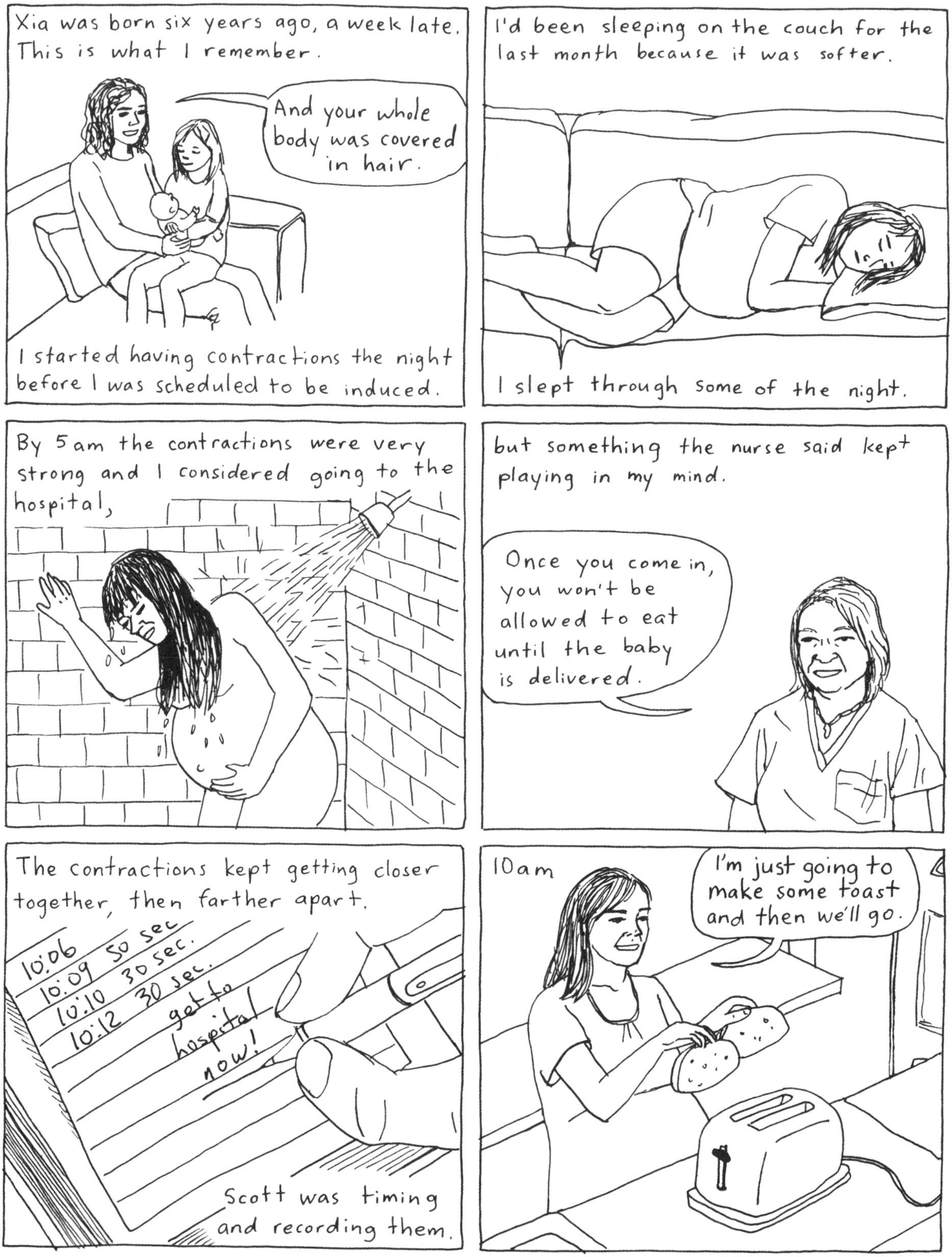
Xia was born six years ago, a week late. This is what I remember.
And your whole body was covered in hair.
I started having contractions the night before I was scheduled to be induced.
I'd been sleeping on the couch for the last month because it was softer.
I slept through some of the night.
By 5am the contractions were very strong and I considered going to the hospital,
but something the nurse said kept playing in my mind.
Once you come in, you won't be allowed to eat until the baby is delivered.
The contractions kept getting closer together, then farther apart.
10:06
10:09 50 sec
10:10 30 sec.
10:12 30 sec.
get to hospital now!
Scott was timing and recording them.
10am
I'm just going to make some toast and then we'll go.

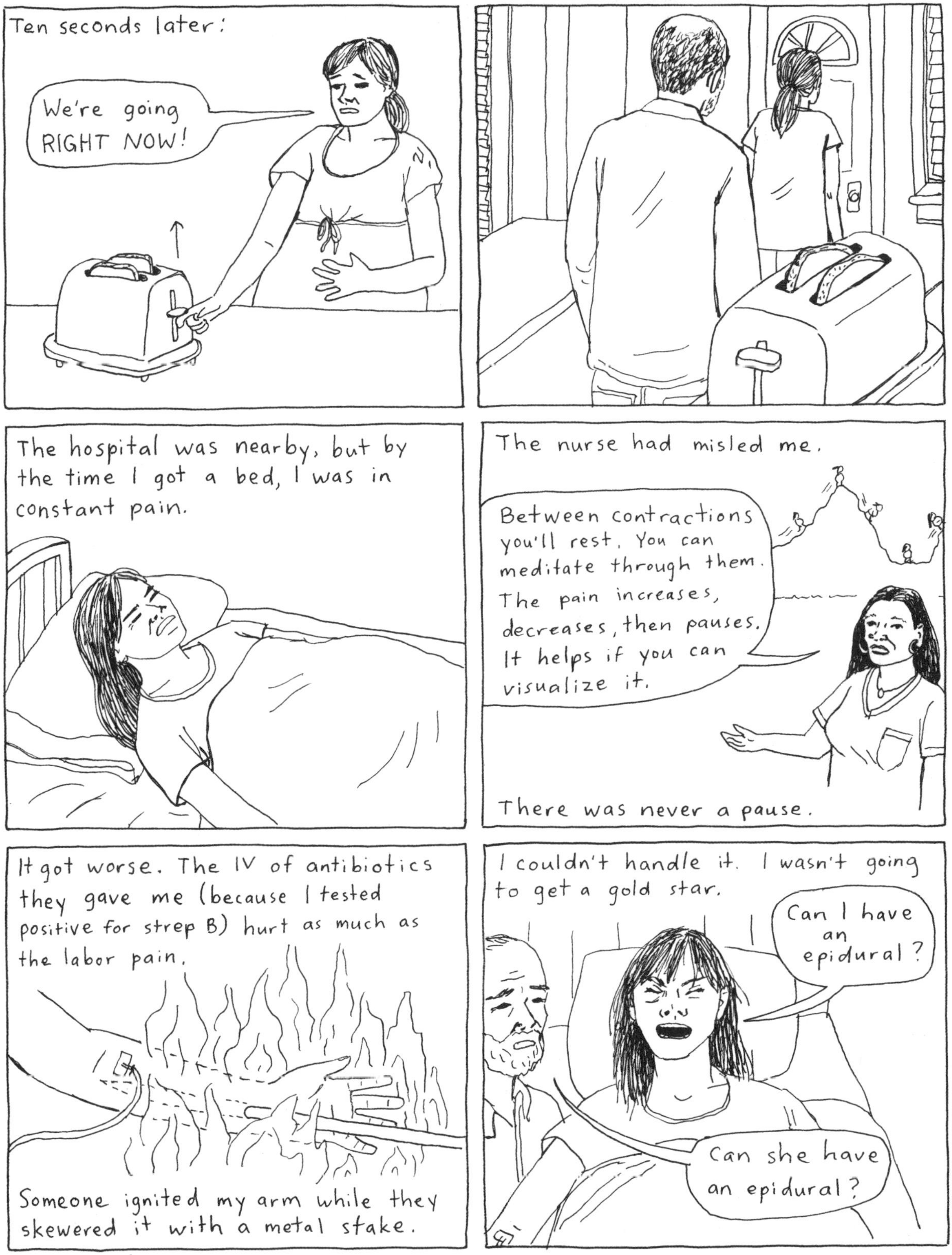
Ten seconds later:
We're going RIGHT NOW!
The hospital was nearby, but by the time I got a bed, I was in constant pain.
The nurse had misled me.
Between contractions you'll rest. You can meditate through them. The pain increases, decreases, then pauses. It helps if you can visualize it.
There was never a pause.
It got worse. The IV of antibiotics they gave me (because I tested positive for strep B) hurt as much as the labor pain.
Someone ignited my arm while they skewered it with a metal stake.
I couldn't handle it. I wasn't going to get a gold star.
Can I have an epidural?
Can she have an epidural?

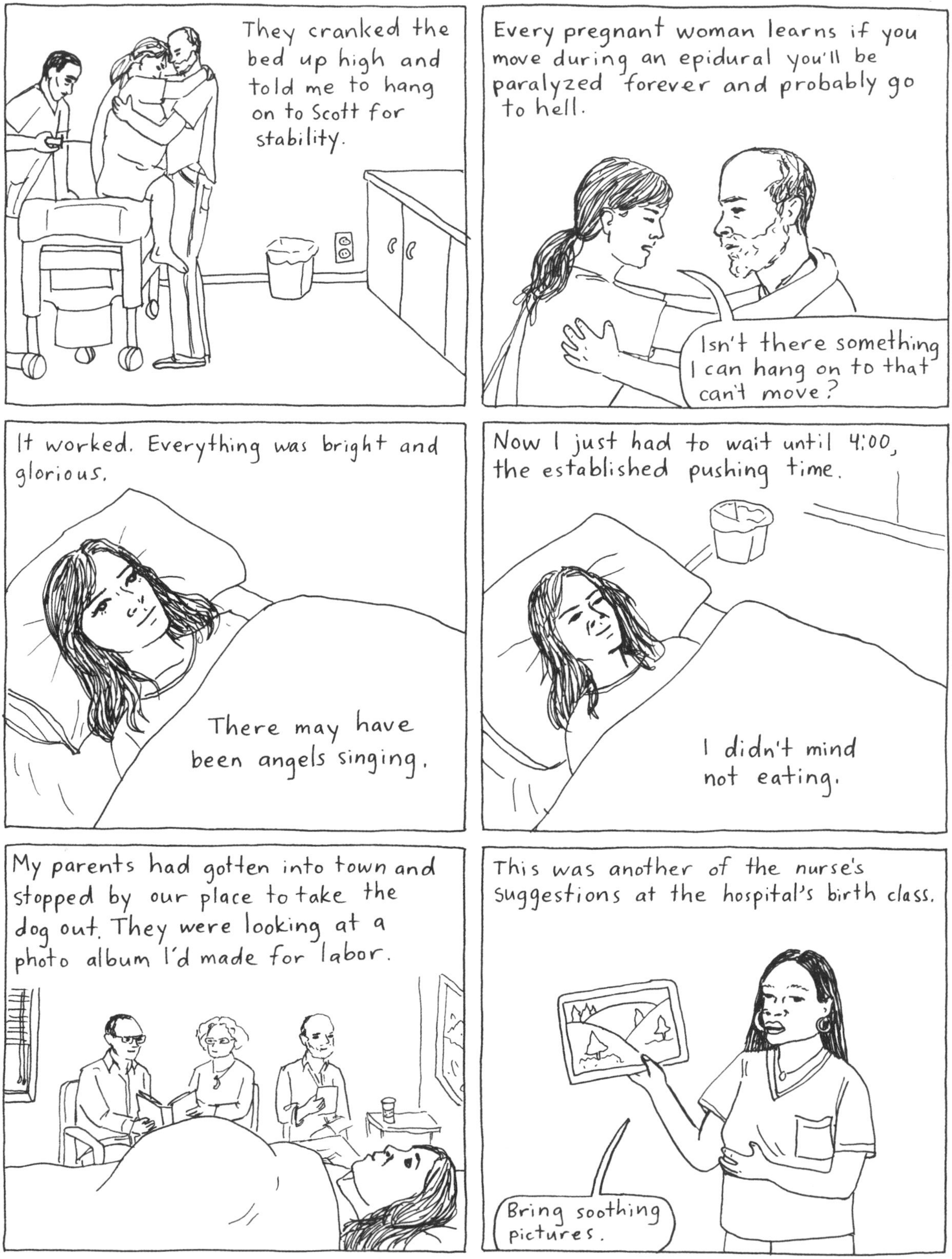
They cranked the bed up high and told me to hang on to Scott for stability.
Every pregnant woman learns if you move during an epidural you'll be paralyzed forever and probably go to hell.
Isn't there something I can hang on to that can't move?
It worked. Everything was bright and glorious.
There may have been angels singing.
Now I just had to wait until 4:00, the established pushing time.
I didn't mind not eating.
My parents had gotten into town and stopped by our place to take the dog out. They were looking at a photo album I'd made for labor.
This was another of the nurse's suggestions at the hospital's birth class.
Bring soothing pictures.

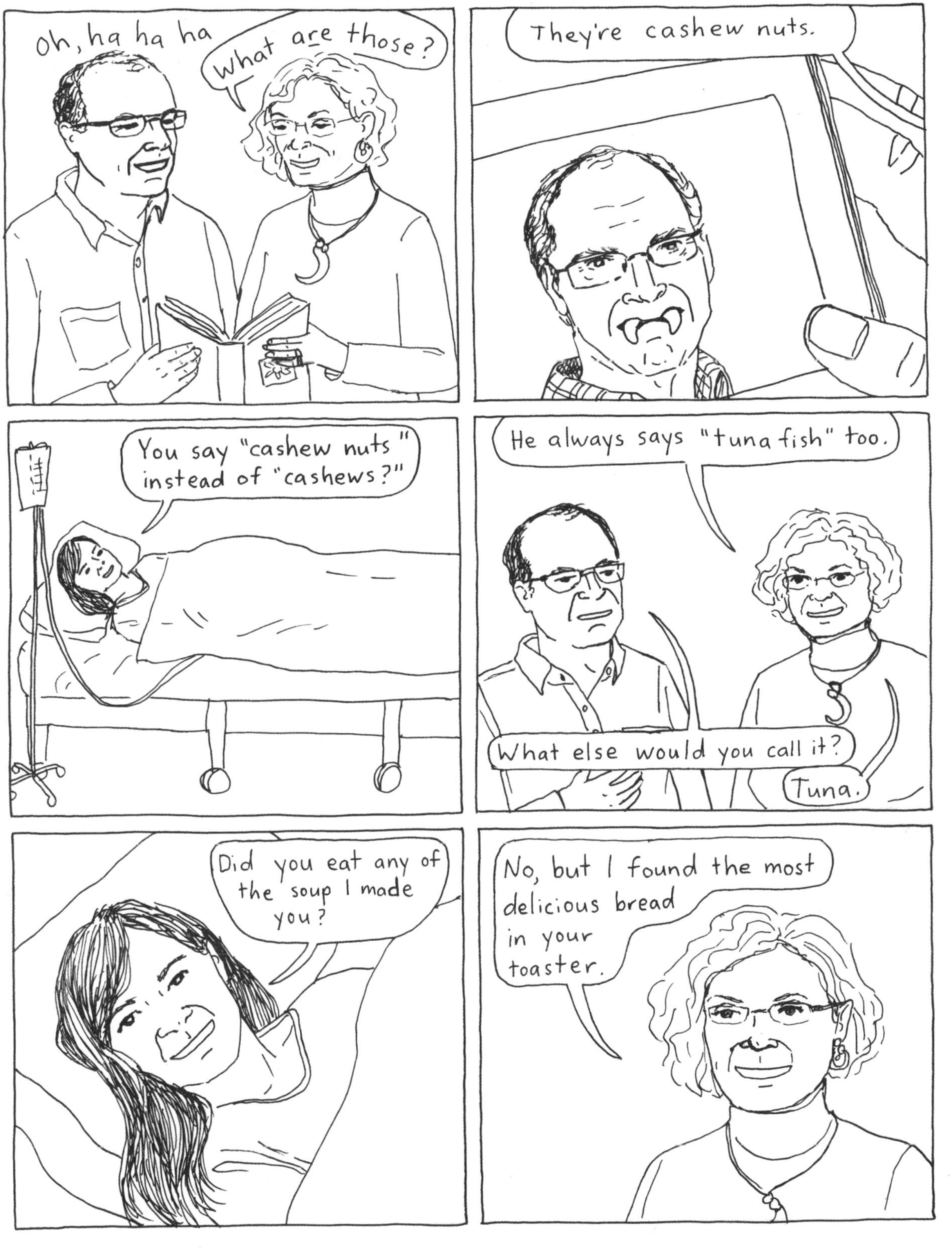
Oh, ha ha ha
What are those?
They're cashew nuts.
You say "cashew nuts" instead of "cashews?"
He always says "tuna fish" too.
What else would you call it?
Tuna.
Did you eat any of the soup I made you?
No, but I found the most delicious bread in your toaster.

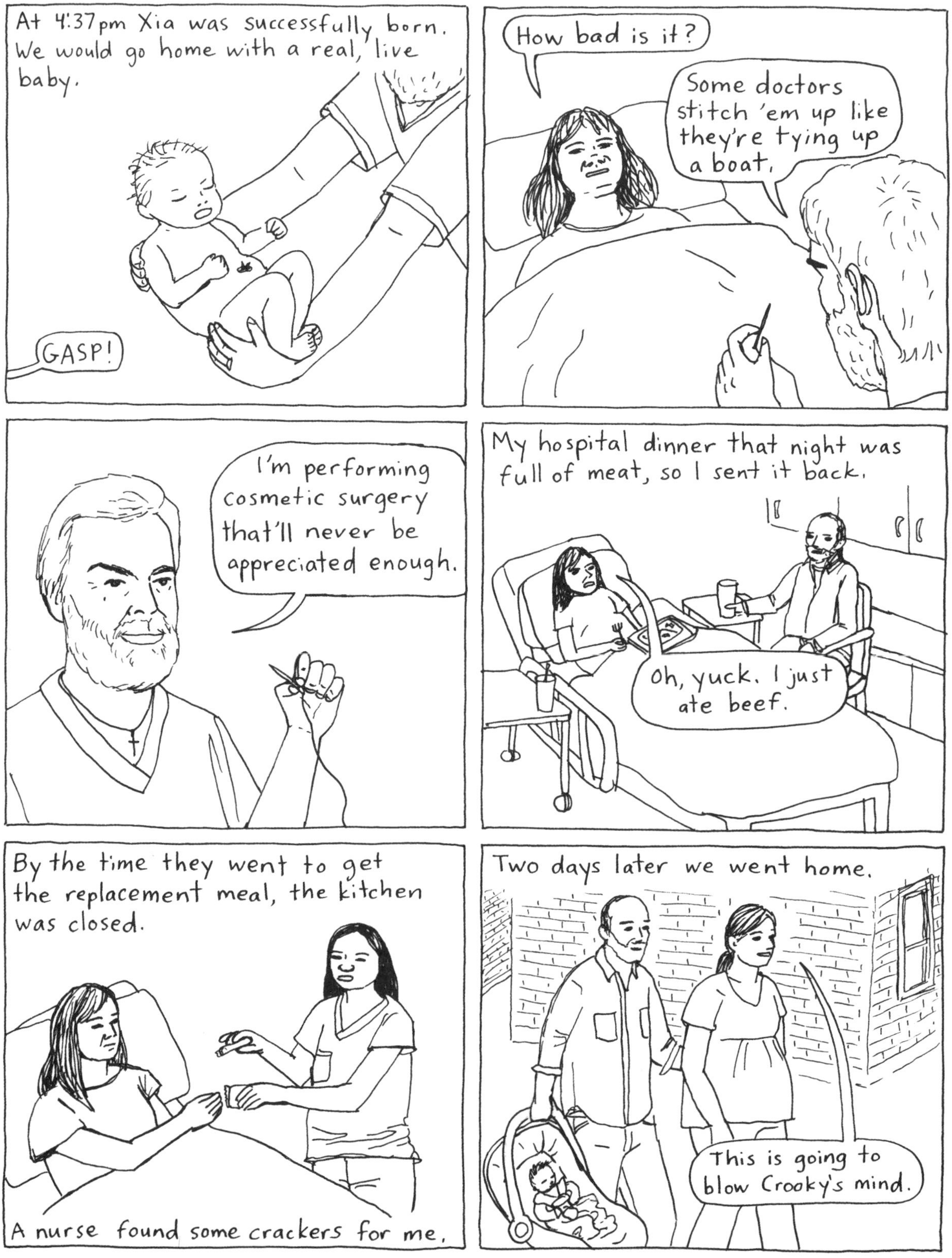
At 4:37pm Xia was successfully born. We would go home with a real, live baby.
GASP!
How bad is it?
Some doctors stitch 'em up like they're tying up a boat.
I'm performing cosmetic surgery that'll never be appreciated enough.
My hospital dinner that night was full of meat, so I sent it back.
Oh, yuck. I just ate beef.
By the time they went to get the replacement meal, the kitchen was closed.
A nurse found some crackers for me.
Two days later we went home.
This is going to blow Crooky's mind.

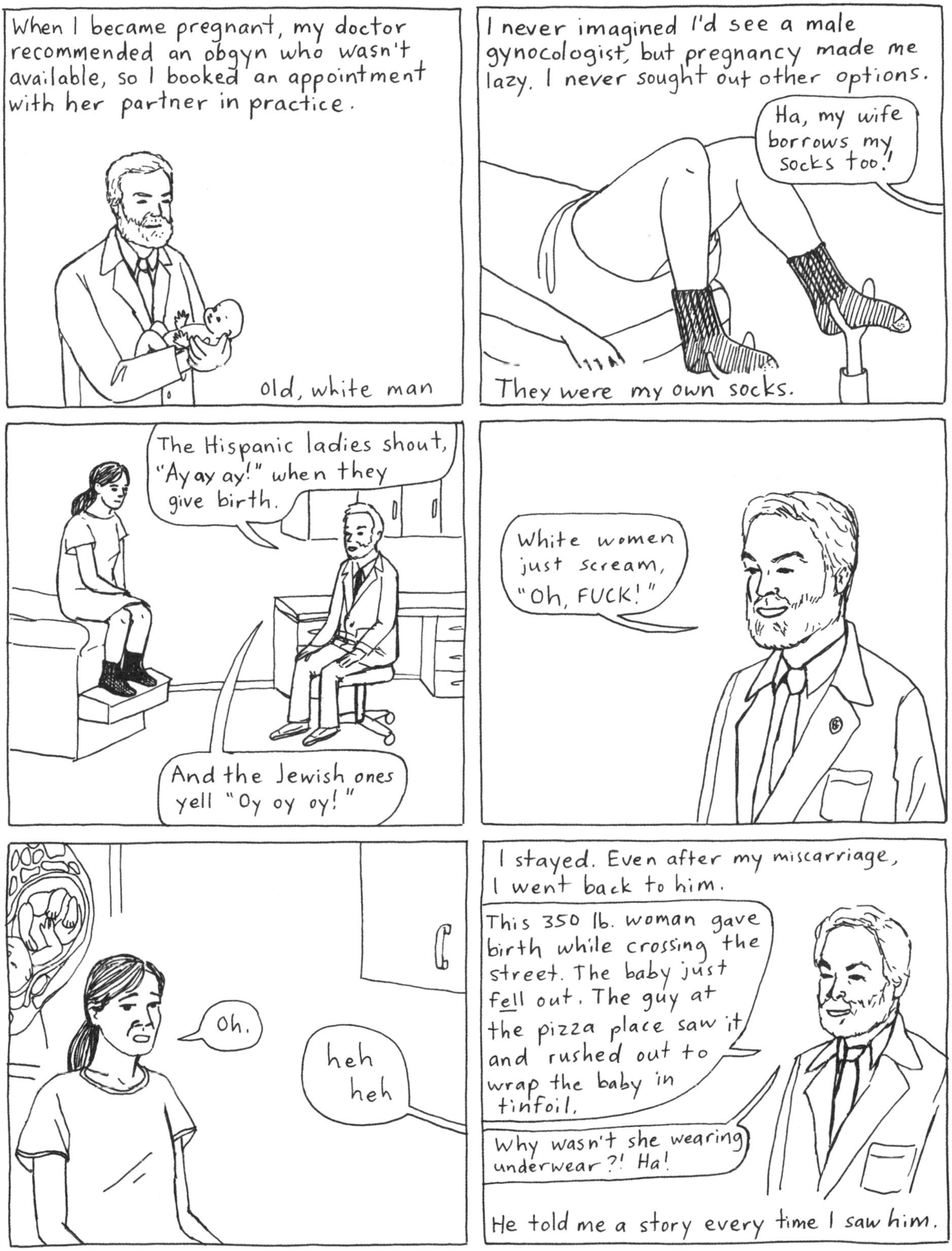
When I became pregnant, my doctor recommended an obgyn who wasn't available, so I booked an appointment with her partner in practice.
old, white man
I never imagined I'd see a male gynocologist, but pregnancy made me lazy. I never sought out other options.
Ha, my wife borrows my socks too!
They were my own socks.
The Hispanic ladies shout, "Ay ay ay!" when they give birth.
And the Jewish ones yell "Oy oy oy!"
White women just scream, "Oh, FUCK!"
Oh.
heh heh
I stayed. Even after my miscarriage, I went back to him.
This 350 lb. woman gave birth while crossing the street. The baby just fell out. The guy at the pizza place saw it and rushed out to wrap the baby in tinfoil.
Why wasn't she wearing underwear?! Ha!
He told me a story every time I saw him.

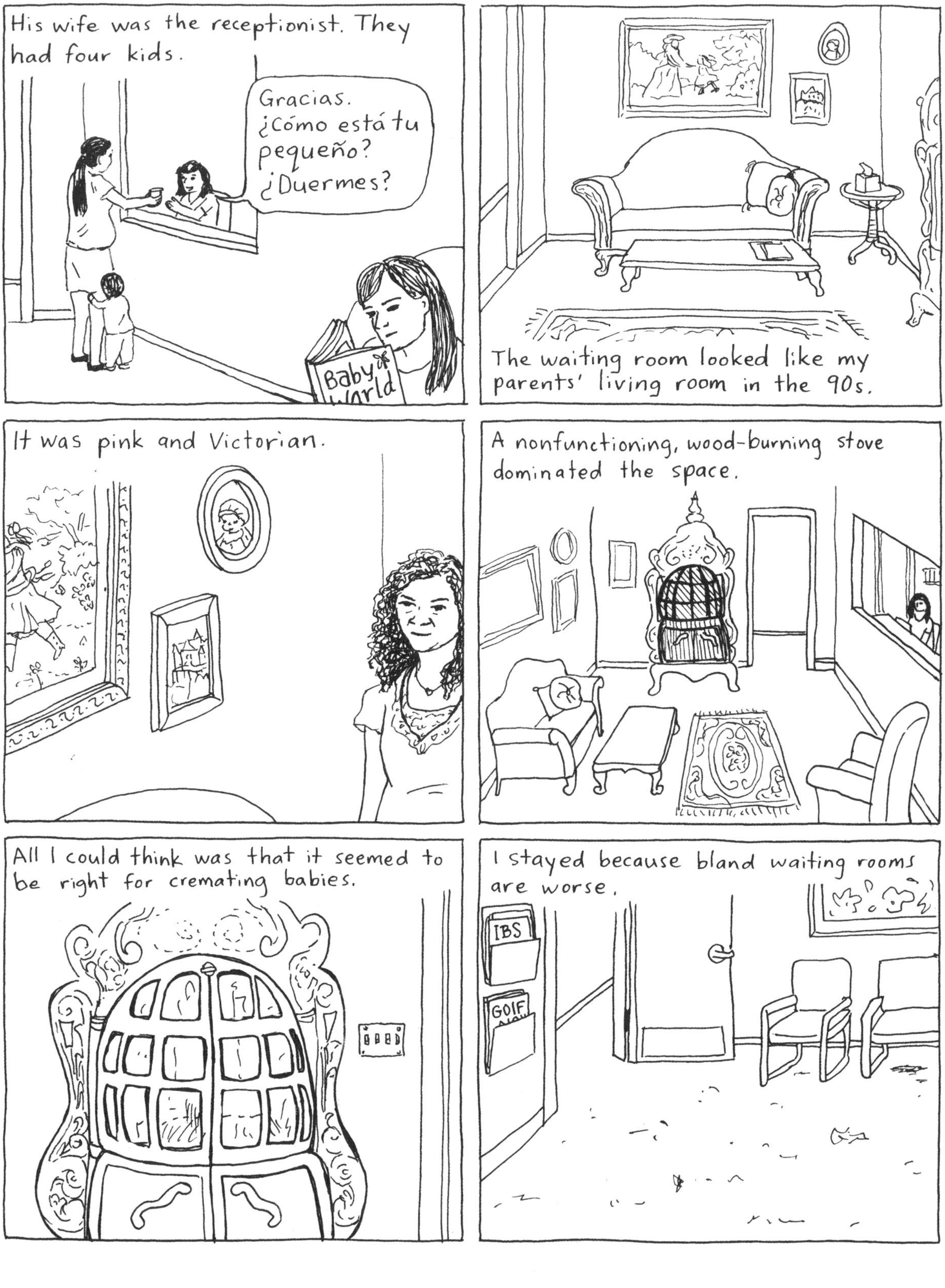
His wife was the receptionist. They had four kids.
Gracias. ¿Cómo está tu pequeño? ¿Duermes?
Baby World
The waiting room looked like my parents' living room in the 90s.
It was pink and Victorian.
A nonfunctioning, wood-burning stove dominated the space.
All I could think was that it seemed to be right for cremating babies.
I stayed because bland waiting rooms are worse.
IBS
GOlF

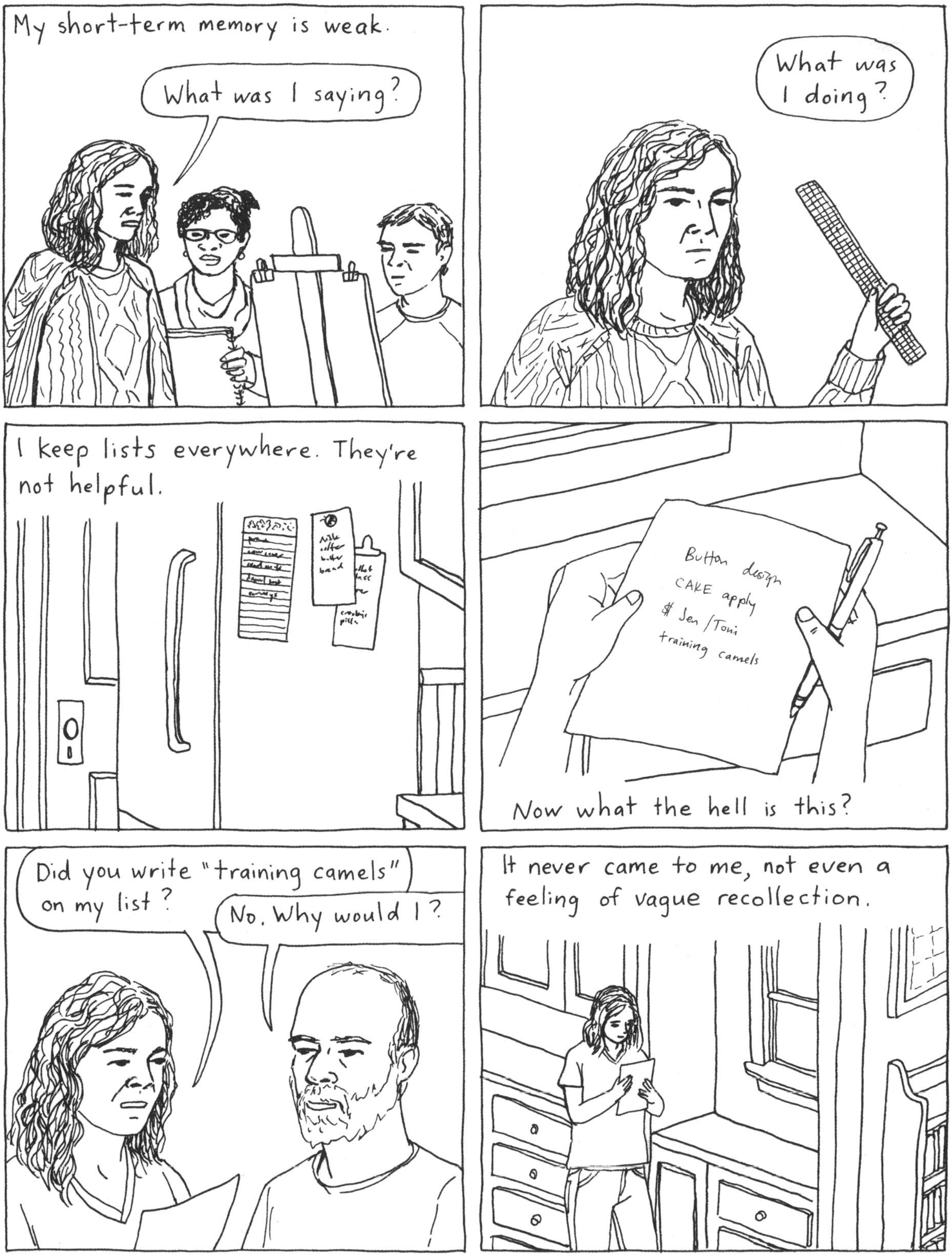
My short-term memory is weak.
What was I saying?
What was I doing?
I keep lists everywhere. They're not helpful.
Button design
CAKE apply
$ Jen / Toni
training camels
Now what the hell is this?
Did you write "training camels" on my list?
No. Why would I?
It never came to me, not even a feeling of vague recollection.

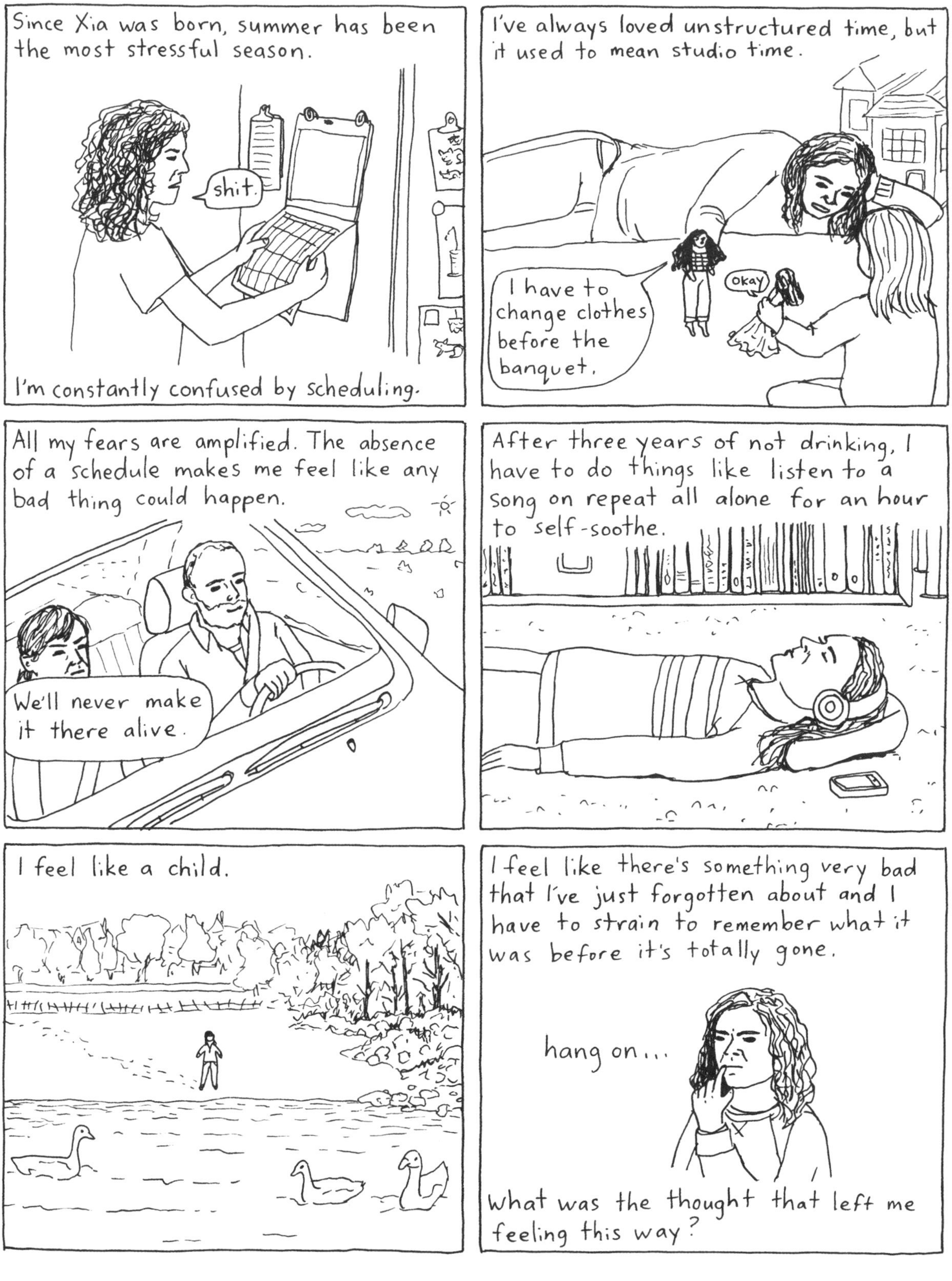

Since Xia was born, summer has been the most stressful season.
shit.
I'm constantly confused by scheduling.
I've always loved unstructured time, but it used to mean studio time.
I have to change clothes before the banquet.
okay
All my fears are amplified. The absence of a schedule makes me feel like any bad thing could happen.
We'll never make it there alive.
After three years of not drinking, I have to do things like listen to a song on repeat all alone for an hour to self-soothe.
I feel like a child.
I feel like there's something very bad that I've just forgotten about and I have to strain to remember what it was before it's totally gone.
hang on...
What was the thought that left me feeling this way?

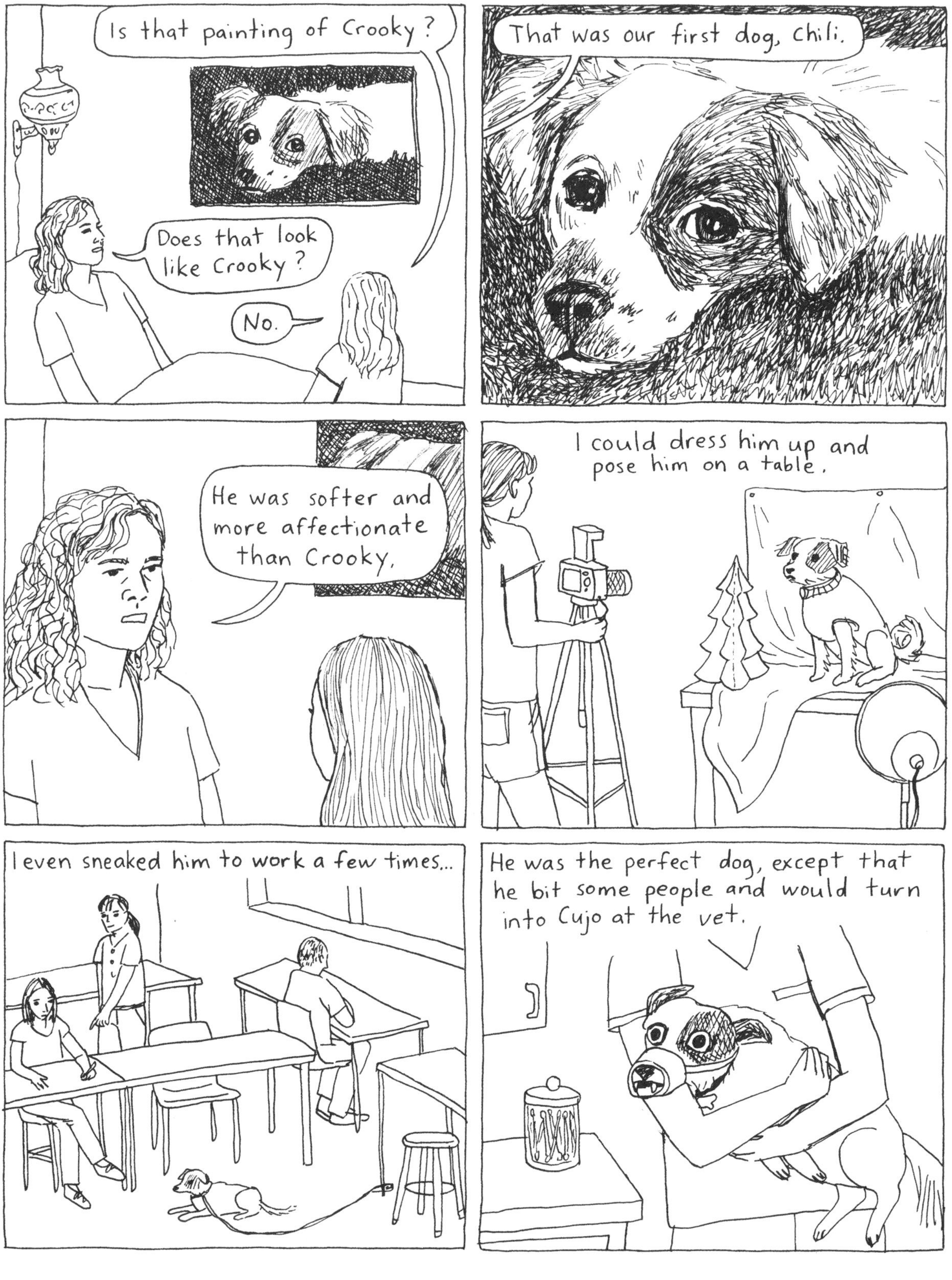
Is that painting of Crooky?
Does that look like Crooky?
No.
That was our first dog, Chili.
He was softer and more affectionate than Crooky.
I could dress him up and pose him on a table.
I even sneaked him to work a few times...
He was the perfect dog, except that he bit some people and would turn into Cujo at the vet.

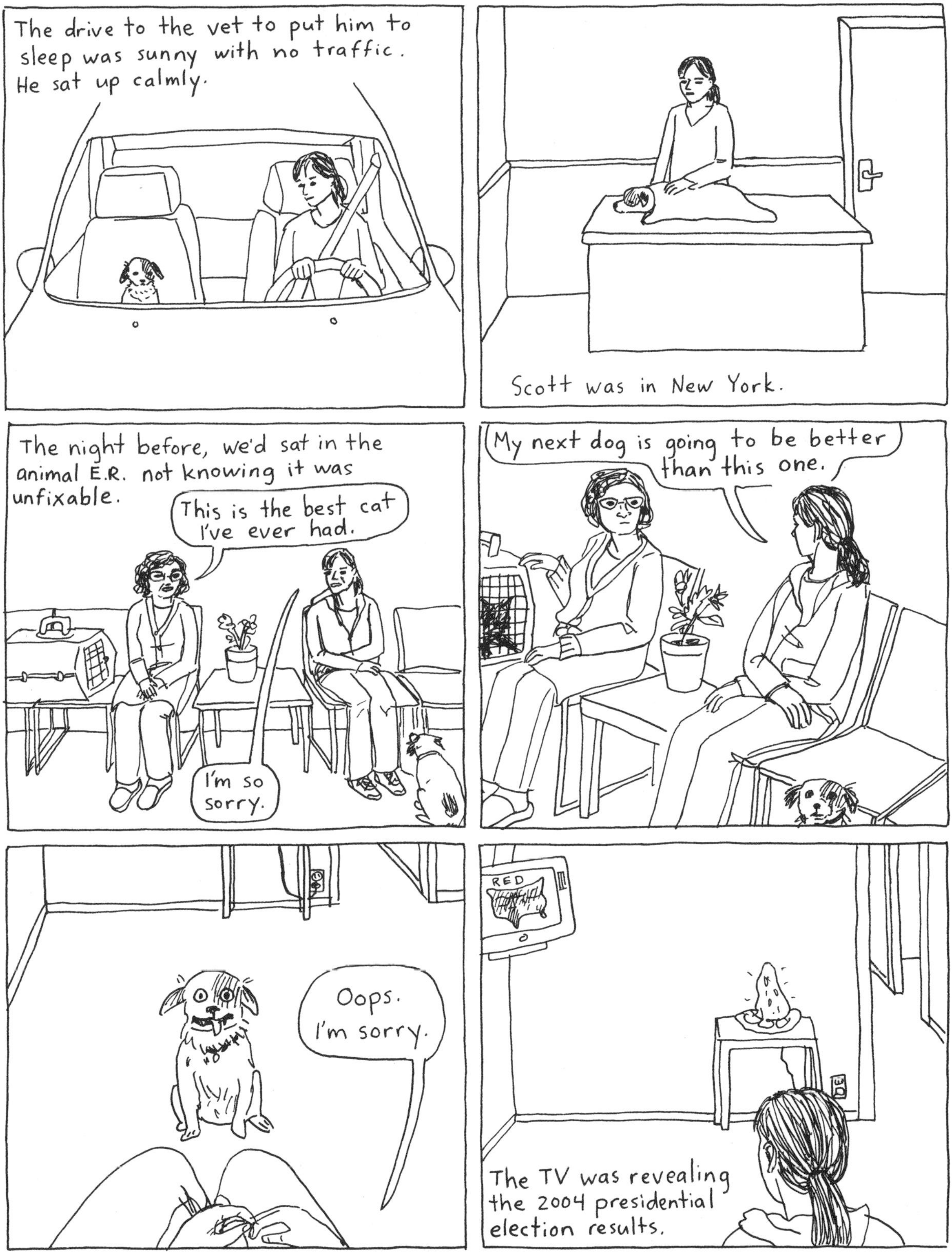
The drive to the vet to put him to sleep was sunny with no traffic. He sat up calmly.
Scott was in New York.
The night before, we'd sat in the animal E.R. not knowing it was unfixable.
This is the best cat I've ever had.
I'm so sorry.
My next dog is going to be better than this one.
Oops. I'm sorry.
RED
The TV was revealing the 2004 presidential election results.

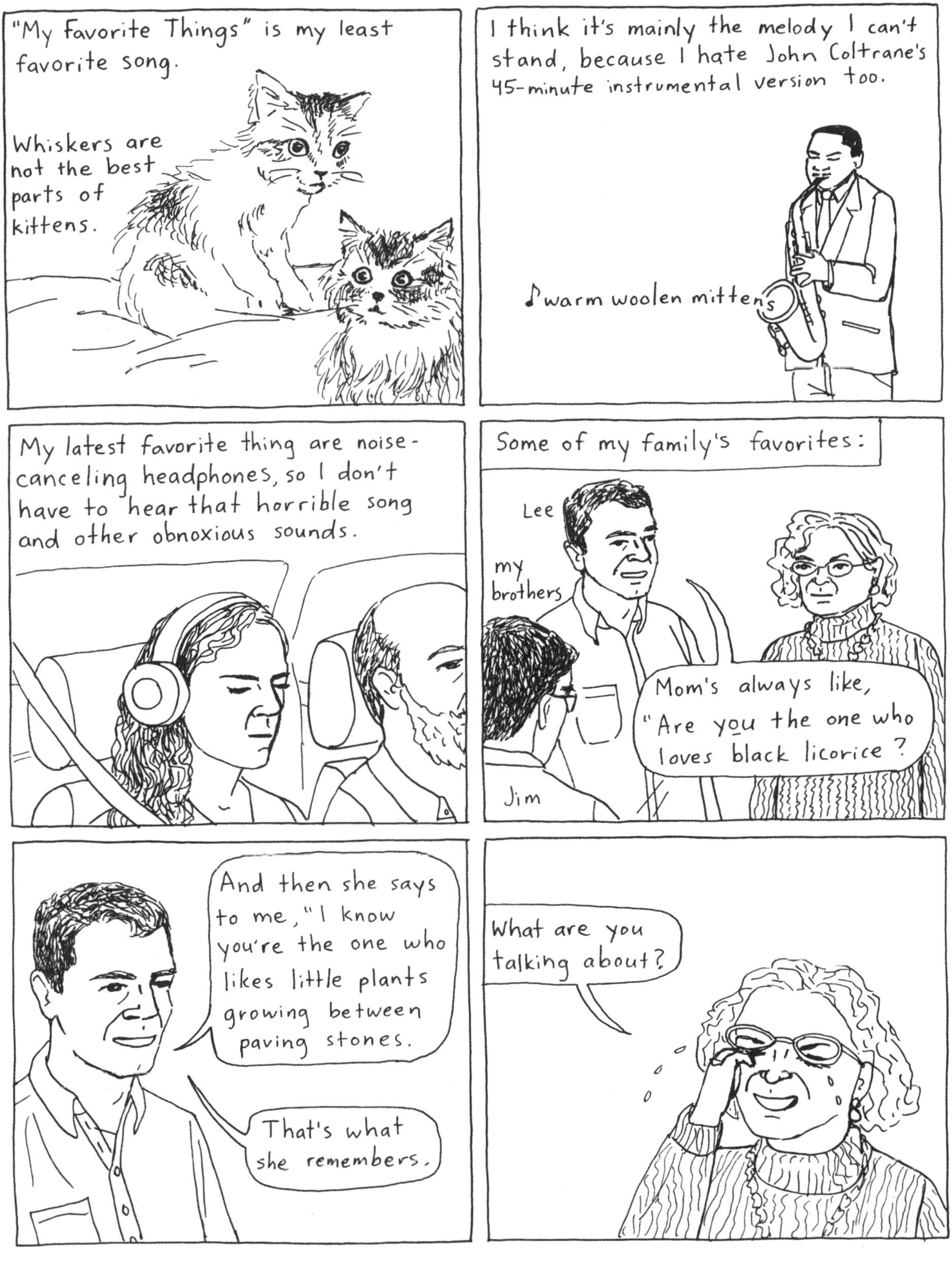
"My Favorite Things" is my least favorite song.
Whiskers are not the best parts of kittens.
I think it's mainly the melody I can't stand, because I hate John Coltrane's 45-minute instrumental version too.
♪warm woolen mittens
My latest favorite thing are noise-canceling headphones, so I don't have to hear that horrible song and other obnoxious sounds.
Some of my family's favorites:
Lee
my brothers
Jim
Mom's always like, "Are you the one who loves black licorice?
And then she says to me, "I know you're the one who likes little plants growing between paving stones.
That's what she remembers.
What are you talking about?

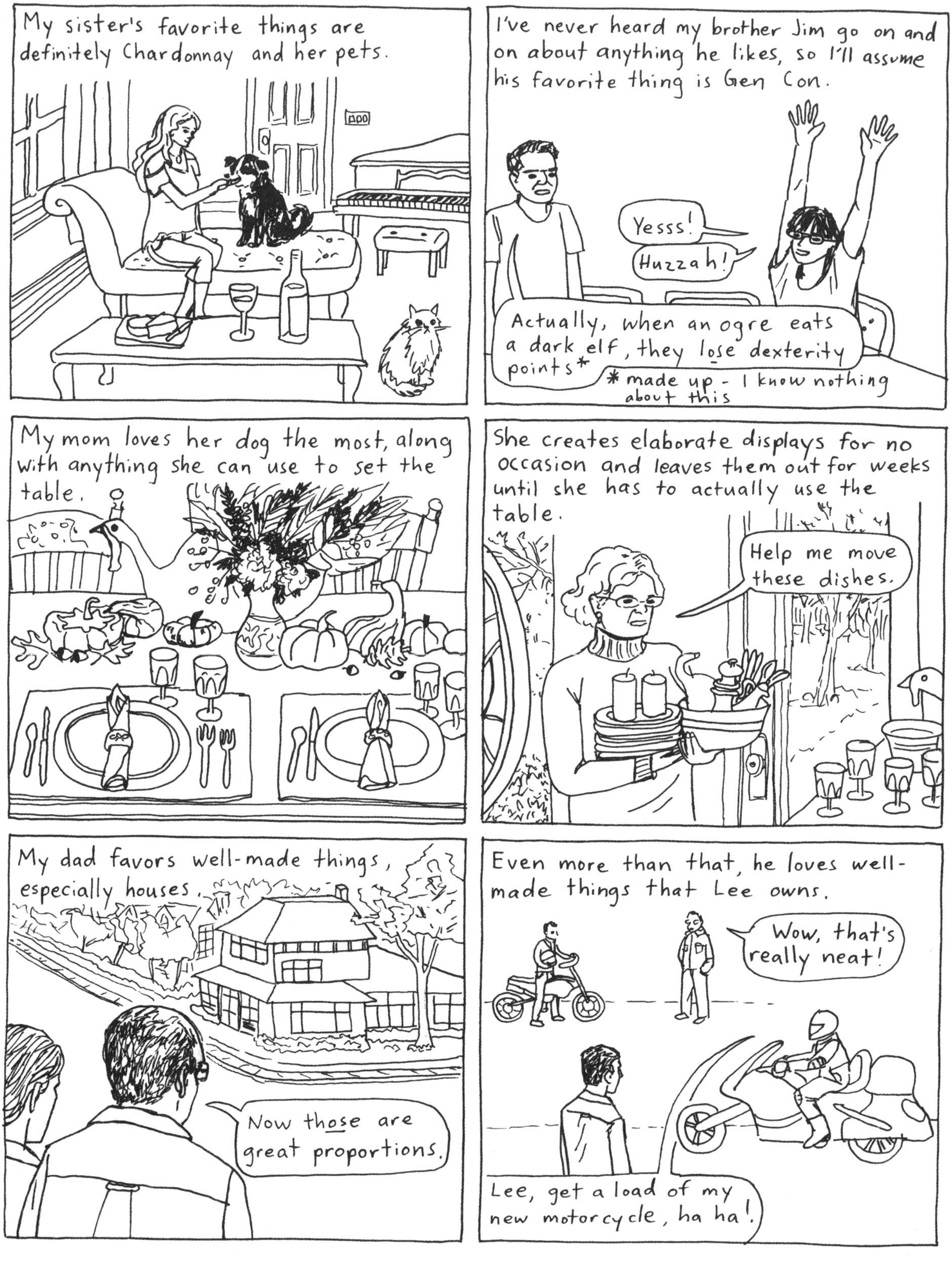
My sister's favorite things are definitely Chardonnay and her pets.
I've never heard my brother Jim go on and on about anything he likes, so I'll assume his favorite thing is Gen Con.
Yesss!
Huzzah!
Actually, when an ogre eats a dark elf, they lose dexterity points*
* made up - I know nothing about this
My mom loves her dog the most, along with anything she can use to set the table.
She creates elaborate displays for no occasion and leaves them out for weeks until she has to actually use the table.
Help me move these dishes.
My dad favors well-made things, especially houses.
Now those are great proportions.
Even more than that, he loves well-made things that Lee owns.
Wow, that's really neat!
Lee, get a load of my new motorcycle, ha ha!

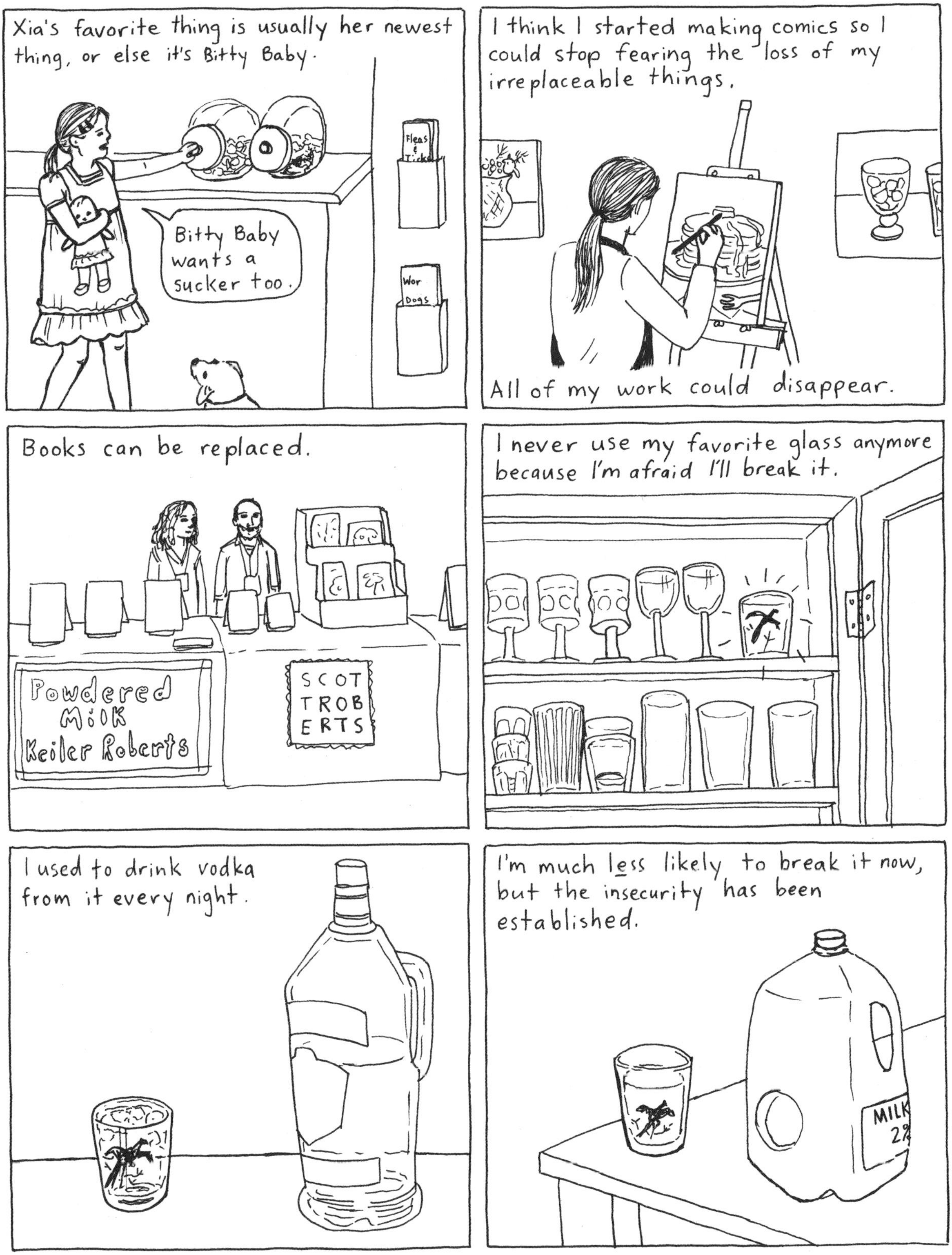

Xia's favorite thing is usually her newest thing, or else it's Bitty Baby.
Bitty Baby wants a sucker too.
Fleas & Ticks
Dogs
I think I started making comics so I could stop fearing the loss of my irreplaceable things.
All of my work could disappear.
Books can be replaced.
Powdered Milk Keiler Roberts
SCOT TROB ERTS
I never use my favorite glass anymore because I'm afraid I'll break it.
I used to drink vodka from it every night.
I'm much less likely to break it now, but the insecurity has been established.
MILK 2%

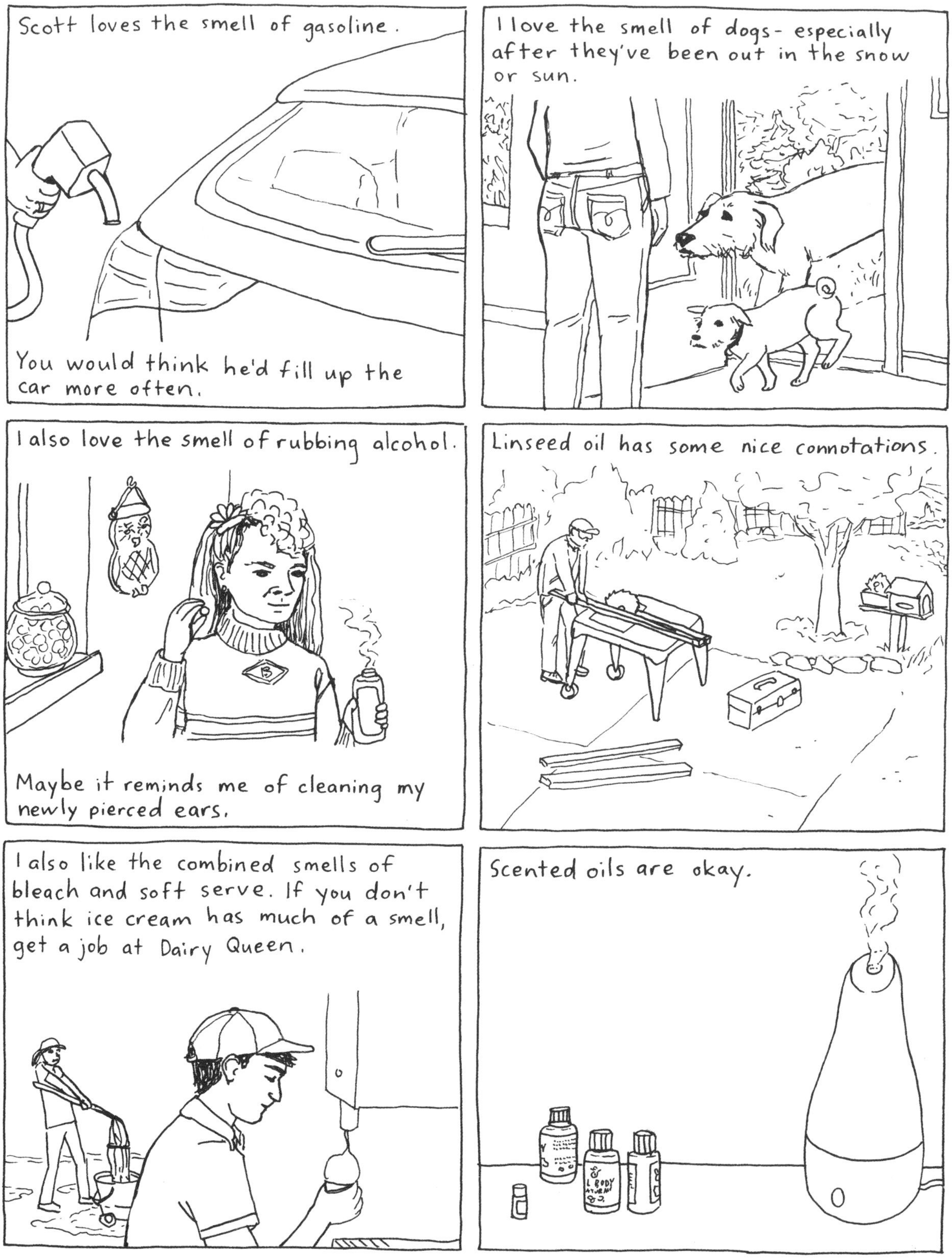
Scott loves the smell of gasoline.
You would think he'd fill up the car more often.
I love the smell of dogs - especially after they've been out in the snow or sun.
I also love the smell of rubbing alcohol.
Maybe it reminds me of cleaning my newly pierced ears.
Linseed oil has some nice connotations.
I also like the combined smells of bleach and soft serve. If you don't think ice cream has much of a smell, get a job at Dairy Queen.
Scented oils are okay.

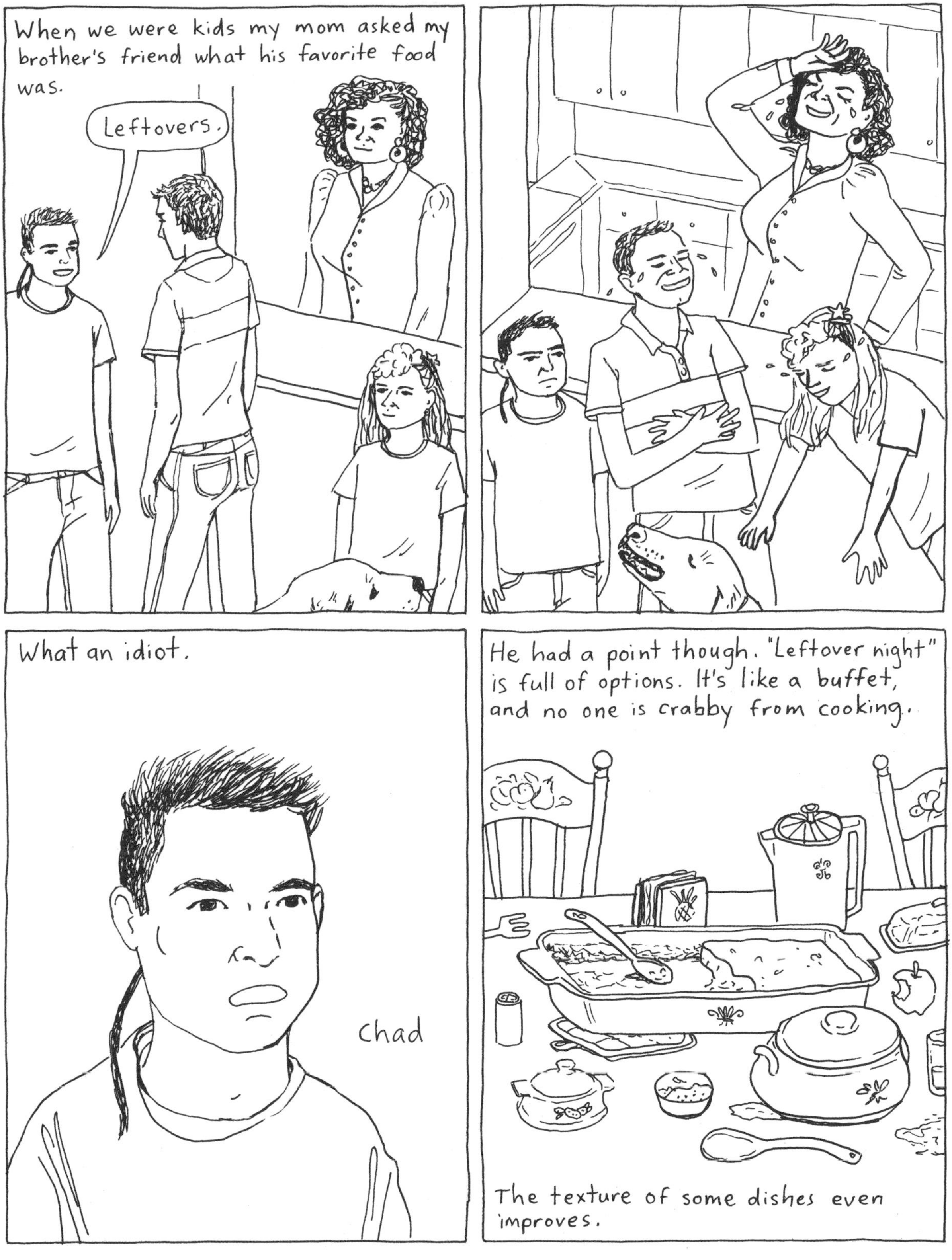
When we were kids my mom asked my brother's friend what his favorite food was.
Leftovers.
What an idiot.
Chad
He had a point though. "Leftover night" is full of options. It's like a buffet, and no one is crabby from cooking.
The texture of some dishes even improves.

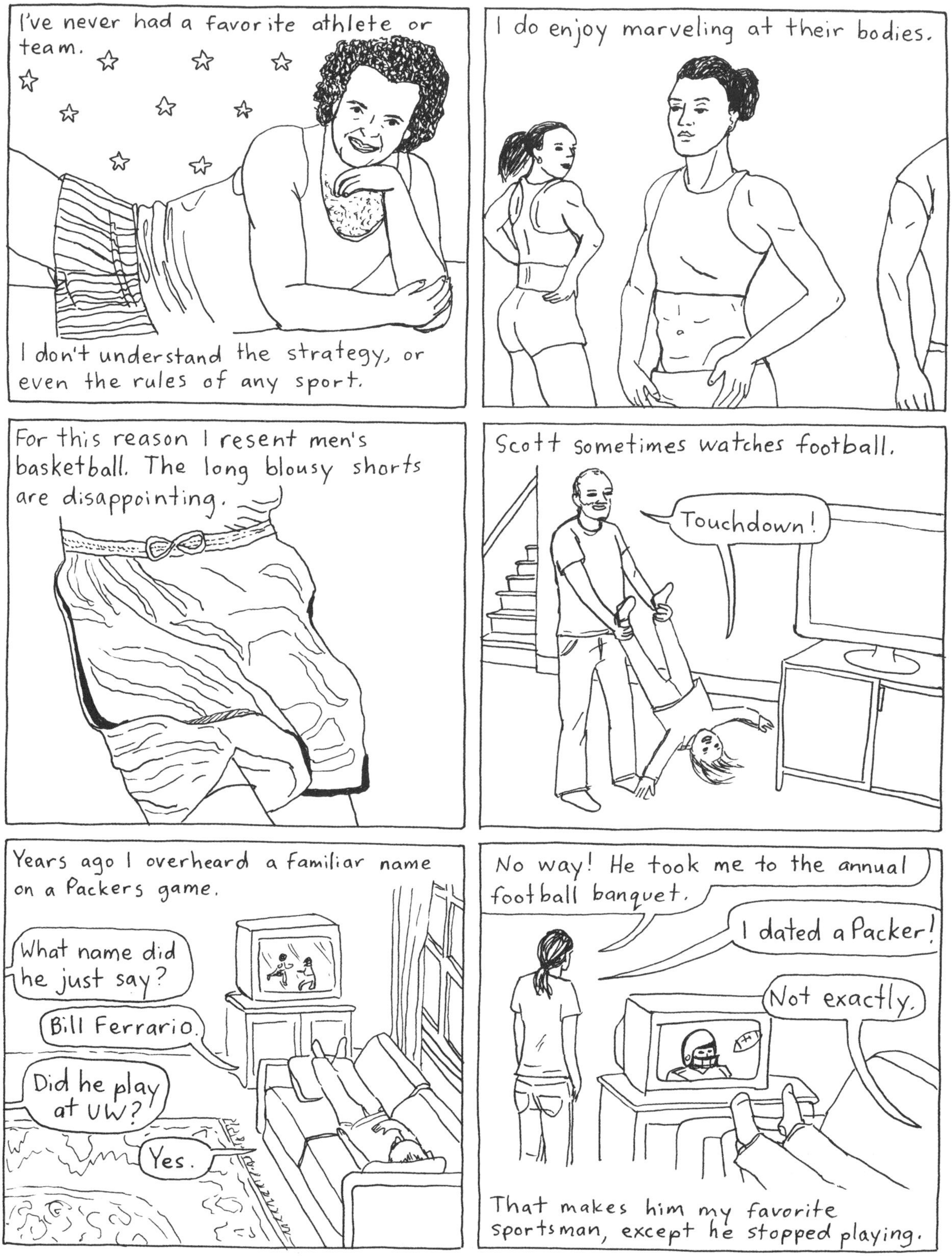
I've never had a favorite athlete or team.
I don't understand the strategy, or even the rules of any sport.
I do enjoy marveling at their bodies.
For this reason I resent men's basketball. The long blousy shorts are disappointing.
Scott sometimes watches football.
Touchdown!
Years ago I overheard a familiar name on a Packers game.
What name did he just say?
Bill Ferrario.
Did he play at UW?
Yes.
No way! He took me to the annual football banquet.
I dated a Packer!
Not exactly.
That makes him my favorite sportsman, except he stopped playing.

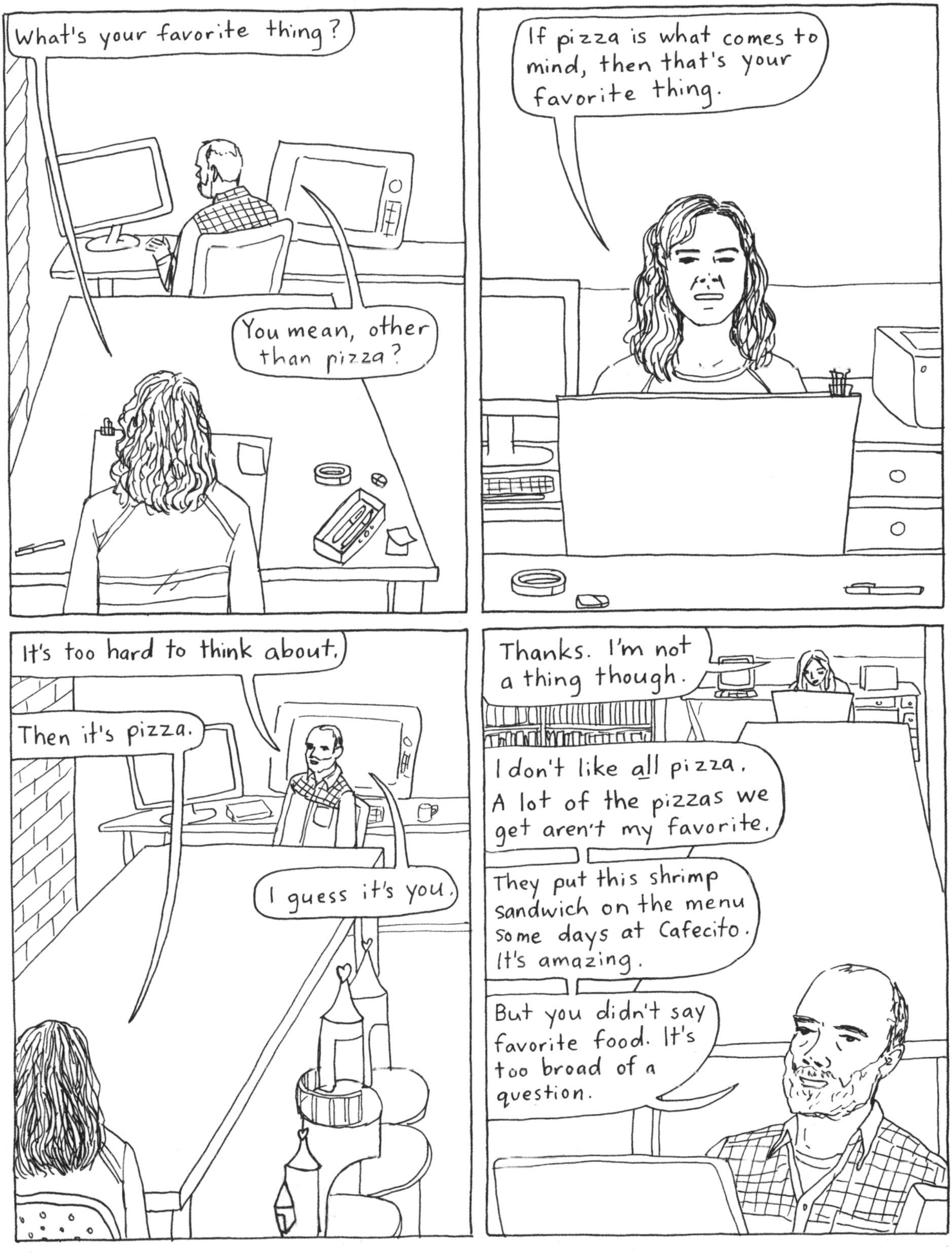
What's your favorite thing?
You mean, other than pizza?
If pizza is what comes to mind, then that's your favorite thing.
It's too hard to think about.
Then it's pizza.
I guess it's you.
Thanks. I'm not a thing though.
I don't like all pizza. A lot of the pizzas we get aren't my favorite.
They put this shrimp sandwich on the menu some days at Cafecito. It's amazing.
But you didn't say favorite food. It's too broad of a question.

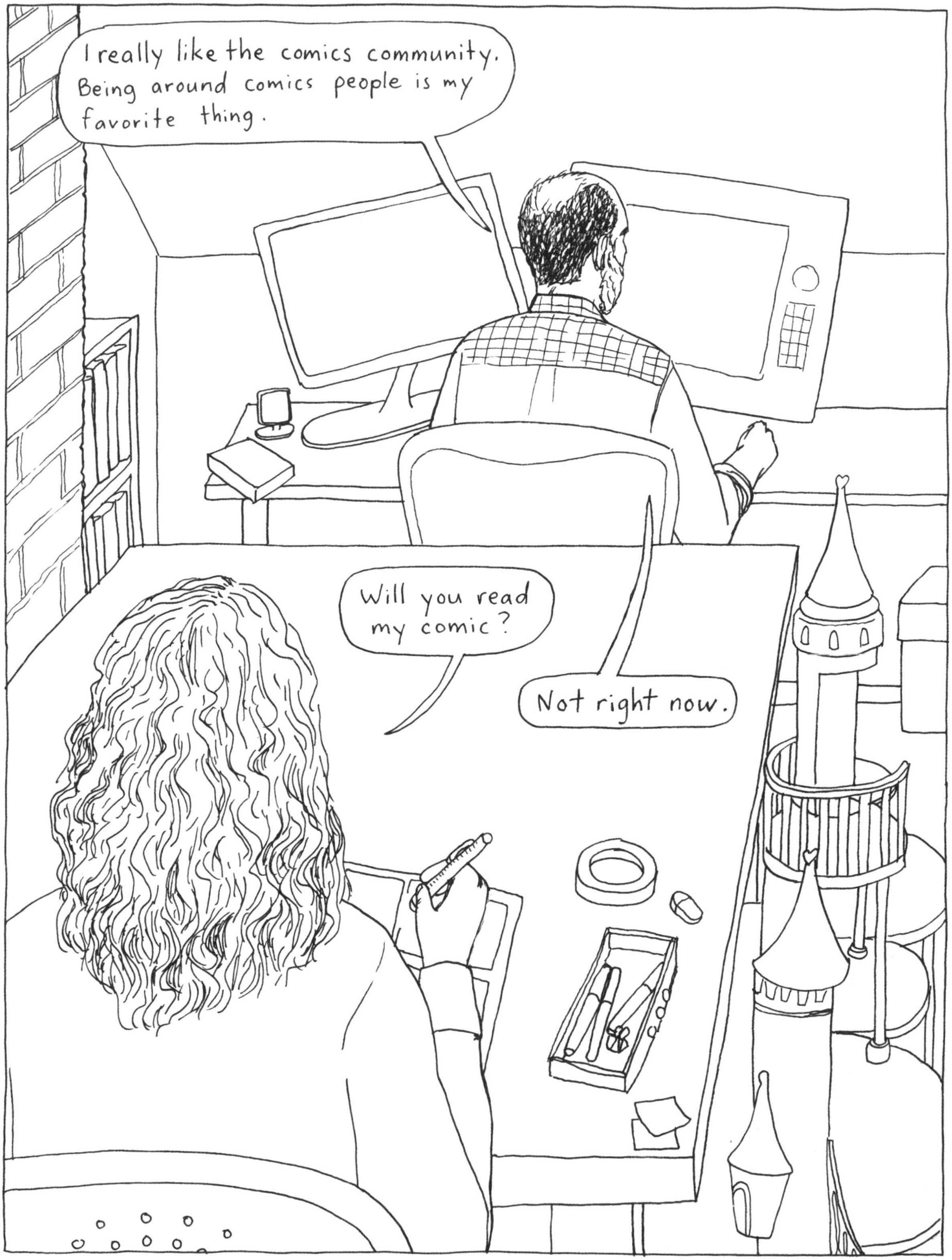
I really like the comics community. Being around comics people is my favorite thing.
Will you read my comic?
Not right now.

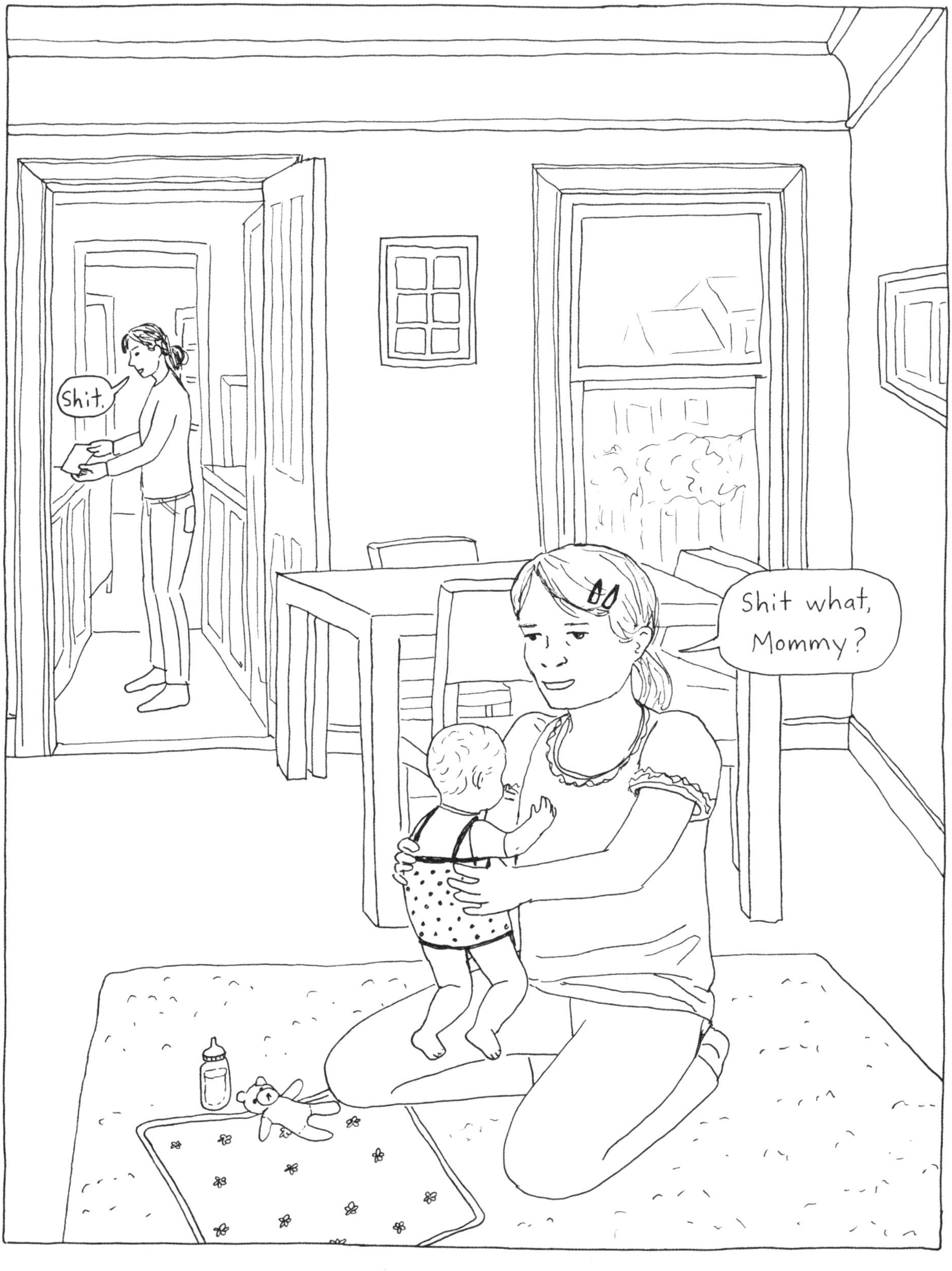
Shit.
Shit what, Mommy?

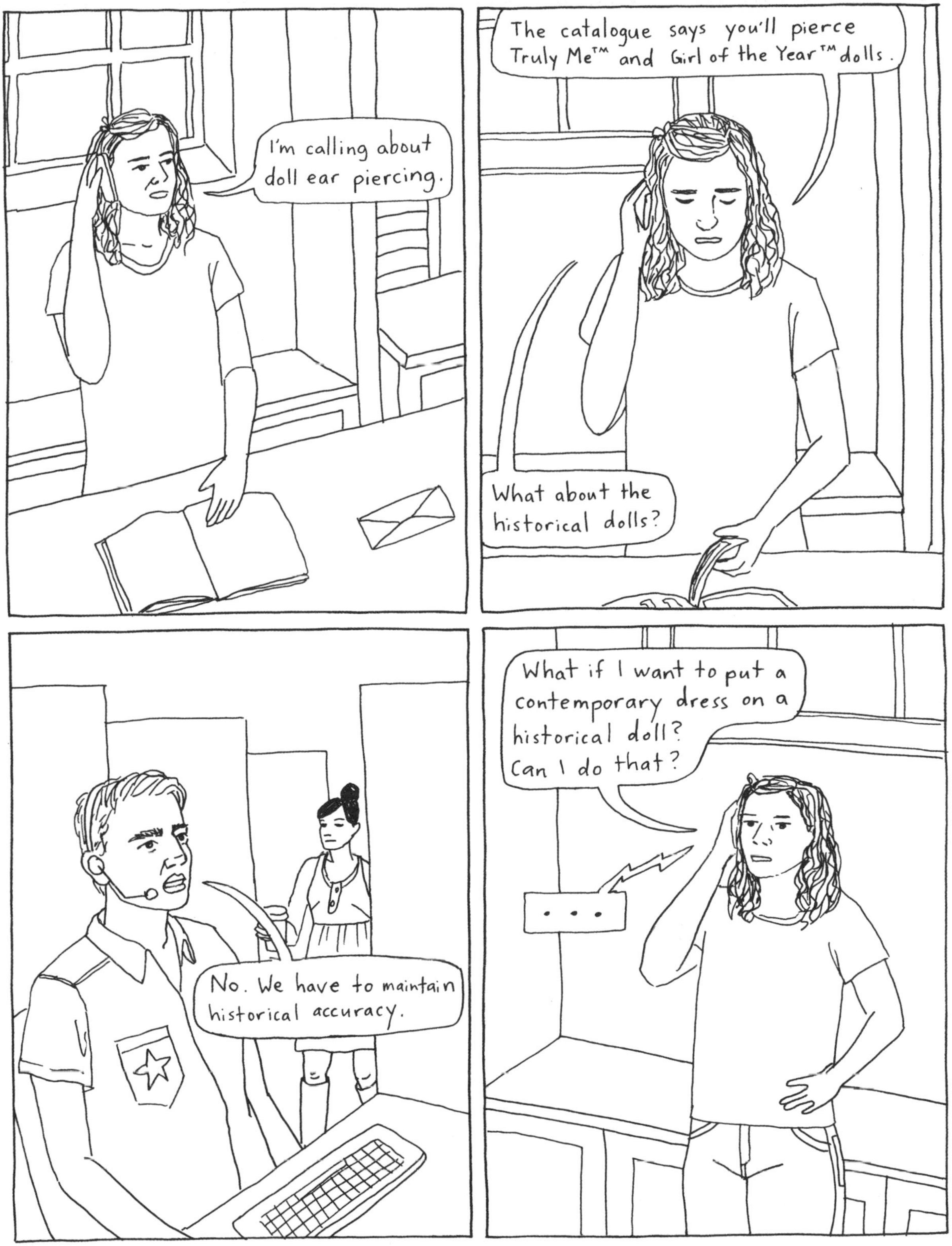
I'm calling about doll ear piercing.
The catalogue says you'll pierce Truly Me™ and Girl of the Year™ dolls.
What about the historical dolls?
No. We have to maintain historical accuracy.
What if I want to put a contemporary dress on a historical doll? Can I do that?
. . .

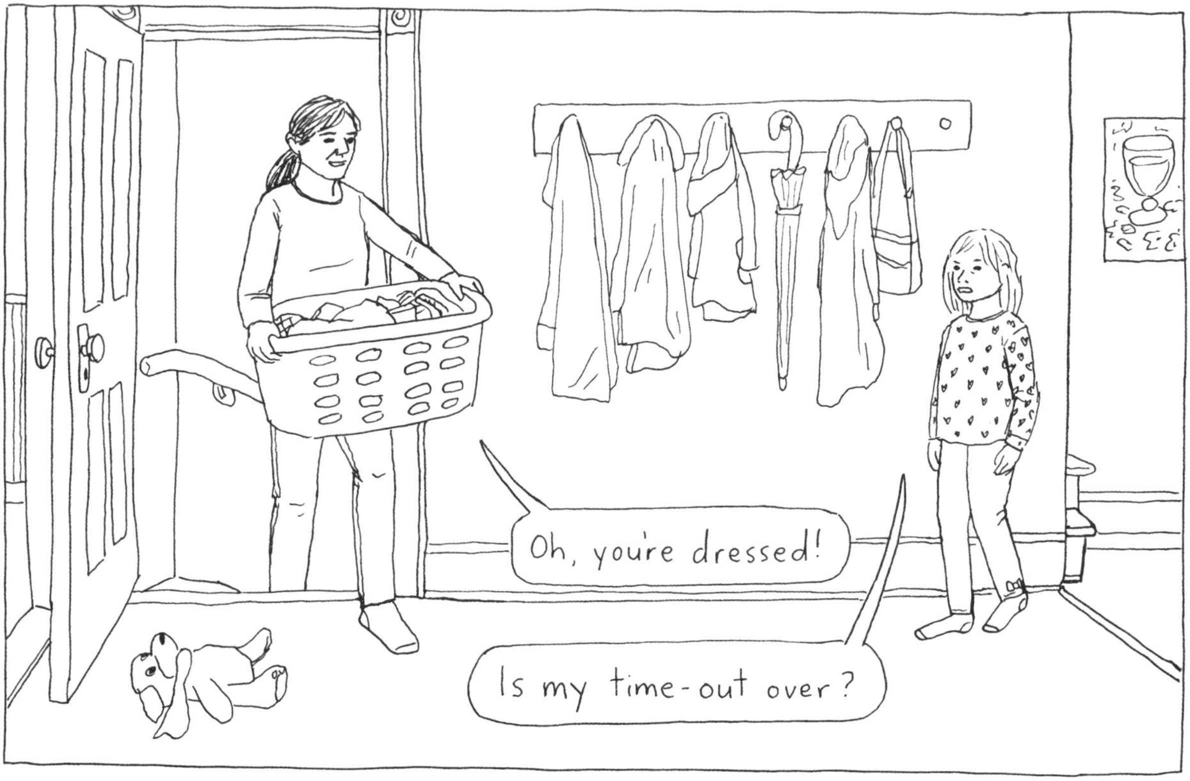
Oh, you're dressed!
Is my time-out over?

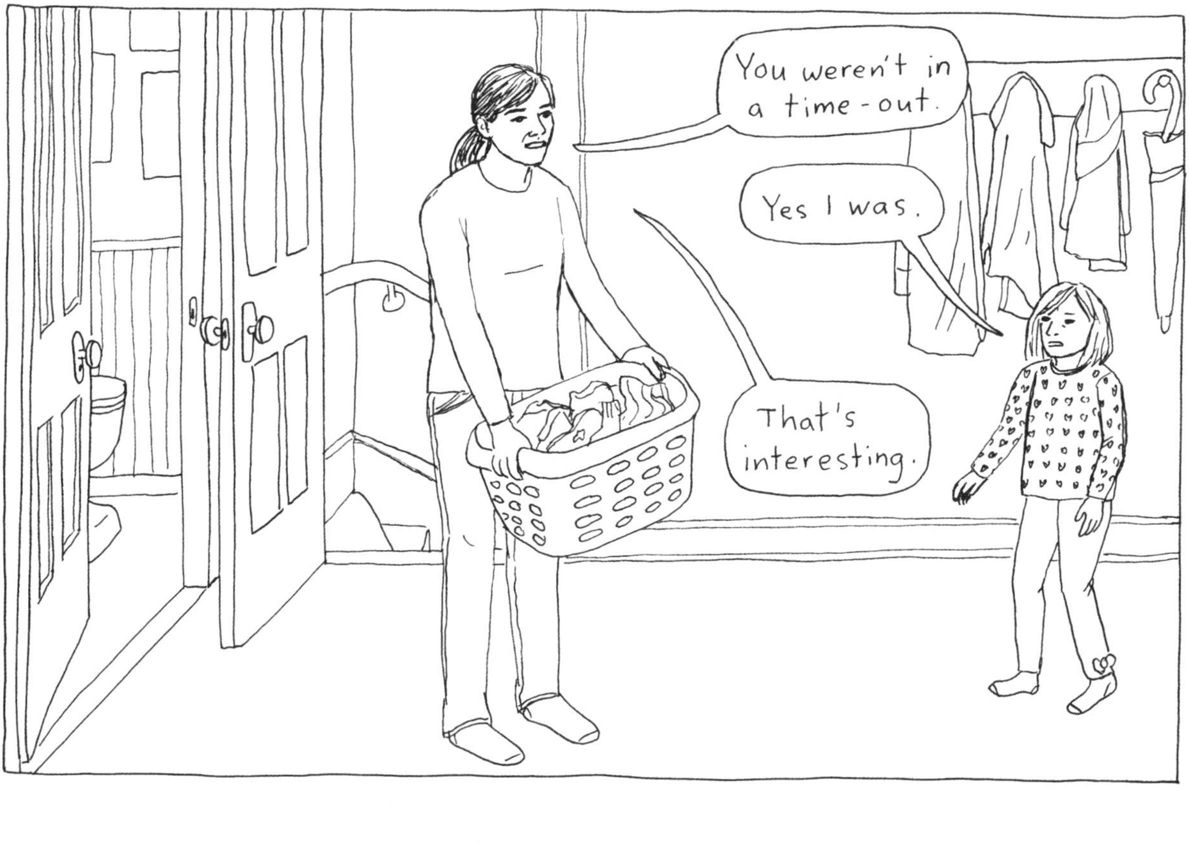
You weren't in a time-out.
Yes I was.
That's interesting.

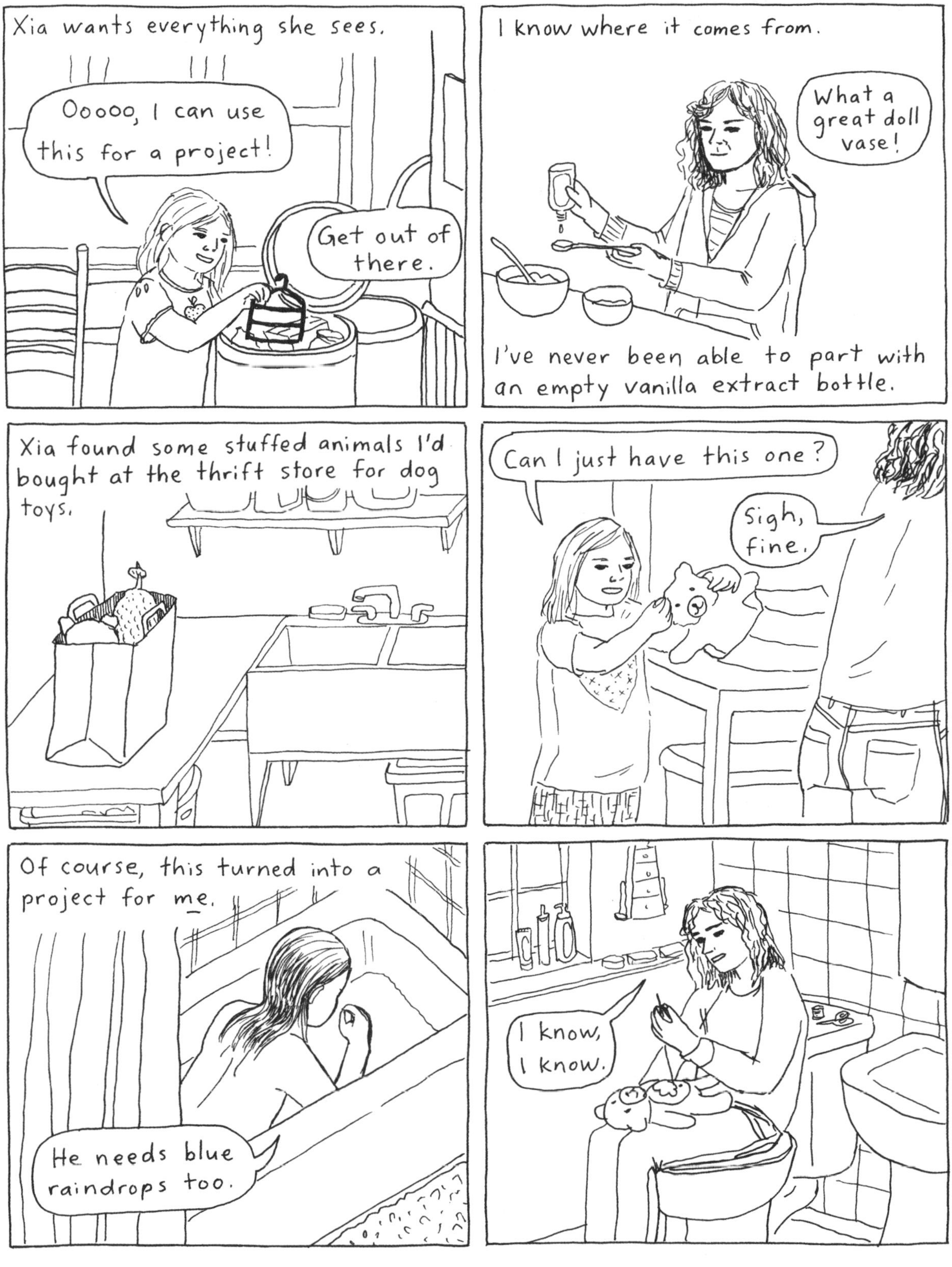
Xia wants everything she sees.
Ooooo, I can use this for a project!
Get out of there.
I know where it comes from.
What a great doll vase!
I've never been able to part with an empty vanilla extract bottle.
Xia found some stuffed animals I'd bought at the thrift store for dog toys.
Can I just have this one?
Sigh, fine.
Of course, this turned into a project for me.
He needs blue raindrops too.
I know, I know.

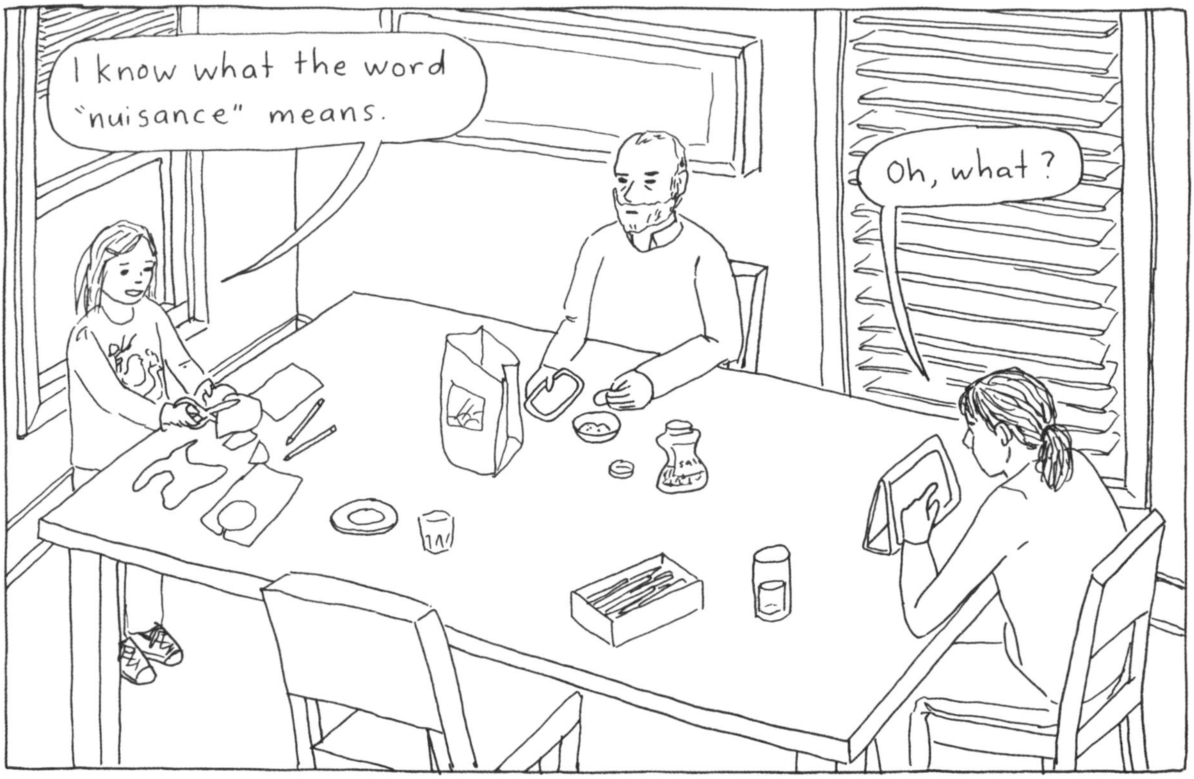
I know what the word "nuisance" means.
Oh, what?
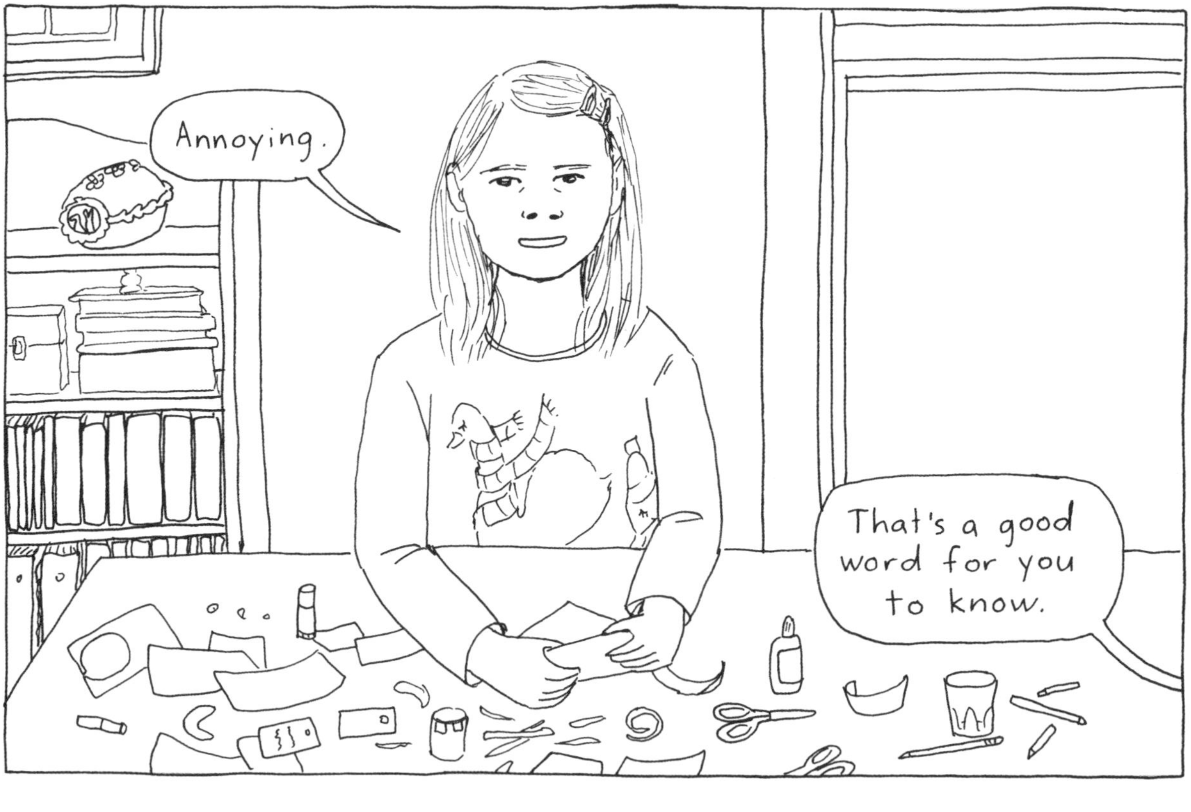
Annoying.
That's a good word for you to know.

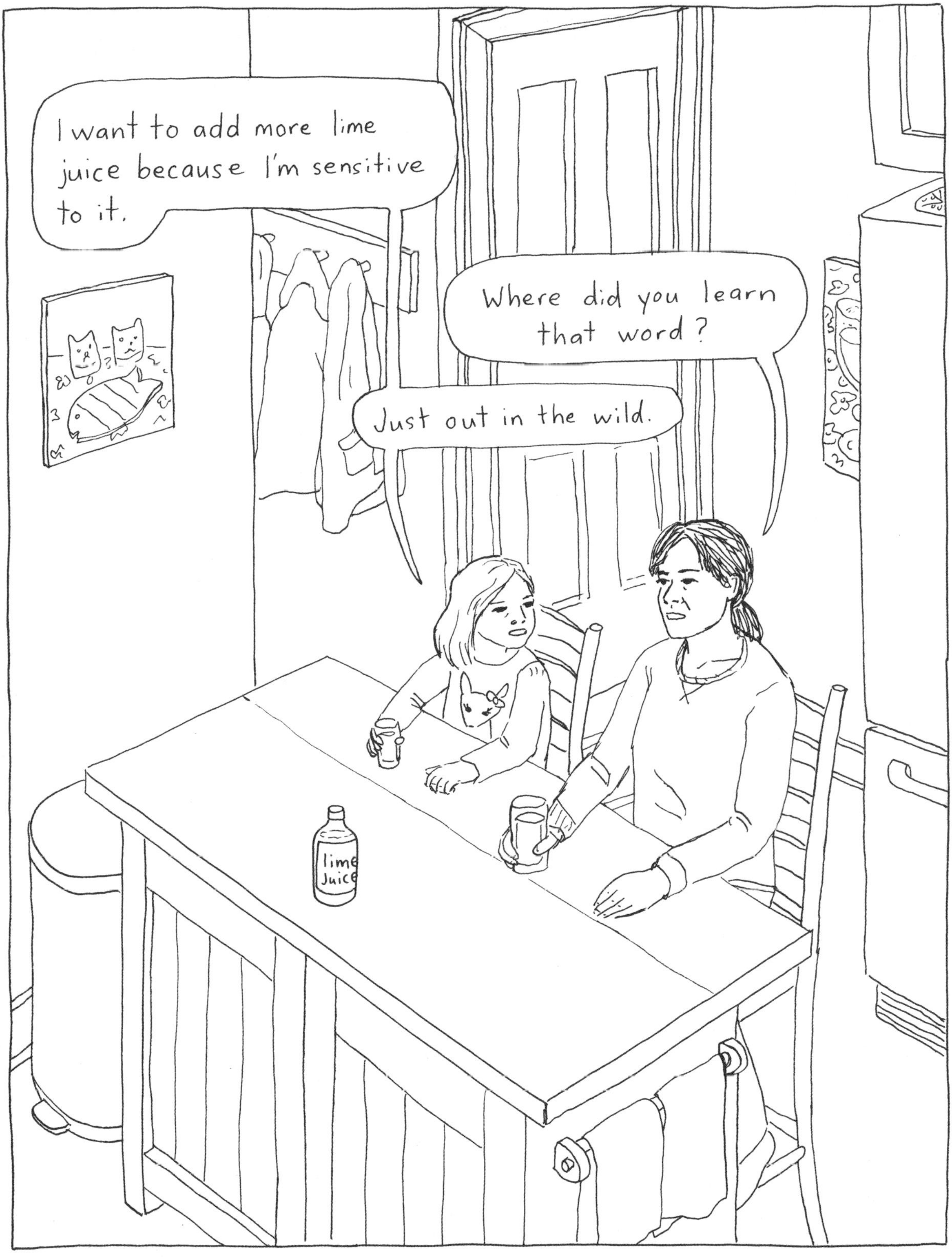
I want to add more lime juice because I'm sensitive to it.
Where did you learn that word?
Just out in the wild.
lime Juice

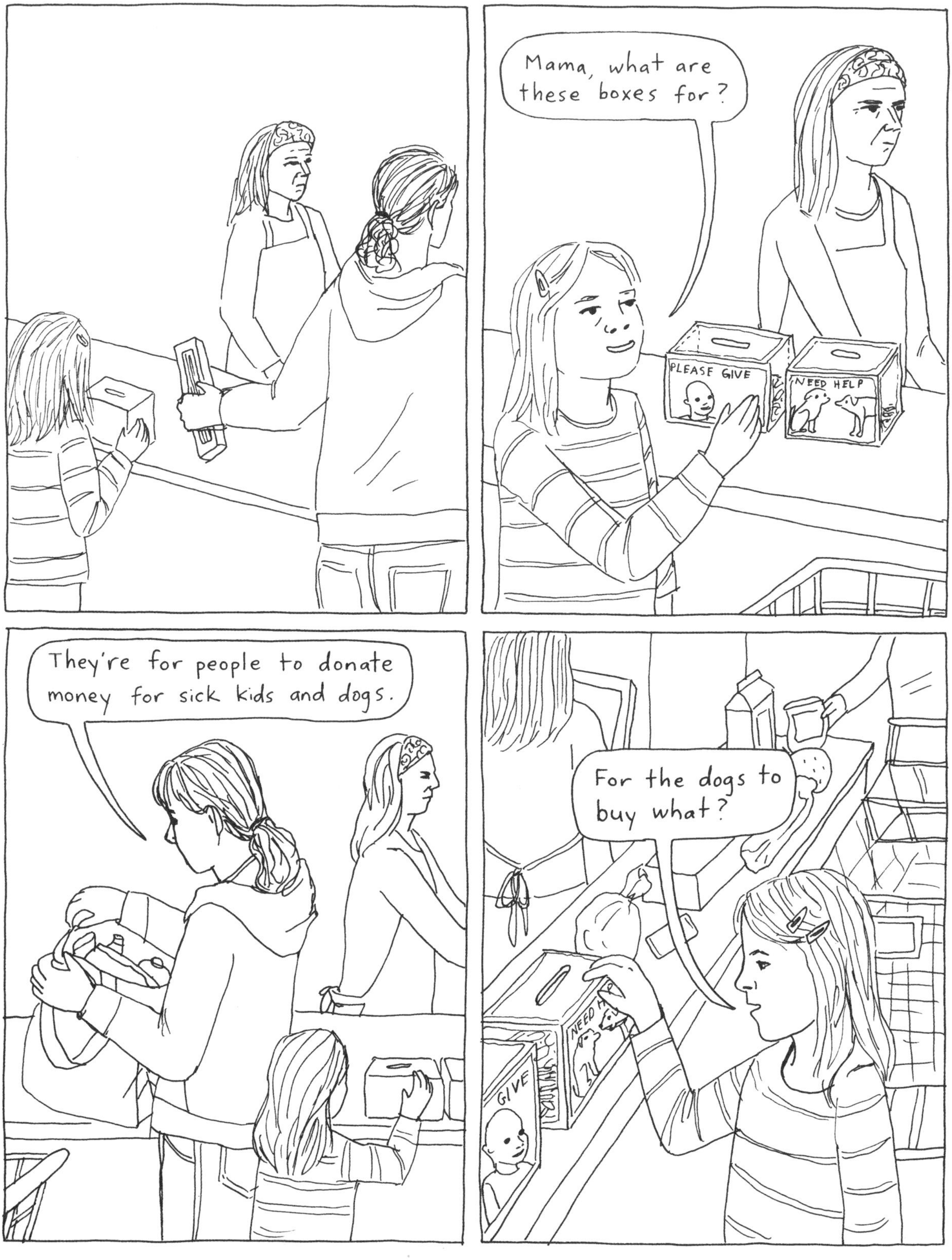
Mama, what are these boxes for?
PLEASE GIVE
NEED HELP
They're for people to donate money for sick kids and dogs.
For the dogs to buy what?
GIVE

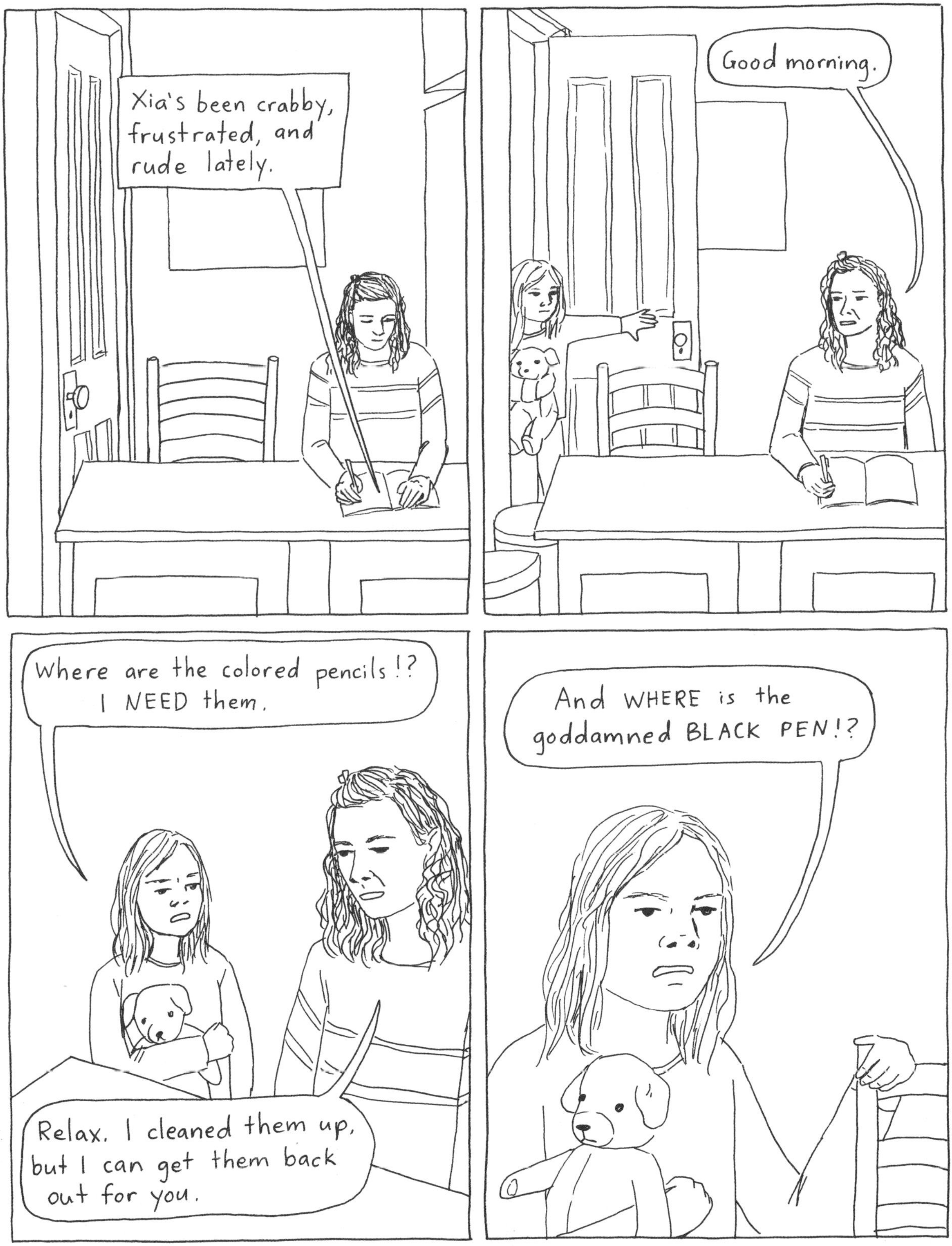
Xia's been crabby, frustrated, and rude lately.
Good morning.
Where are the colored pencils!? I NEED them.
Relax. I cleaned them up, but I can get them back out for you.
And WHERE is the goddamned BLACK PEN!?

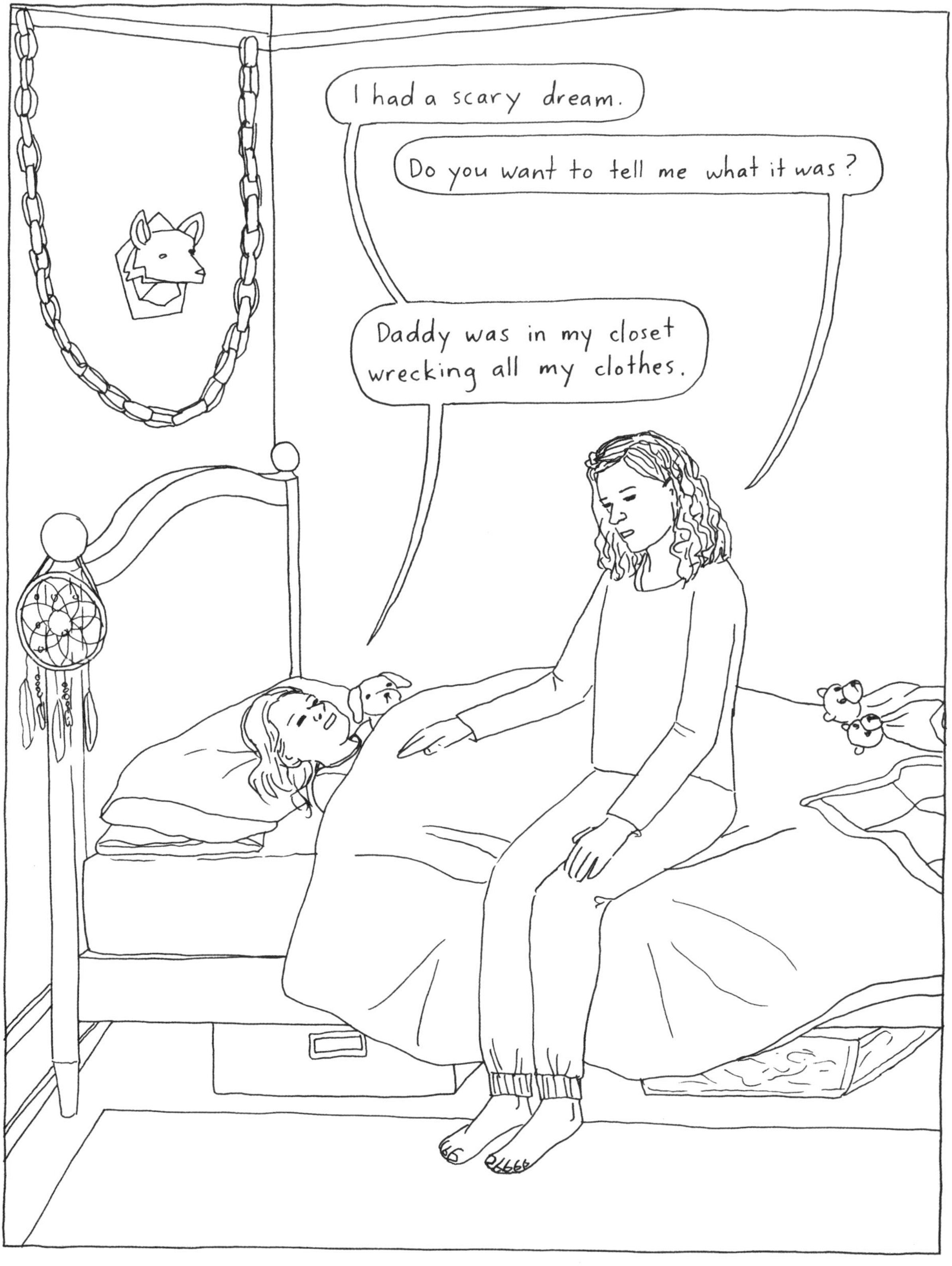
I had a scary dream.
Do you want to tell me what it was?
Daddy was in my closet wrecking all my clothes.

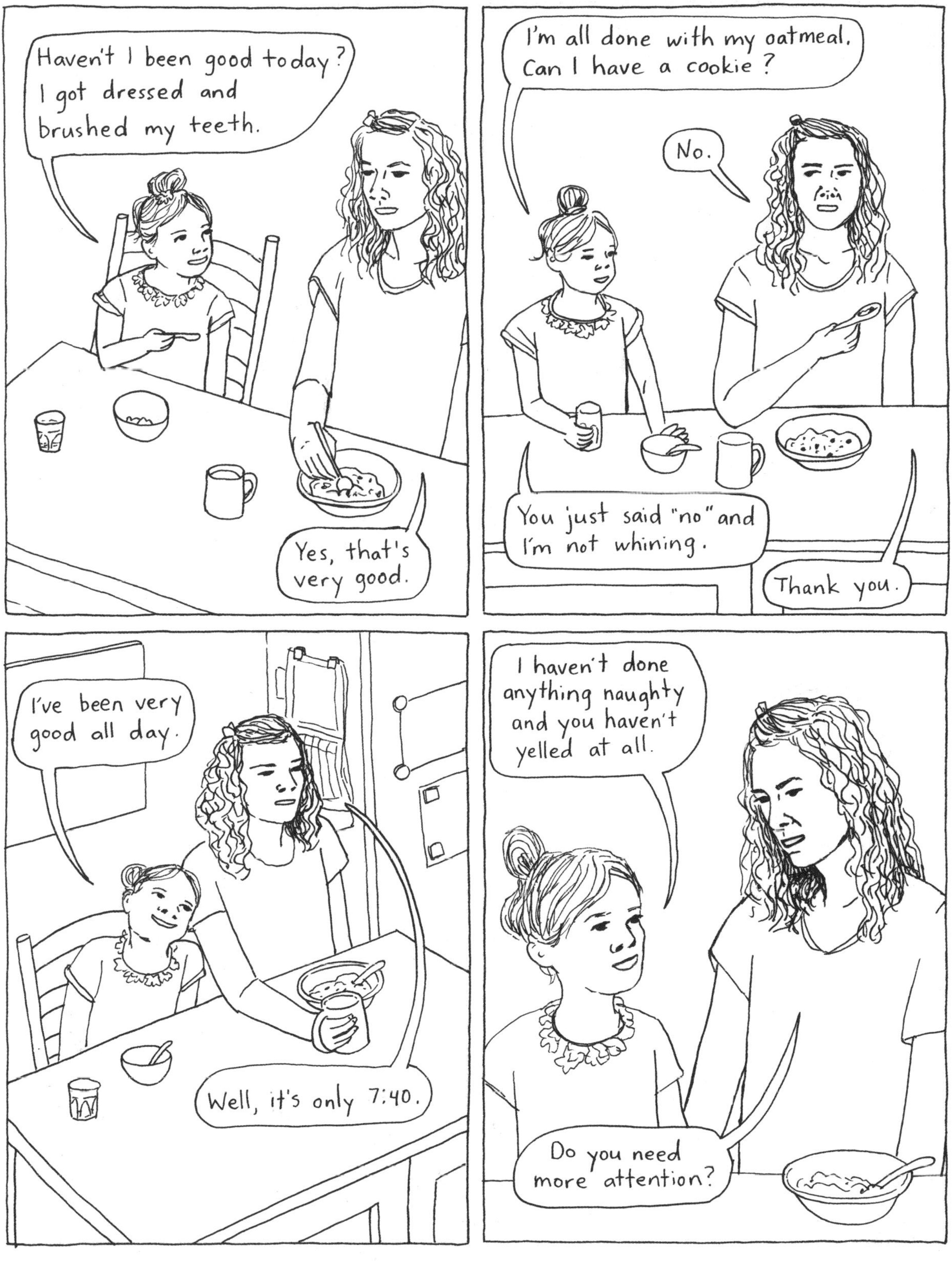
Haven't I been good today? I got dressed and brushed my teeth.
Yes, that's very good.
I'm all done with my oatmeal. Can I have a cookie?
No.
You just said "no" and I'm not whining.
Thank you.
I've been very good all day.
Well, it's only 7:40.
I haven't done anything naughty and you haven't yelled at all.
Do you need more attention?

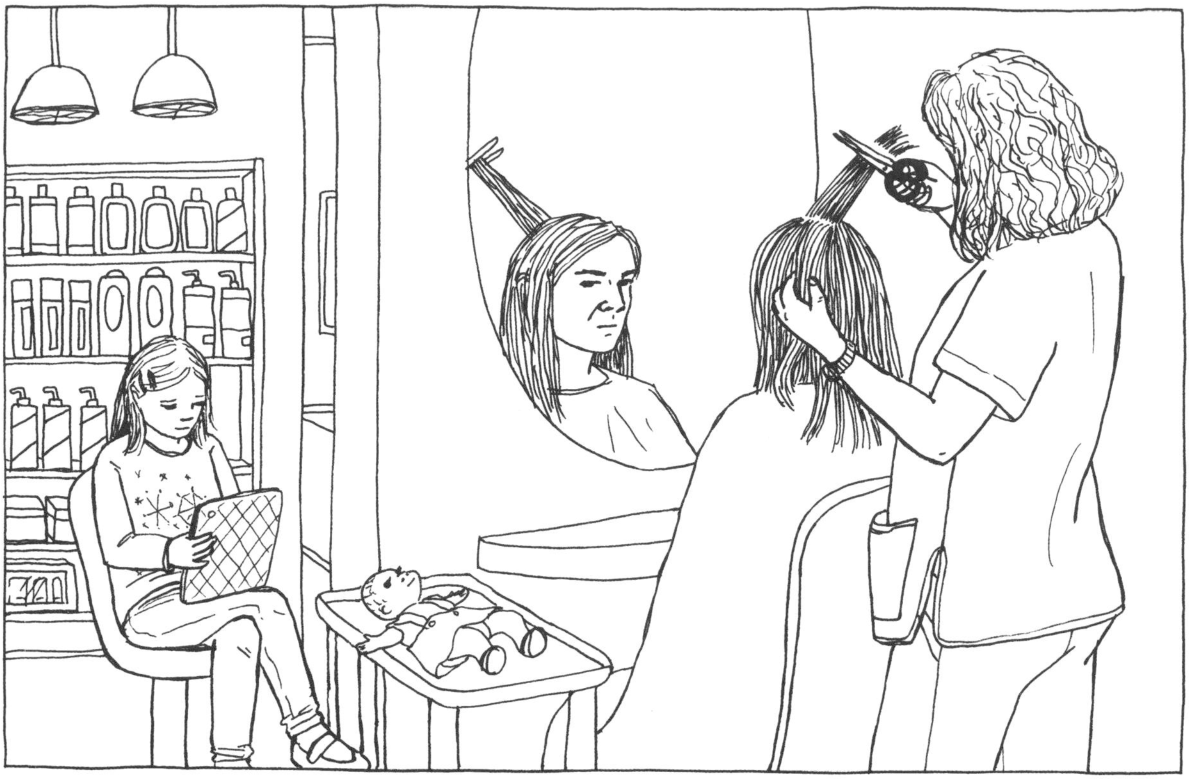

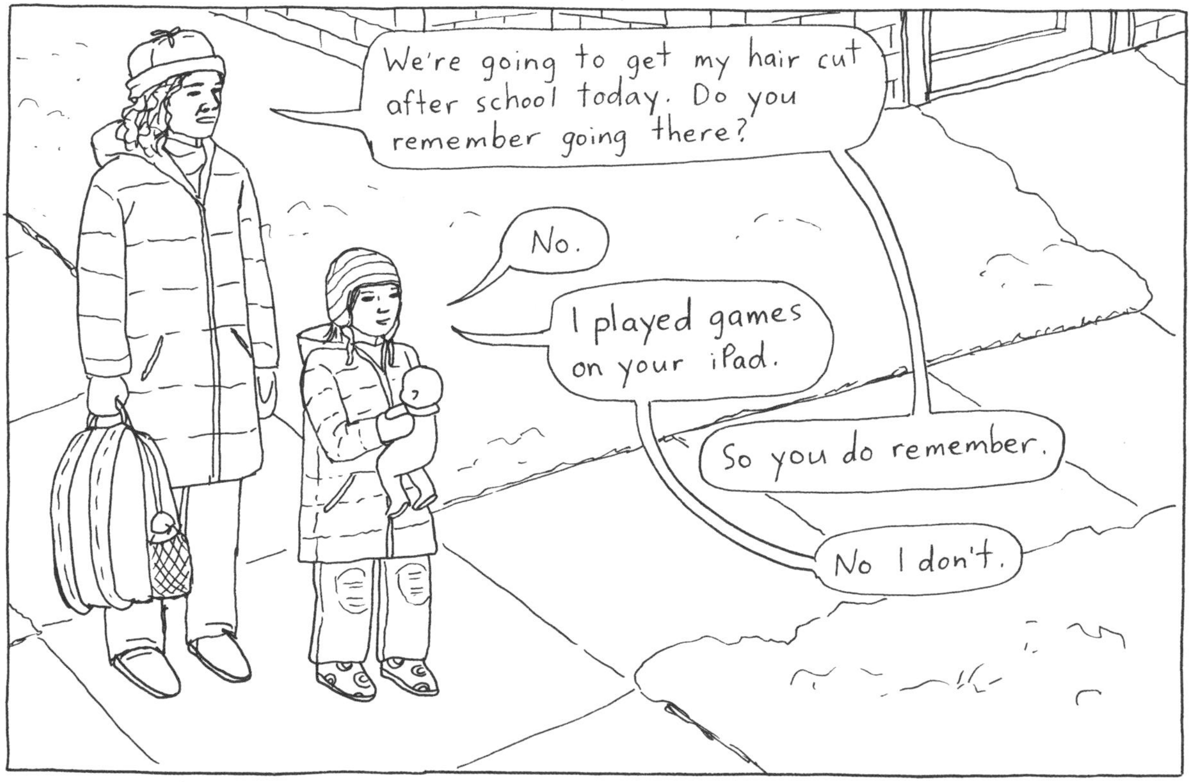
We're going to get my hair cut after school today. Do you remember going there?
No.
I played games on your iPad.
So you do remember.
No I don't.

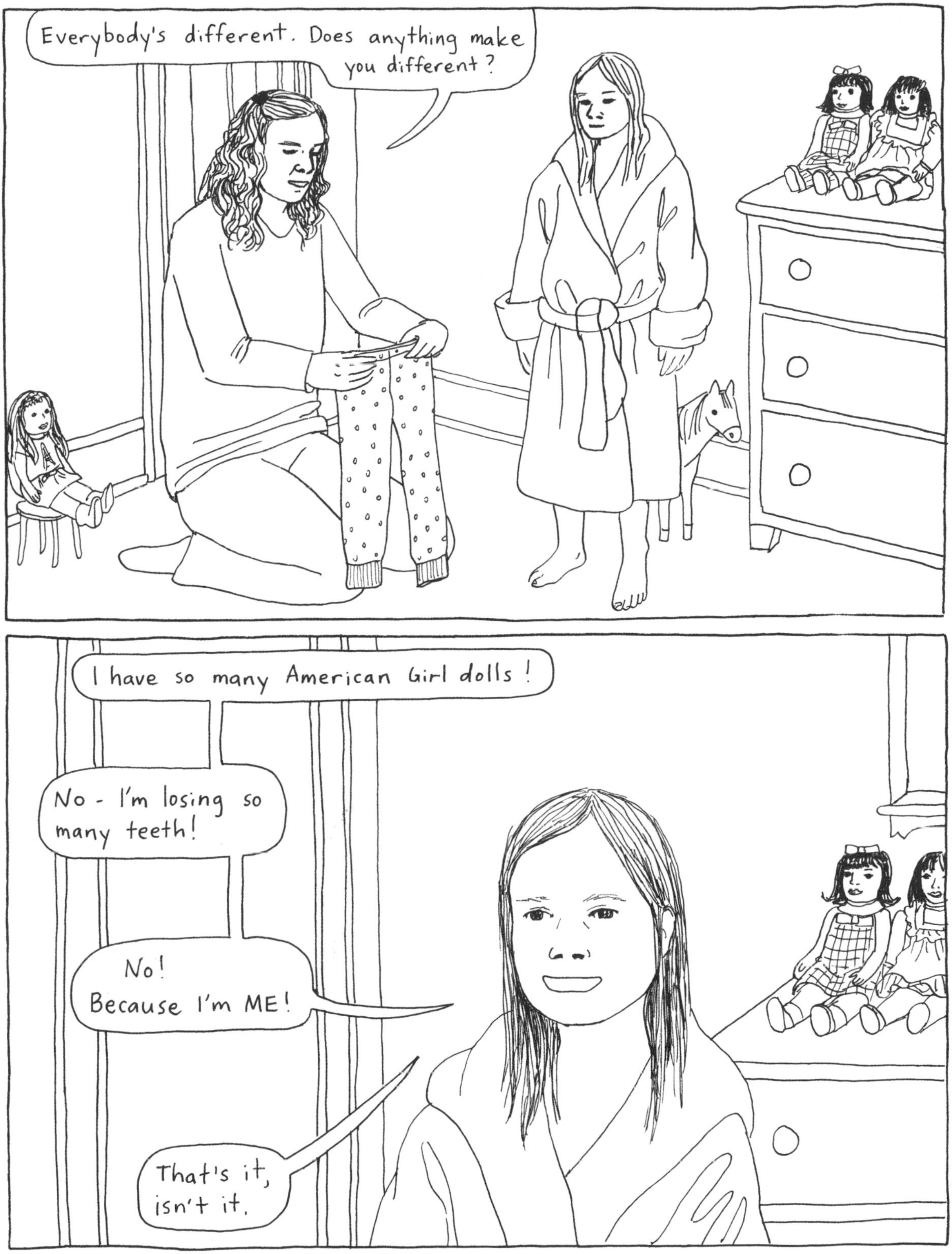
Everybody's different. Does anything make you different?
I have so many American Girl dolls!
No - I'm losing so many teeth!
No! Because I'm ME!
That's it, isn't it.

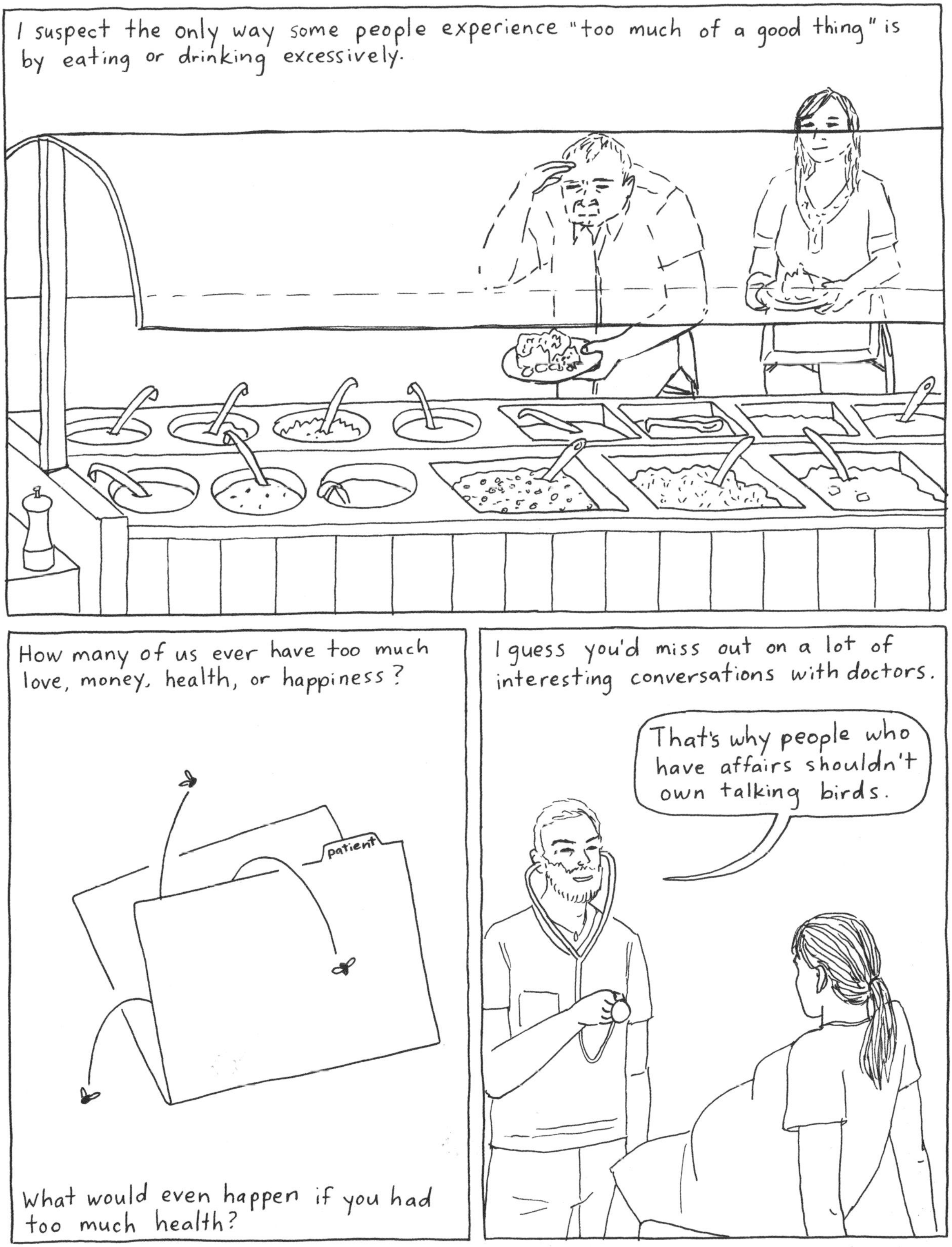
I suspect the only way some people experience "too much of a good thing" is by eating or drinking excessively.
How many of us ever have too much love, money, health, or happiness?
patient
What would even happen if you had too much health?
I guess you'd miss out on a lot of interesting conversations with doctors.
That's why people who have affairs shouldn't own talking birds.

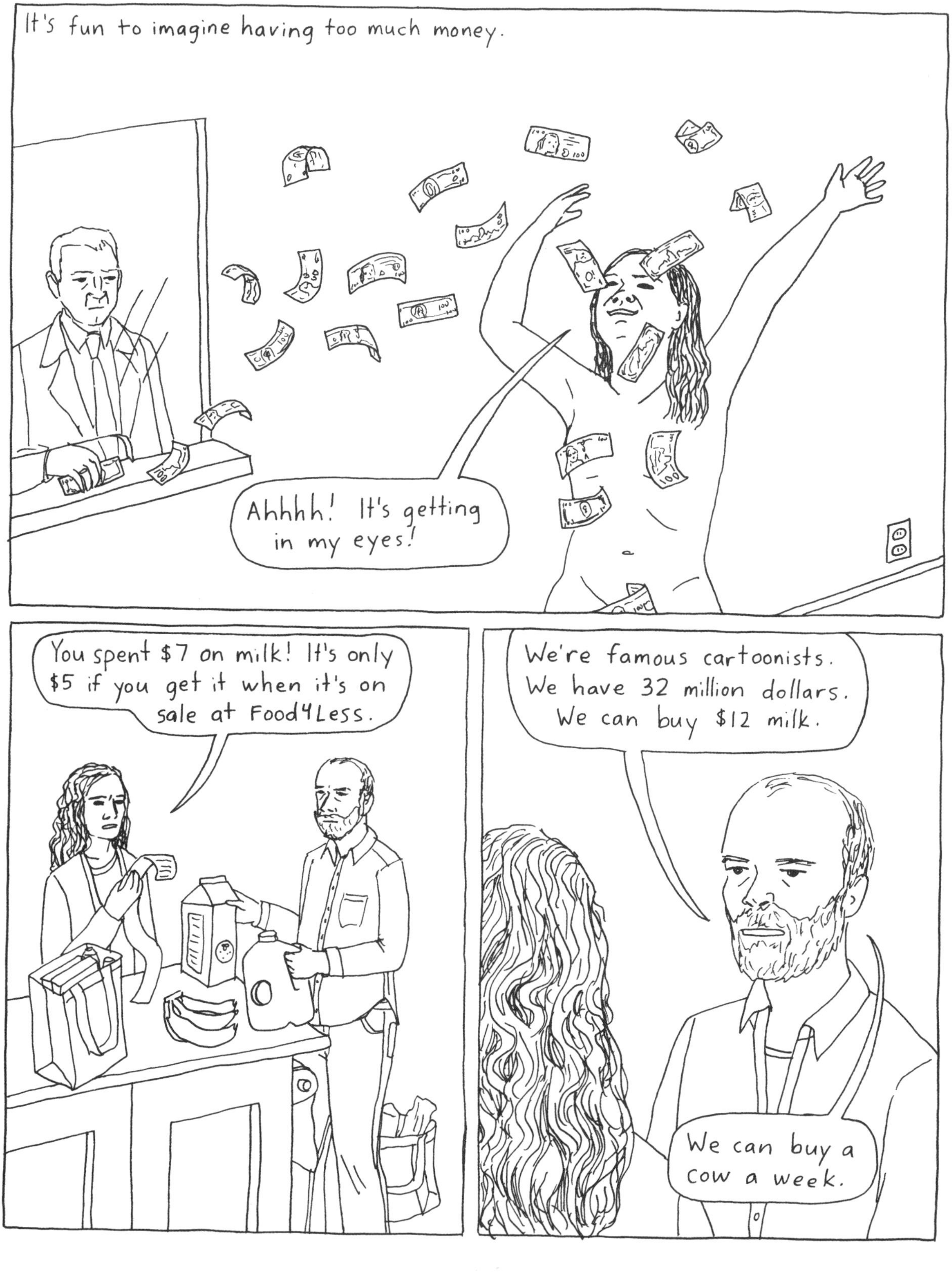
It's fun to imagine having too much money.
Ahhhh! It's getting in my eyes!
You spent $7 on milk! It's only $5 if you get it when it's on sale at Food4Less.
We're famous cartoonists. We have 32 million dollars. We can buy $12 milk.
We can buy a cow a week.

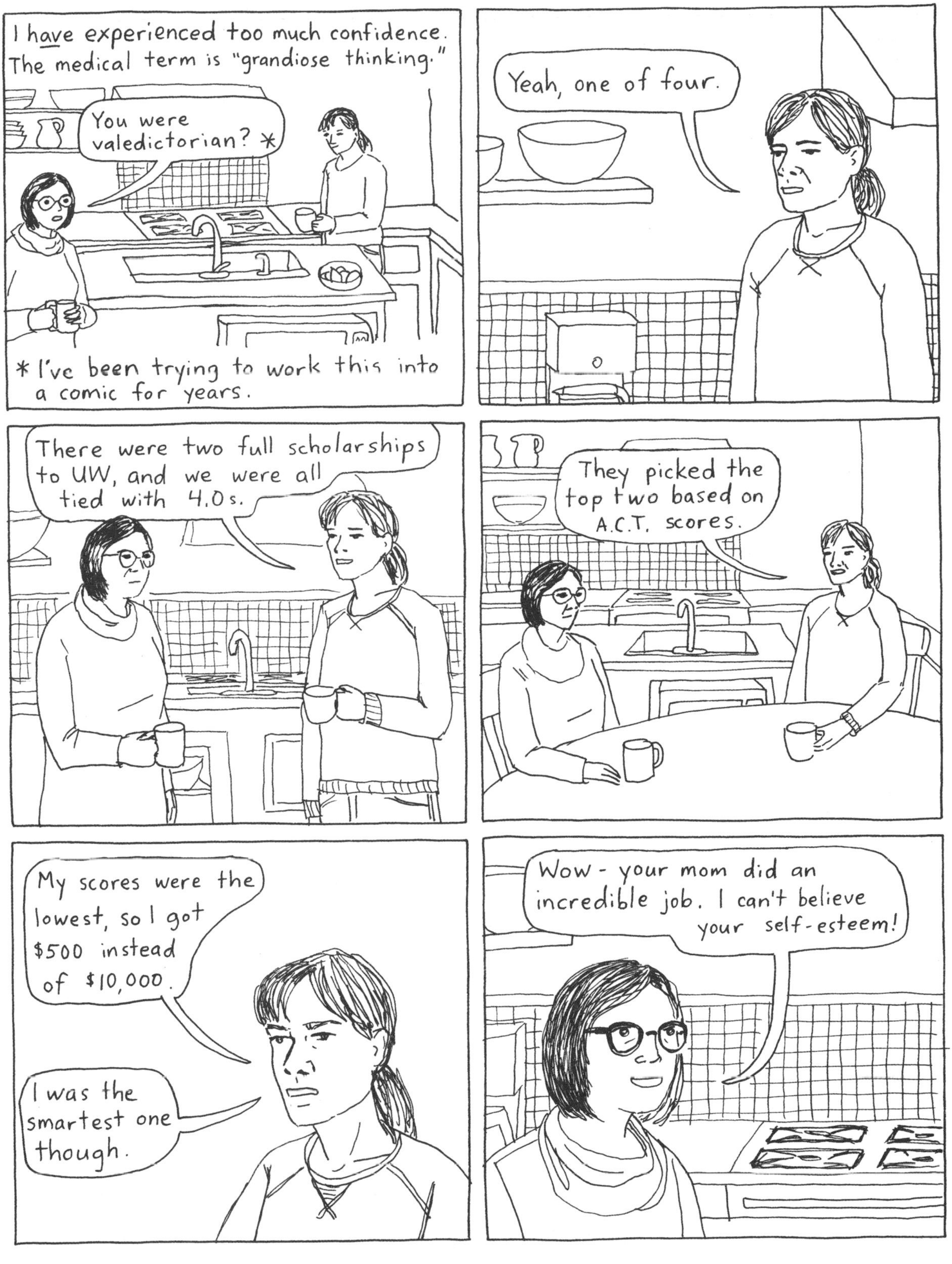
I have experienced too much confidence. The medical term is "grandiose thinking."
You were valedictorian? *
* I've been trying to work this into a comic for years.
Yeah, one of four.
There were two full scholarships to UW, and we were all tied with 4.0s.
They picked the top two based on A.C.T. scores.
My scores were the lowest, so I got $500 instead of $10,000.
I was the smartest one though.
Wow - your mom did an incredible job. I can't believe your self-esteem!

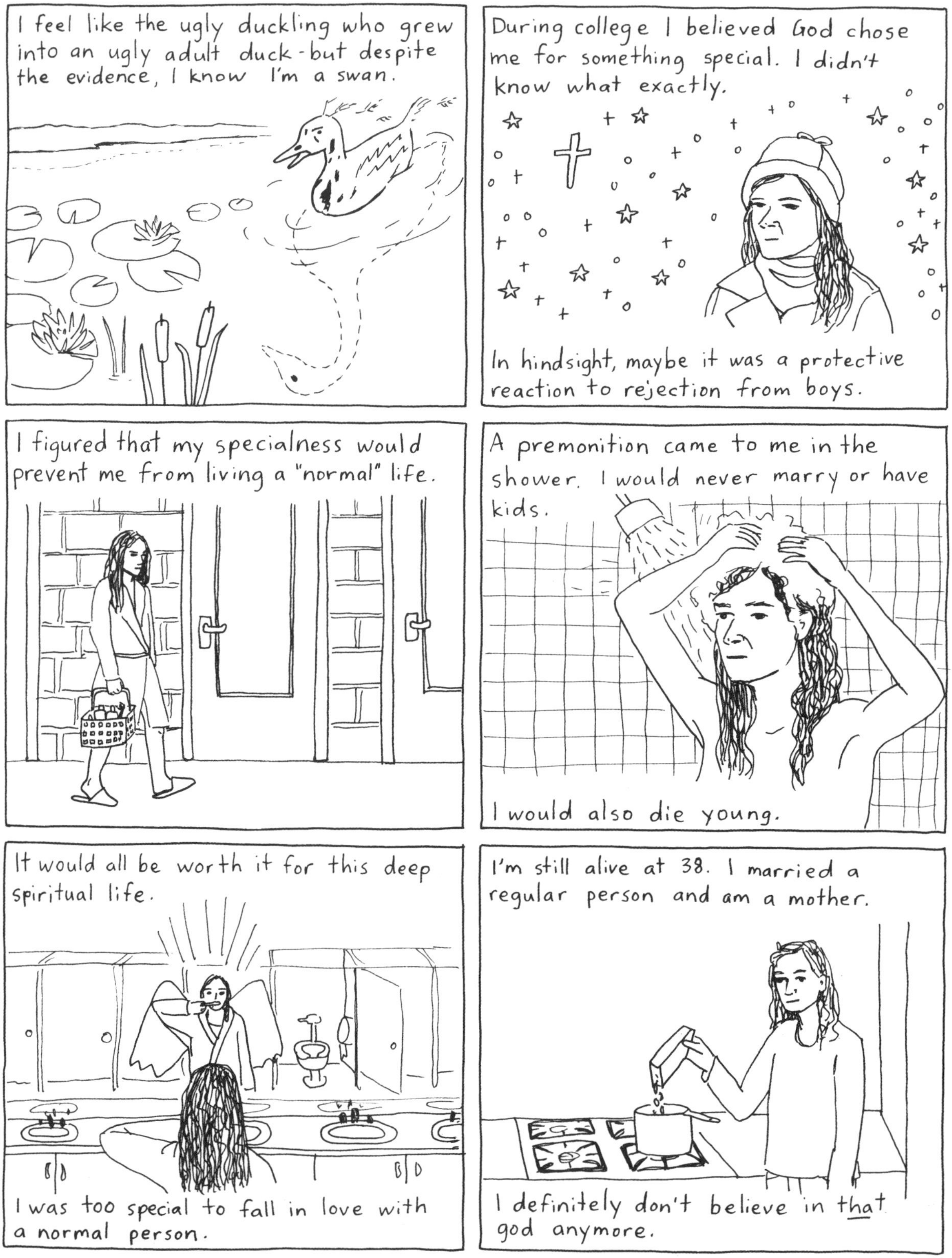
I feel like the ugly duckling who grew into an ugly adult duck - but despite the evidence, I know I'm a swan.
During college I believed God chose me for something special. I didn't know what exactly.
In hindsight, maybe it was a protective reaction to rejection from boys.
I figured that my specialness would prevent me from living a "normal" life.
A premonition came to me in the shower. I would never marry or have kids.
I would also die young.
It would all be worth it for this deep spiritual life.
I was too special to fall in love with a normal person.
I'm still alive at 38. I married a regular person and am a mother.
I definitely don't believe in that god anymore.

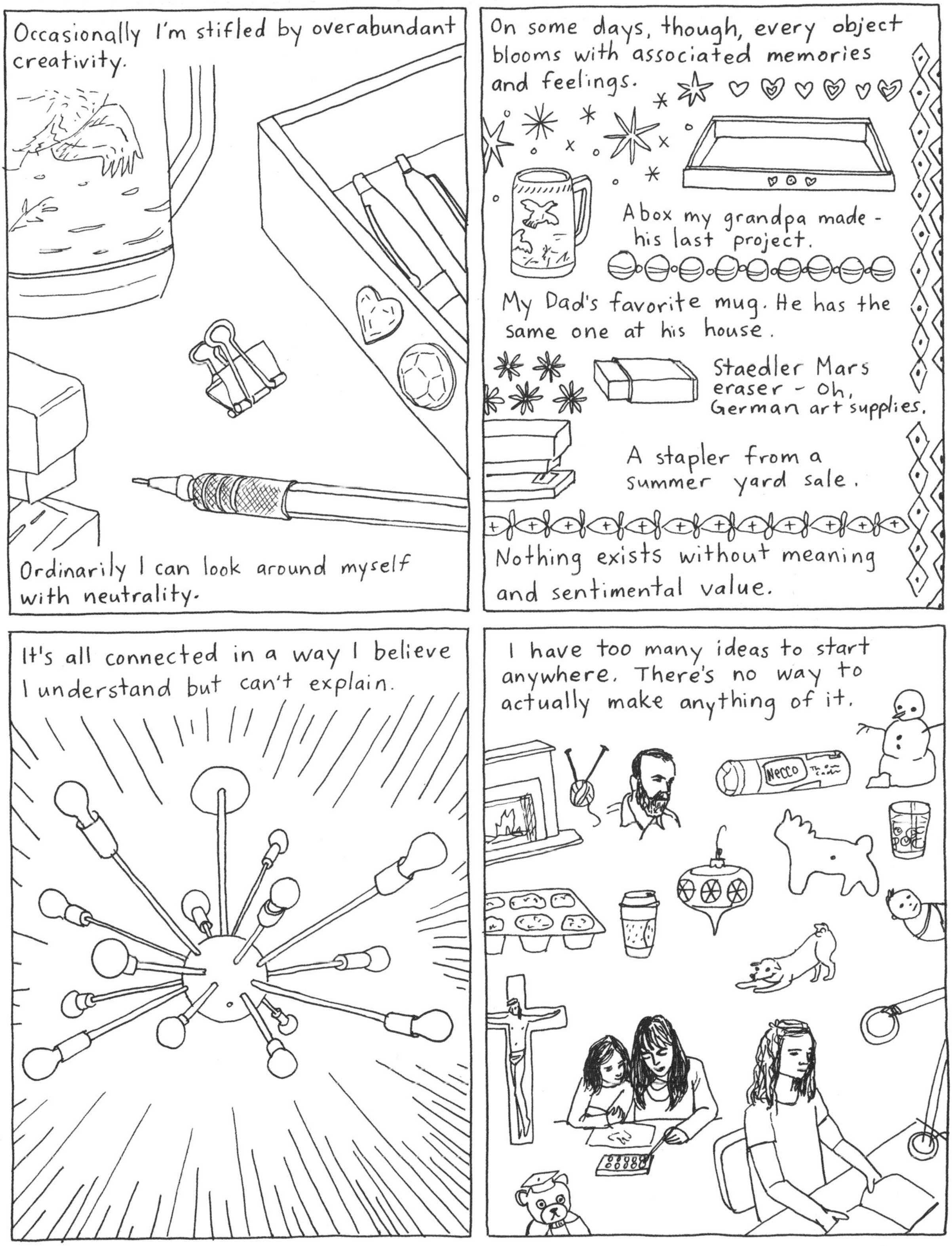
Occasionally I'm stifled by overabundant creativity.
Ordinarily I can look around myself with neutrality.
On some days, though, every object blooms with associated memories and feelings.
A box my grandpa made - his last project.
My Dad's favorite mug. He has the same one at his house.
Staedler Mars eraser - Oh, German art supplies.
A stapler from a summer yard sale.
Nothing exists without meaning and sentimental value.
It's all connected in a way I believe I understand but can't explain.
I have too many ideas to start anywhere. There's no way to actually make anything of it.
Necco

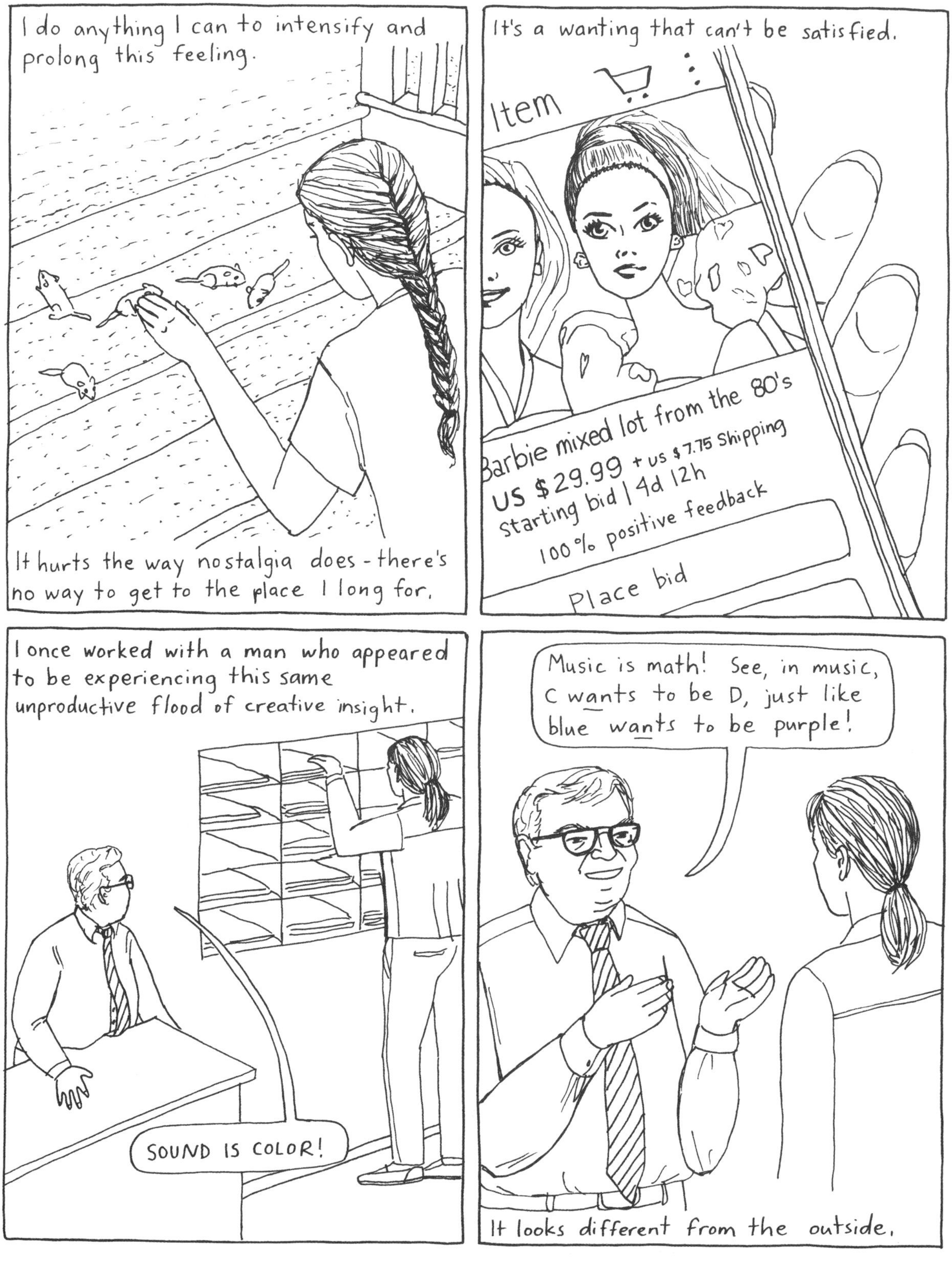

I do anything I can to intensify and prolong this feeling.
It hurts the way nostalgia does - there's no way to get to the place I long for.
It's a wanting that can't be satisfied.
Item
Barbie mixed lot from the 80's
US $29.99 + US $7.75 Shipping
Starting bid | 4d 12h
100% positive feedback
Place bid
I once worked with a man who appeared to be experiencing this same unproductive flood of creative insight.
SOUND IS COLOR!
Music is math! See, in music, C wants to be D, just like blue wants to be purple!
It looks different from the outside.

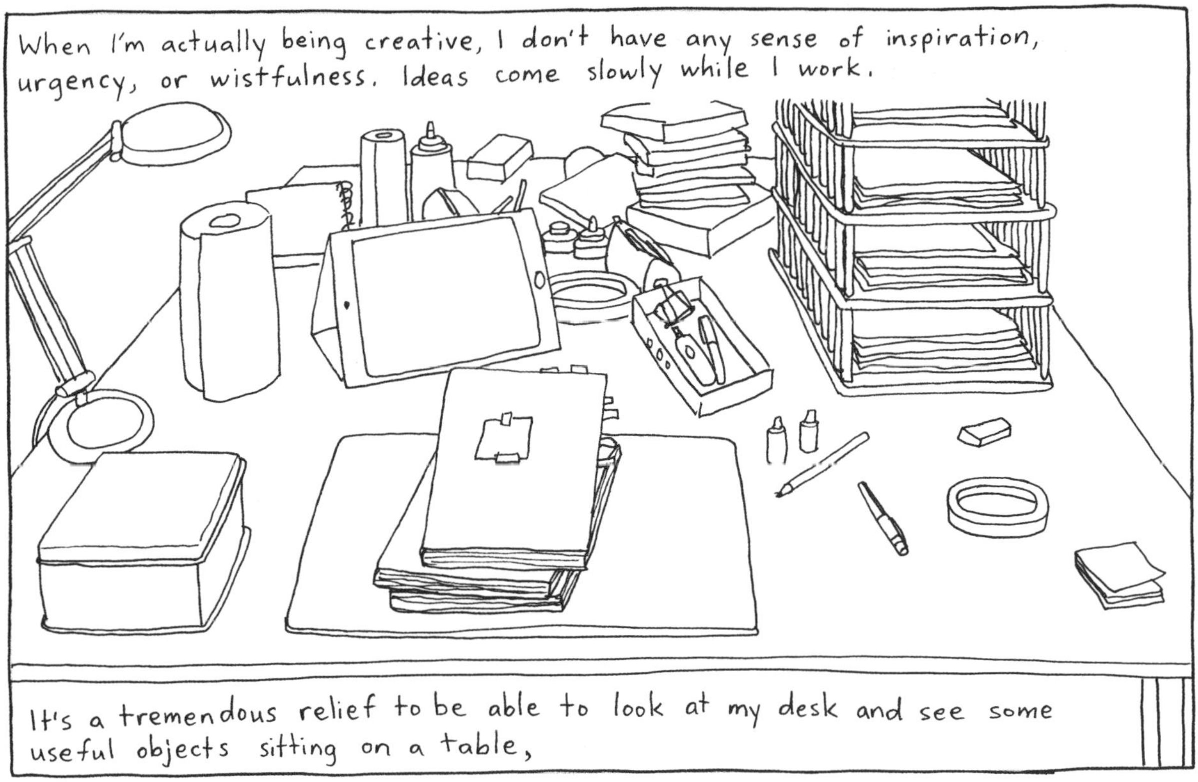
When I'm actually being creative, I don't have any sense of inspiration, urgency, or wistfulness. Ideas come slowly while I work.
It's a tremendous relief to be able to look at my desk and see some useful objects sitting on a table,

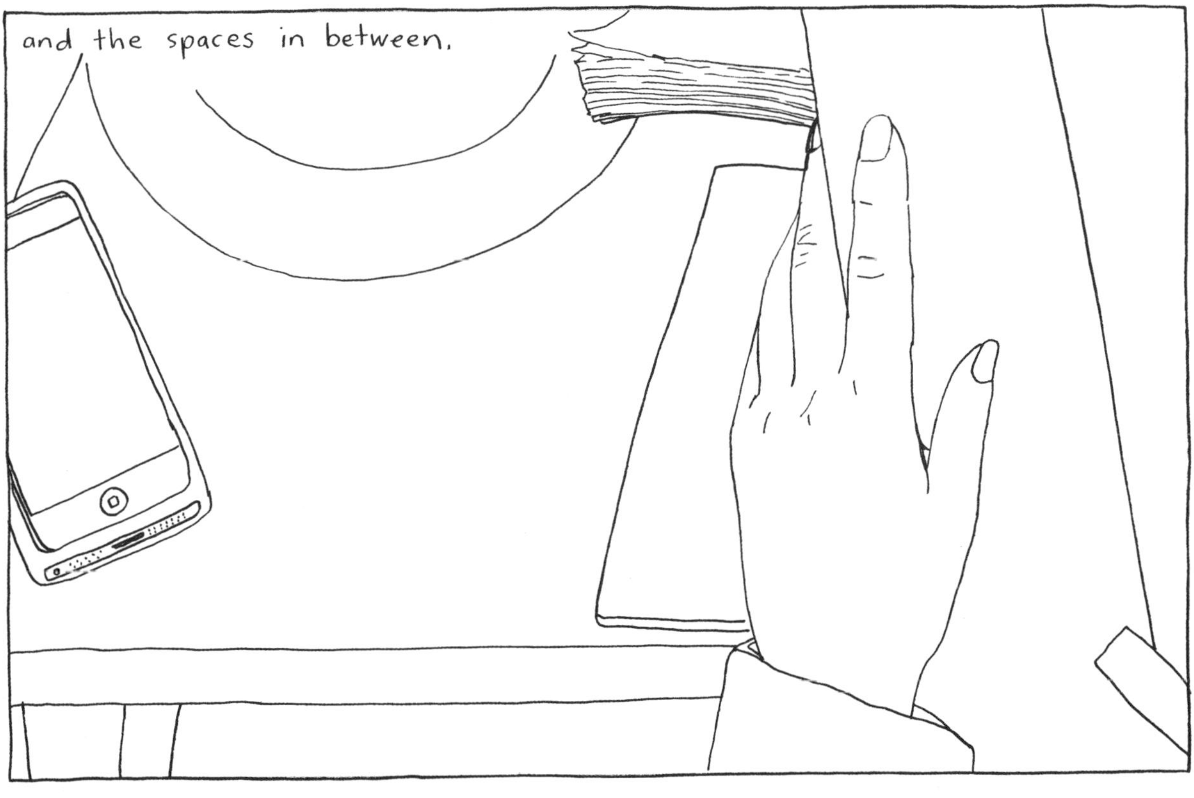
and the spaces in between.

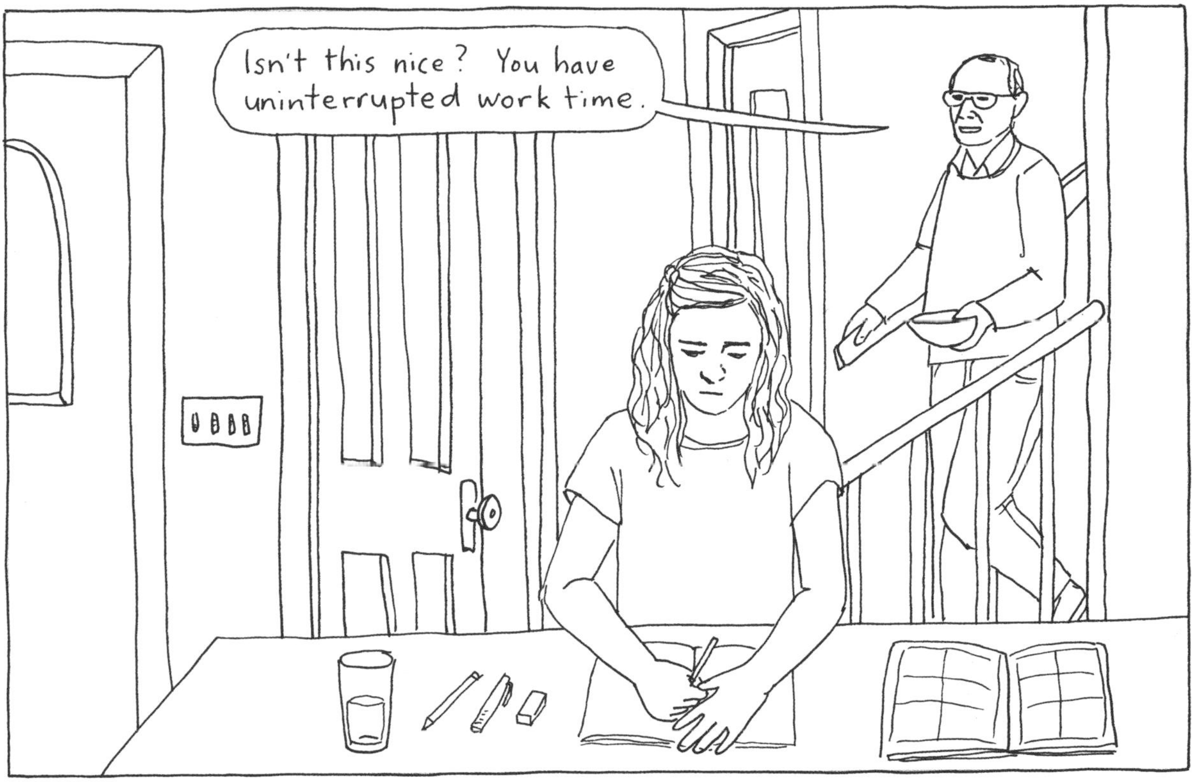
Isn't this nice? You have uninterrupted work time.

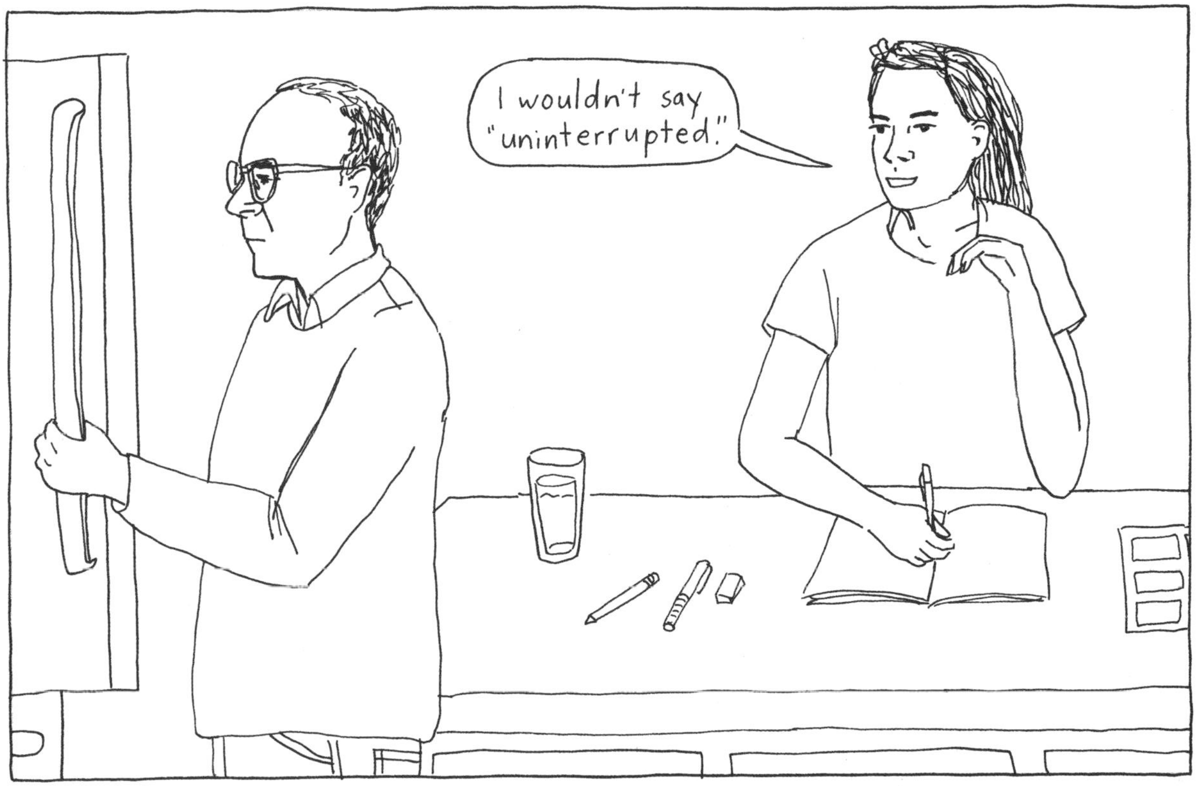
I wouldn't say "uninterrupted."

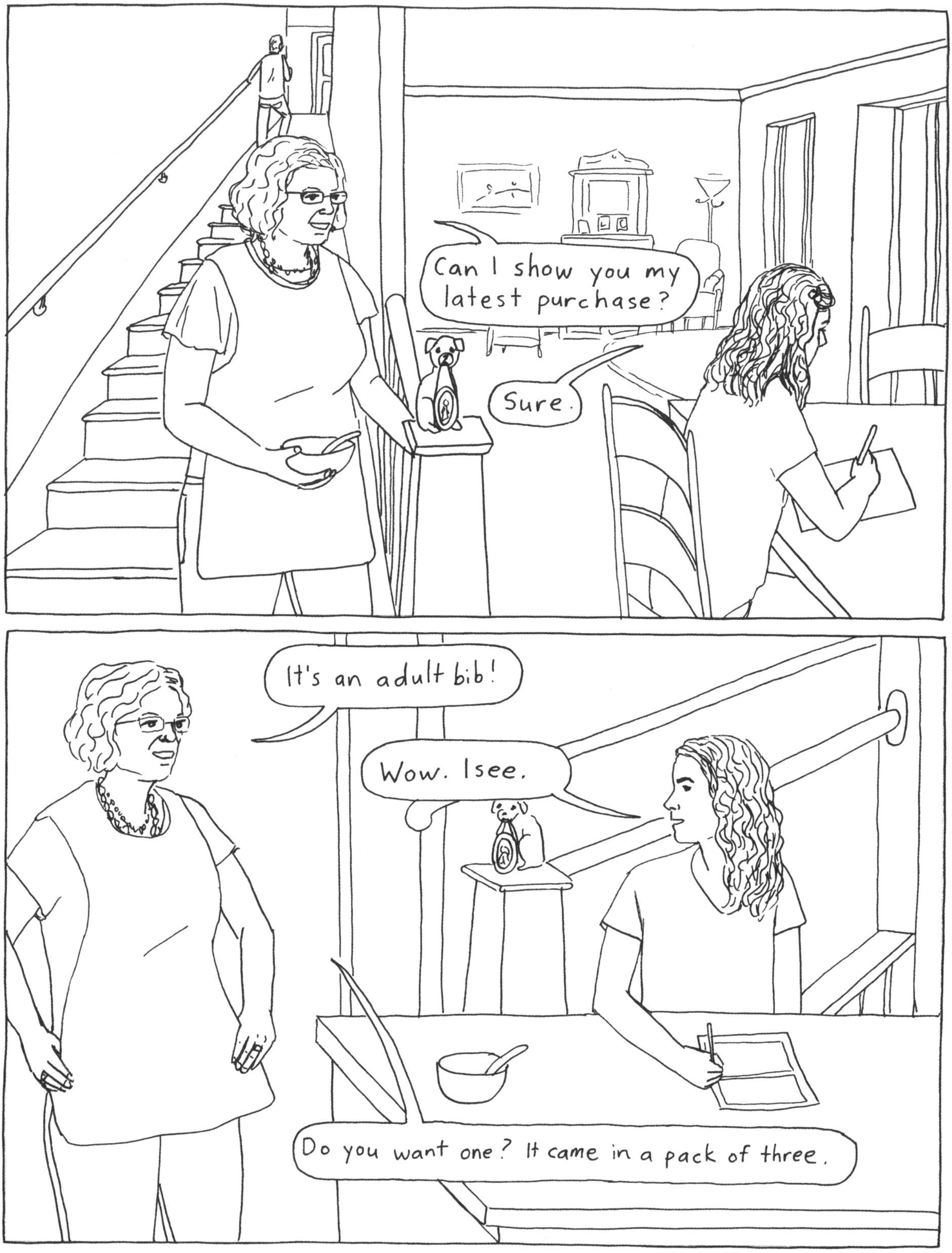
Can I show you my latest purchase?
Sure.
It's an adult bib!
Wow. Isee.
Do you want one? It came in a pack of three.

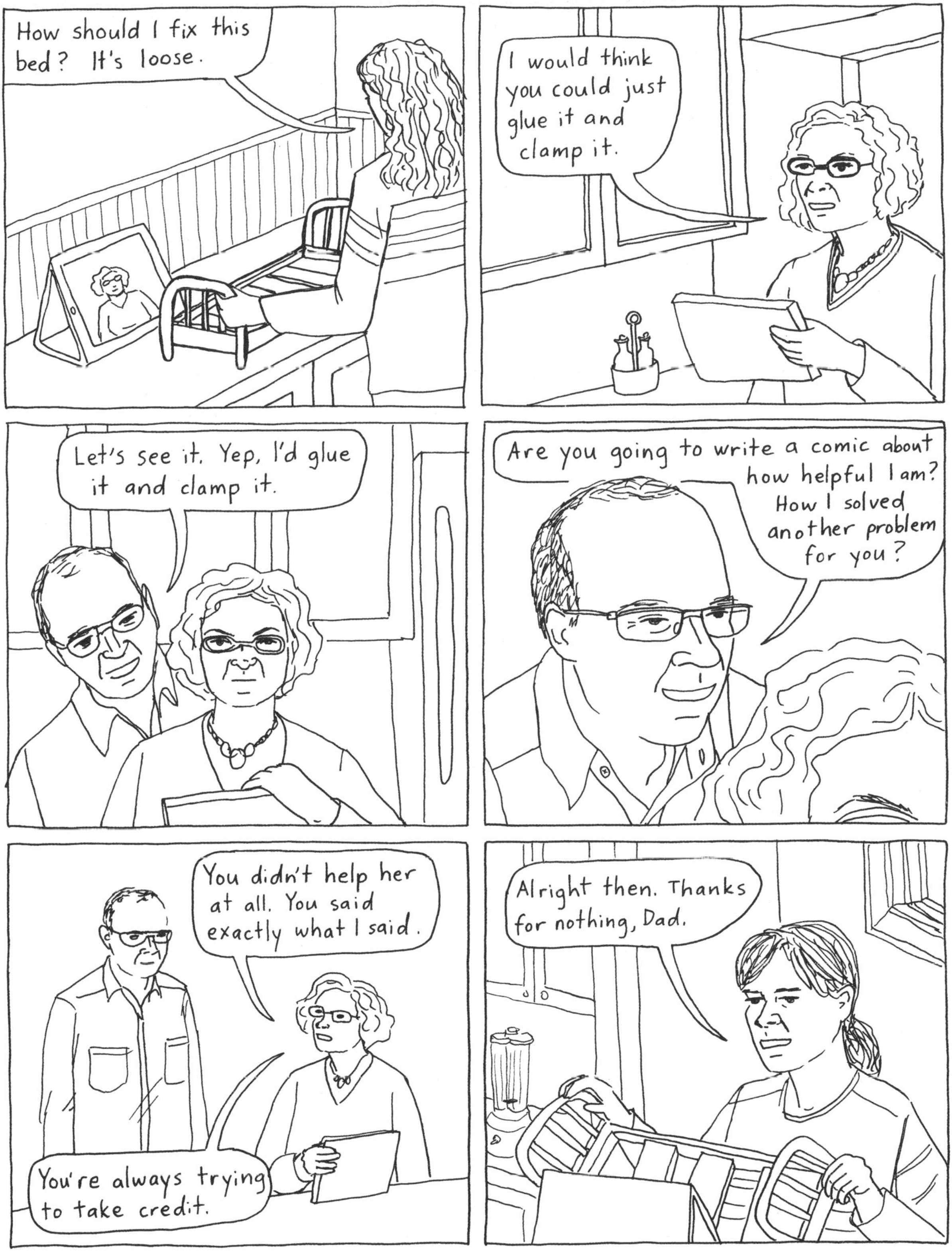
How should I fix this bed? It's loose.
I would think you could just glue it and clamp it.
Let's see it. Yep, I'd glue it and clamp it.
Are you going to write a comic about how helpful I am? How I solved another problem for you?
You didn't help her at all. You said exactly what I said.
You're always trying to take credit.
Alright then. Thanks for nothing, Dad.

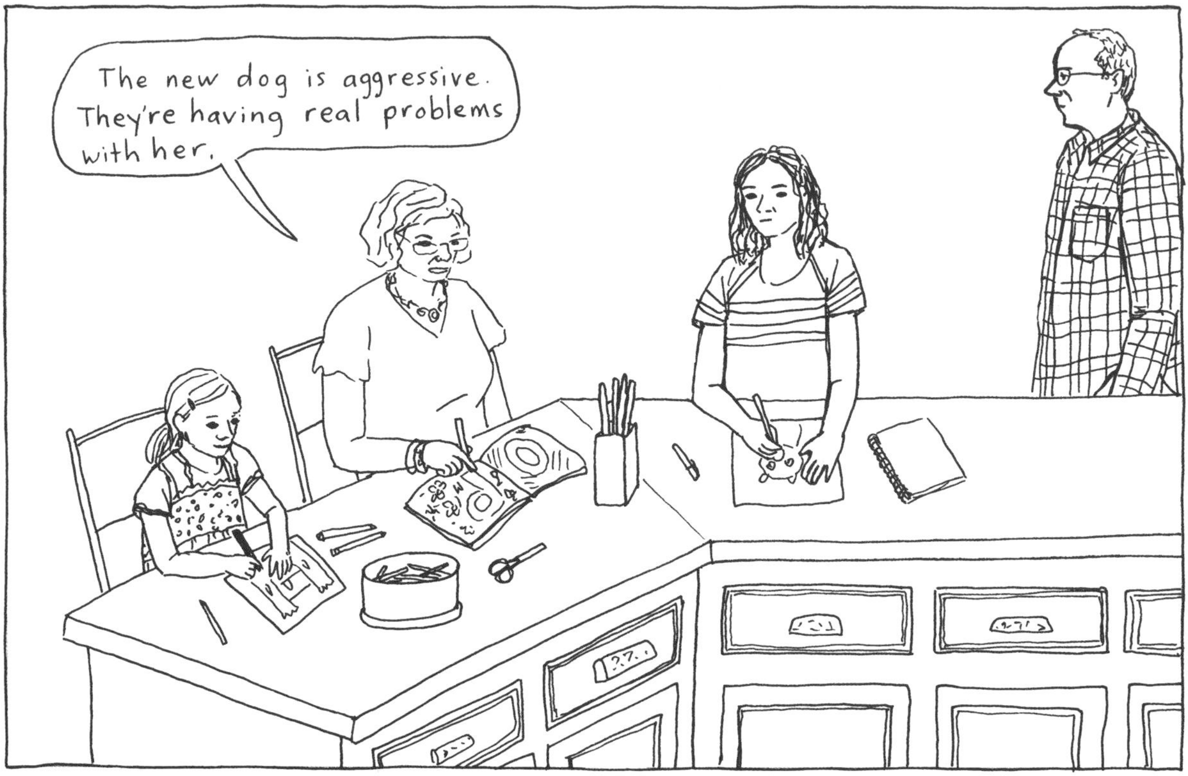
The new dog is aggressive. They're having real problems with her.

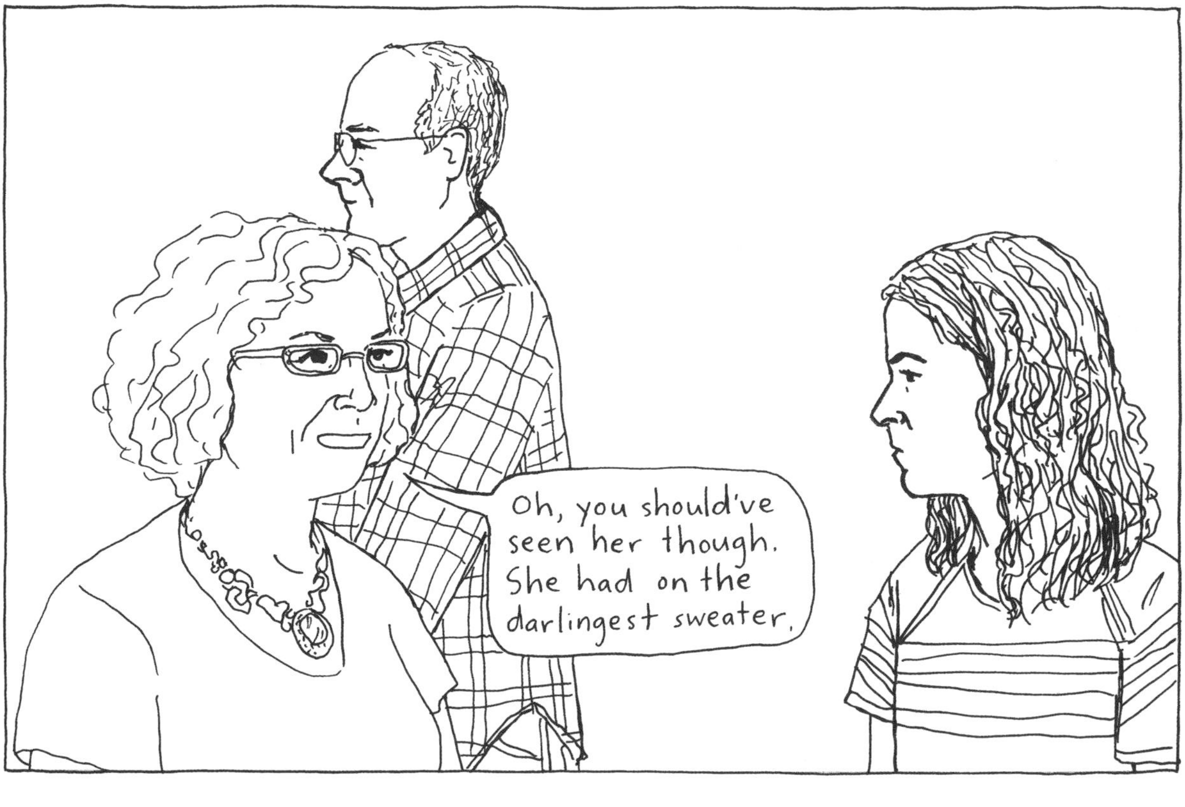
Oh, you should've seen her though. She had on the darlingest sweater.

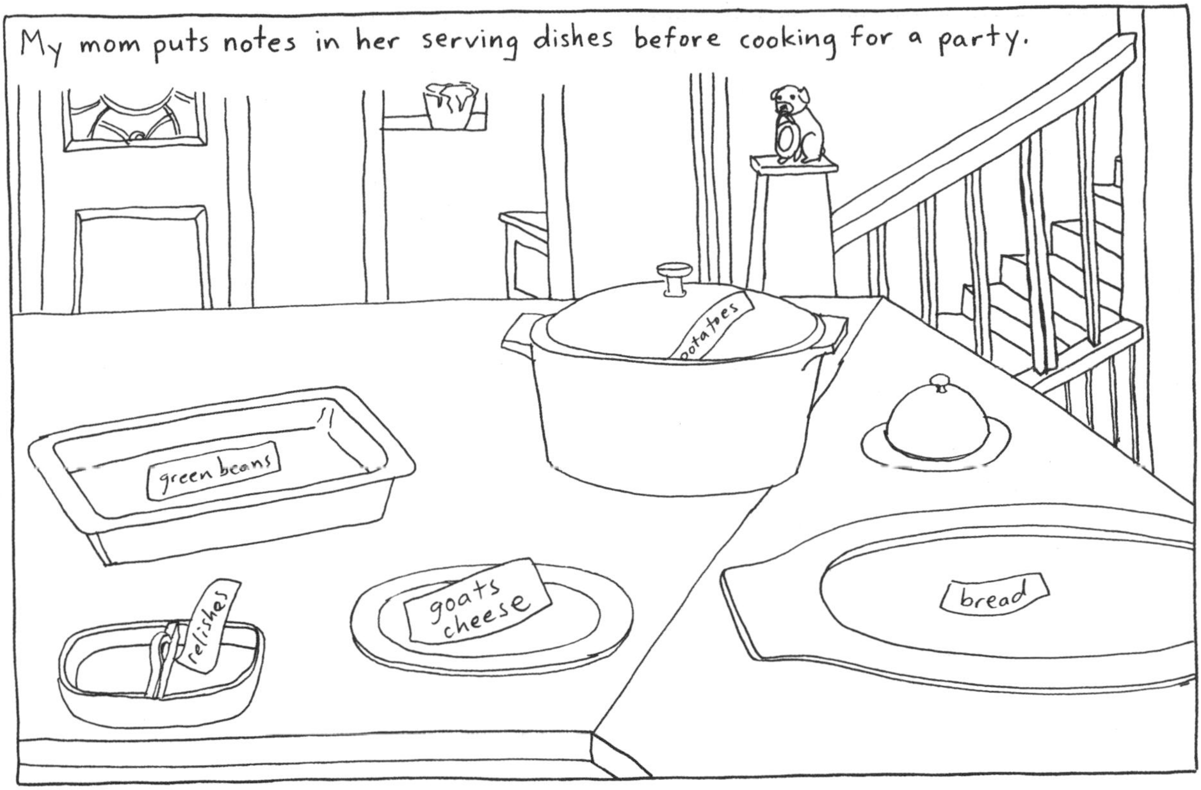
My mom puts notes in her serving dishes before cooking for a party.
potatoes
green beans
relishes
goats cheese
bread

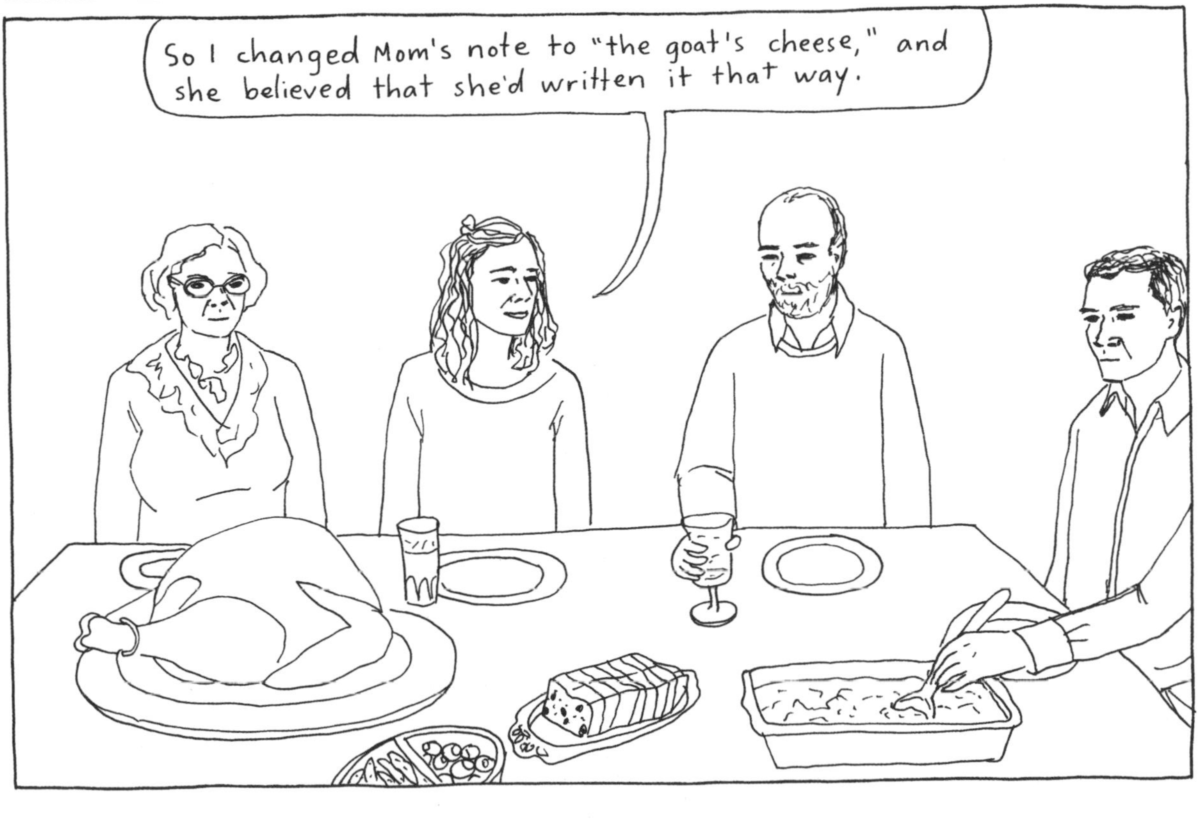
So I changed Mom's note to "the goat's cheese," and she believed that she'd written it that way.

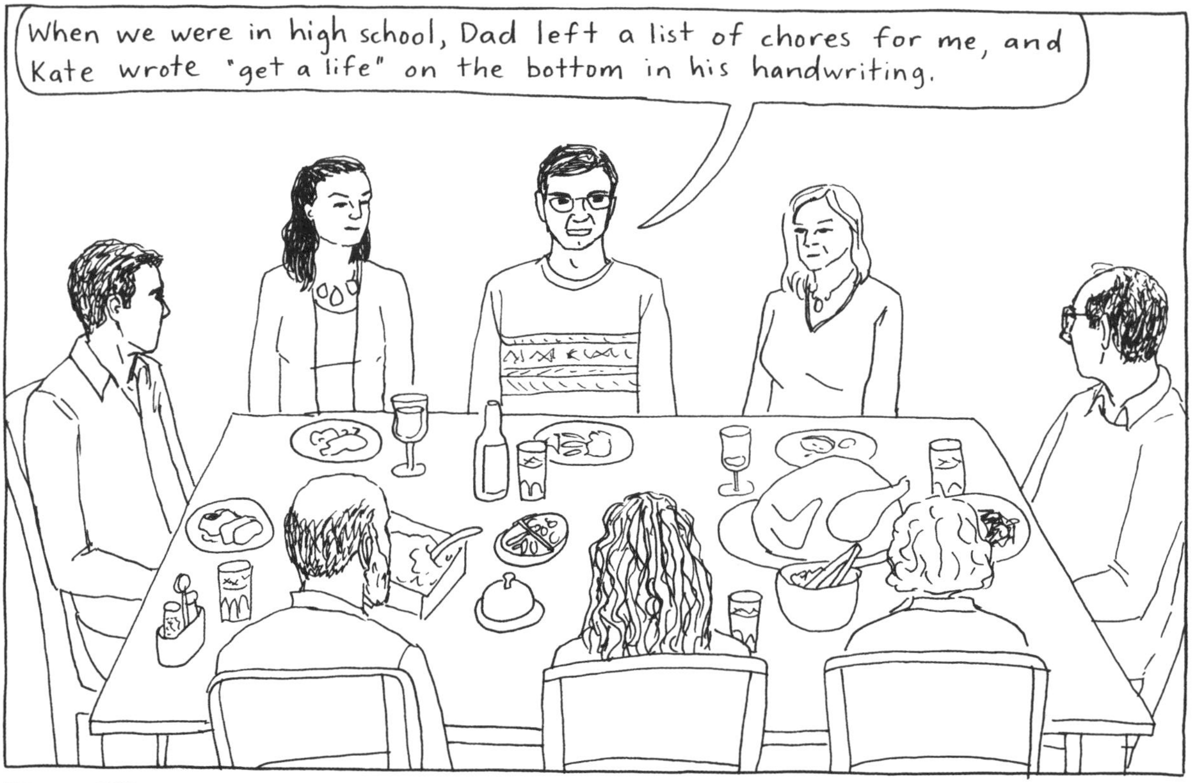
When we were in high school, Dad left a list of chores for me, and Kate wrote "get a life" on the bottom in his handwriting.

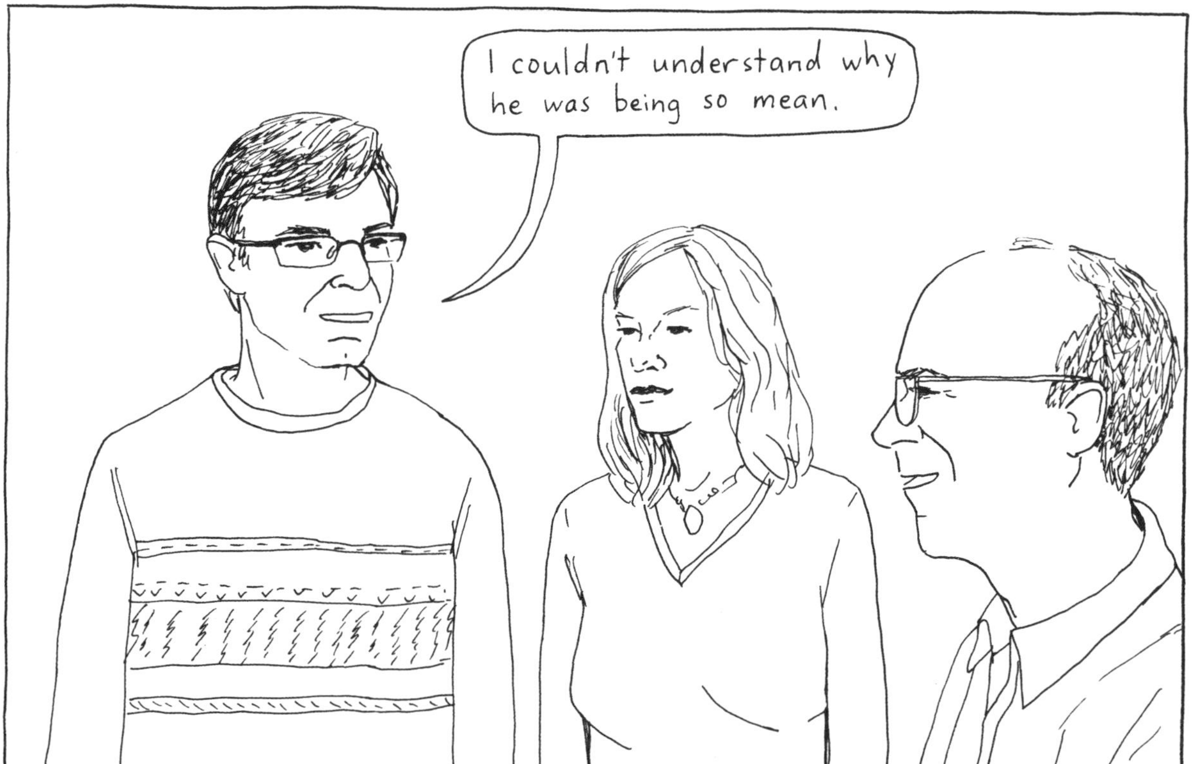
I couldn't understand why he was being so mean.

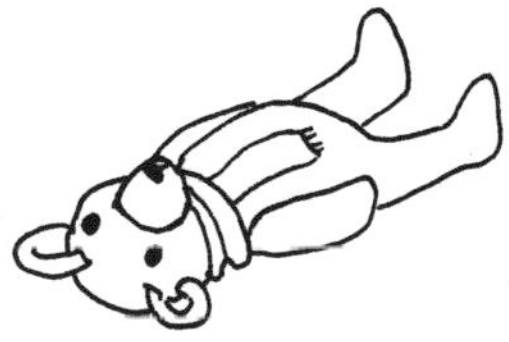

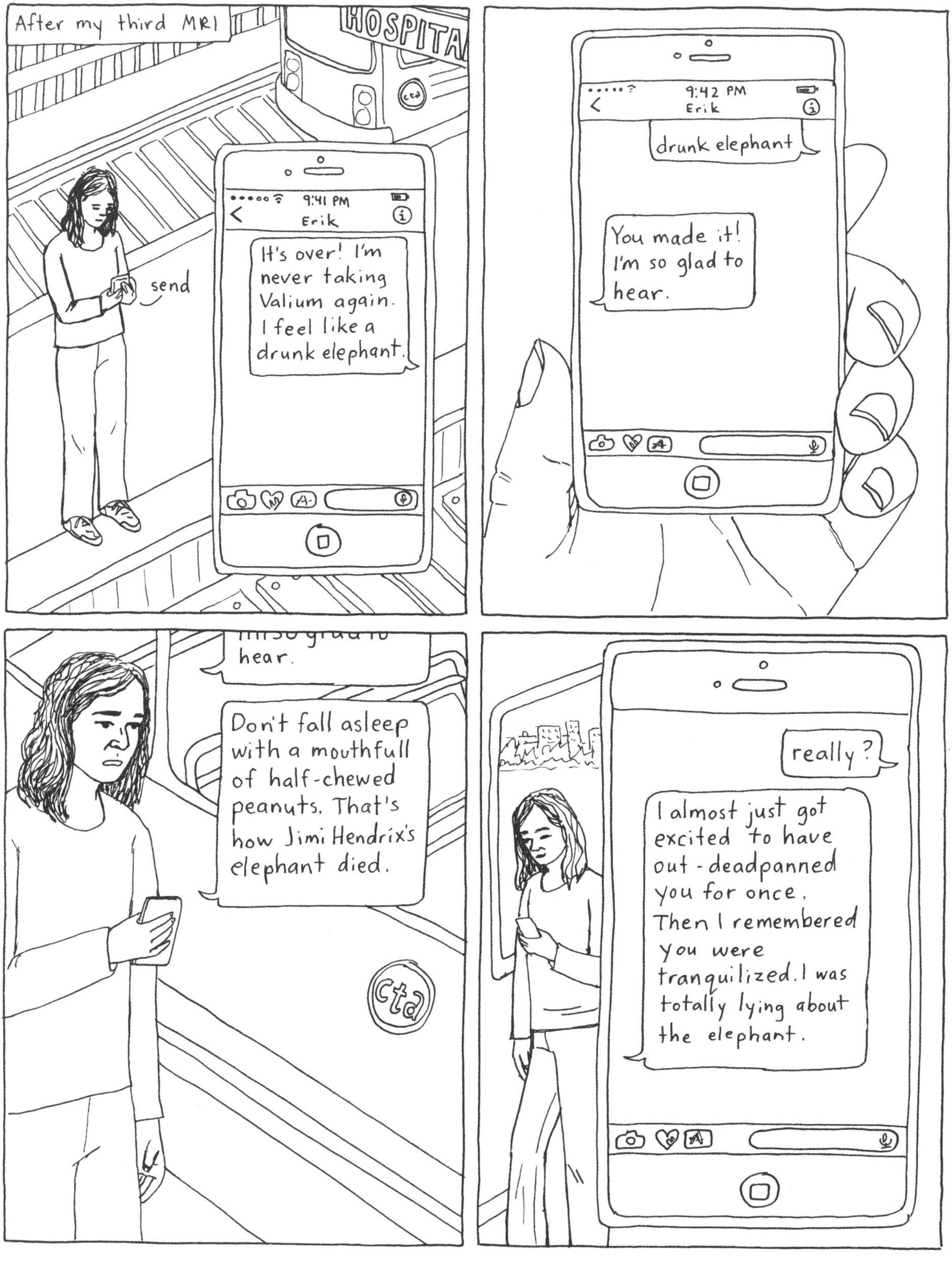
After my third MRI
HOSPITA
cta
send
9:41 PM
Erik
It's over! I'm never taking Valium again. I feel like a drunk elephant.
9:42 PM
Erik
drunk elephant
You made it! I'm so glad to hear.
hear.
Don't fall asleep with a mouthfull of half-chewed peanuts. That's how Jimi Hendrix's elephant died.
cta
really?
I almost just got excited to have out-deadpanned you for once. Then I remembered you were tranquilized. I was totally lying about the elephant.

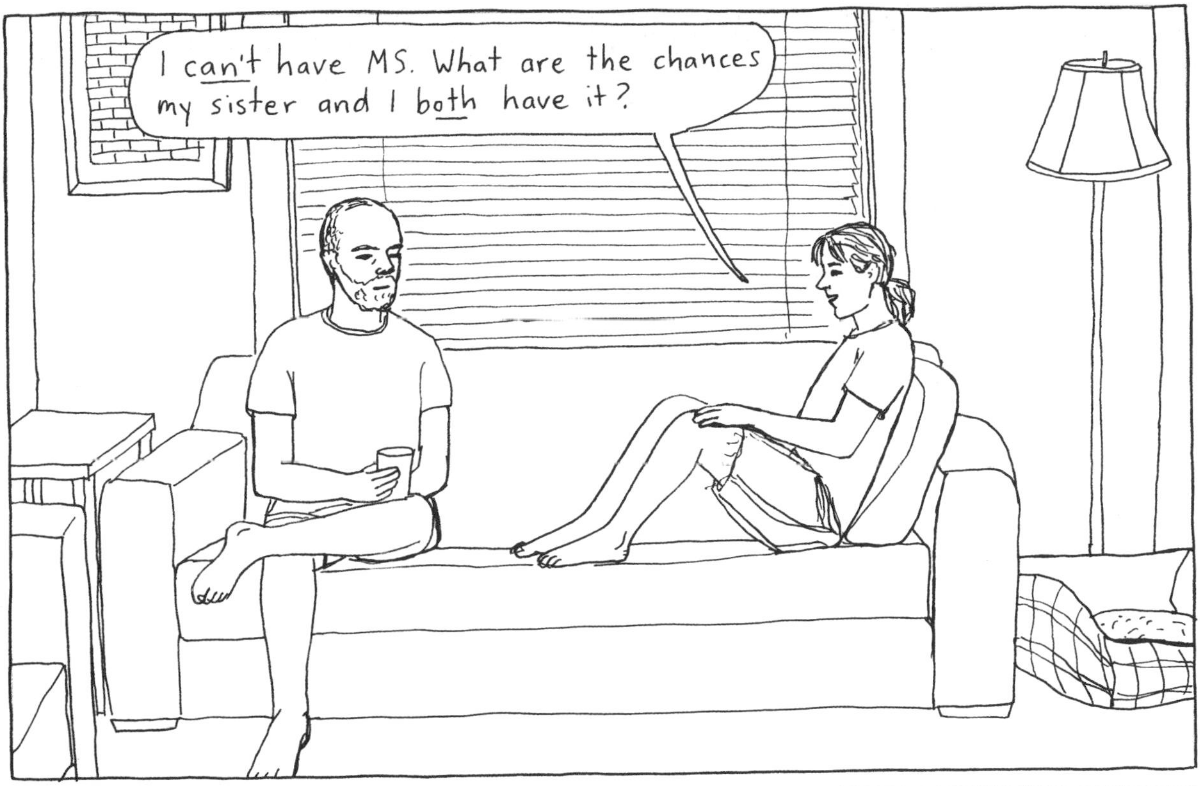
I can't have MS. What are the chances my sister and I both have it?

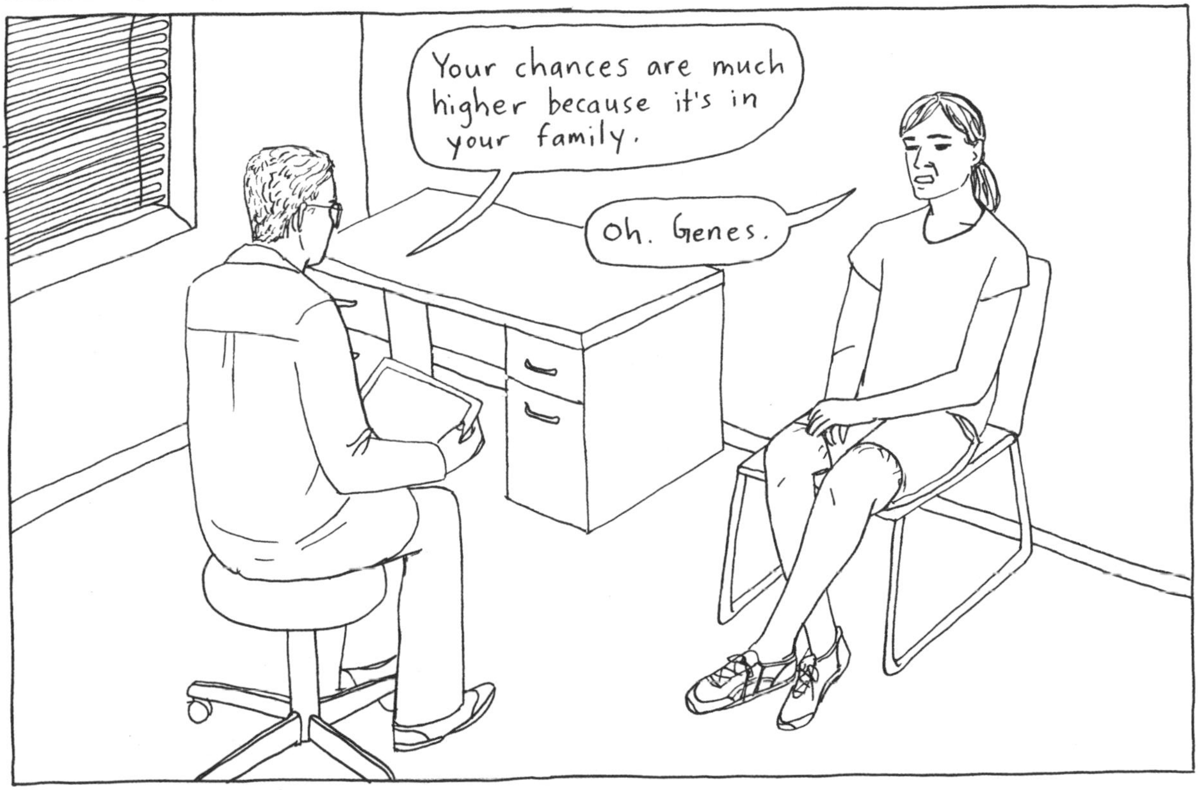
Your chances are much higher because it's in your family.
Oh. Genes.

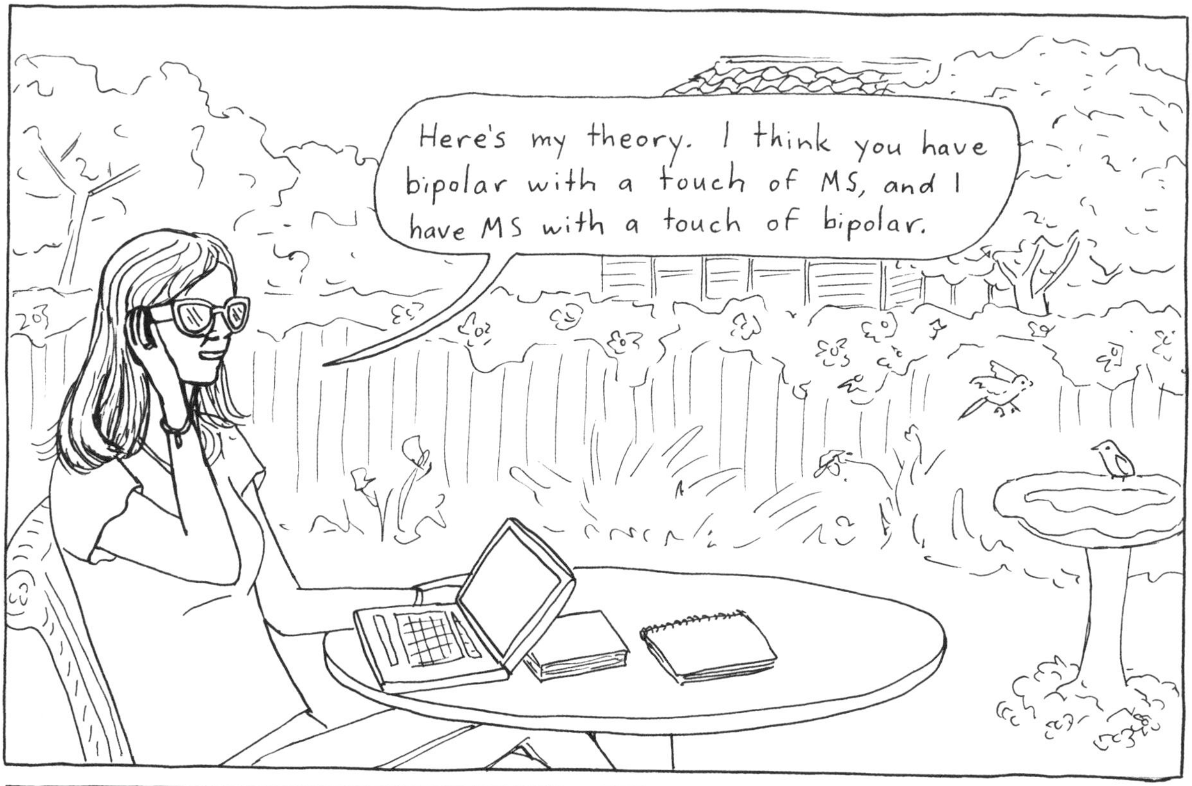
Here's my theory. I think you have bipolar with a touch of MS, and I have MS with a touch of bipolar.

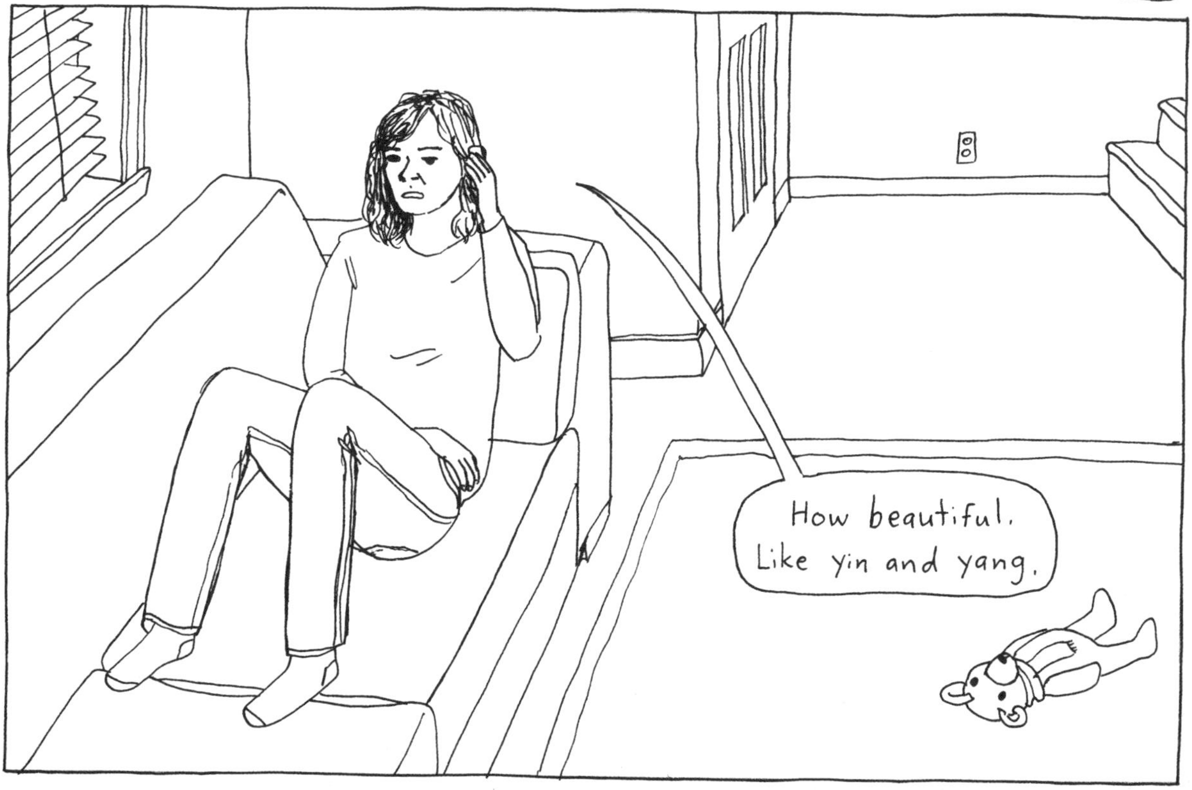
How beautiful. Like yin and yang.

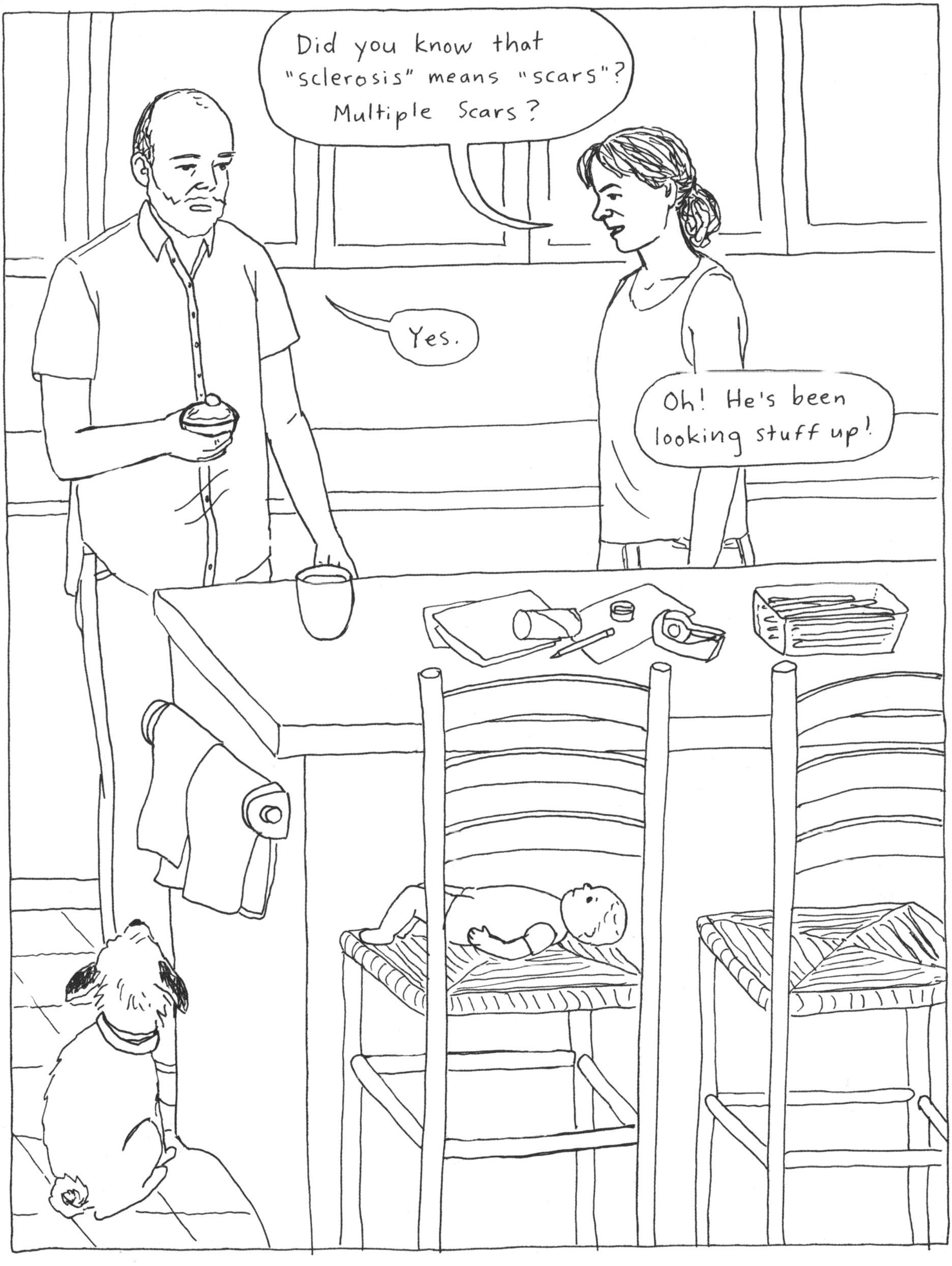
Did you know that "sclerosis" means "scars"? Multiple Scars?
Yes.
Oh! He's been looking stuff up!

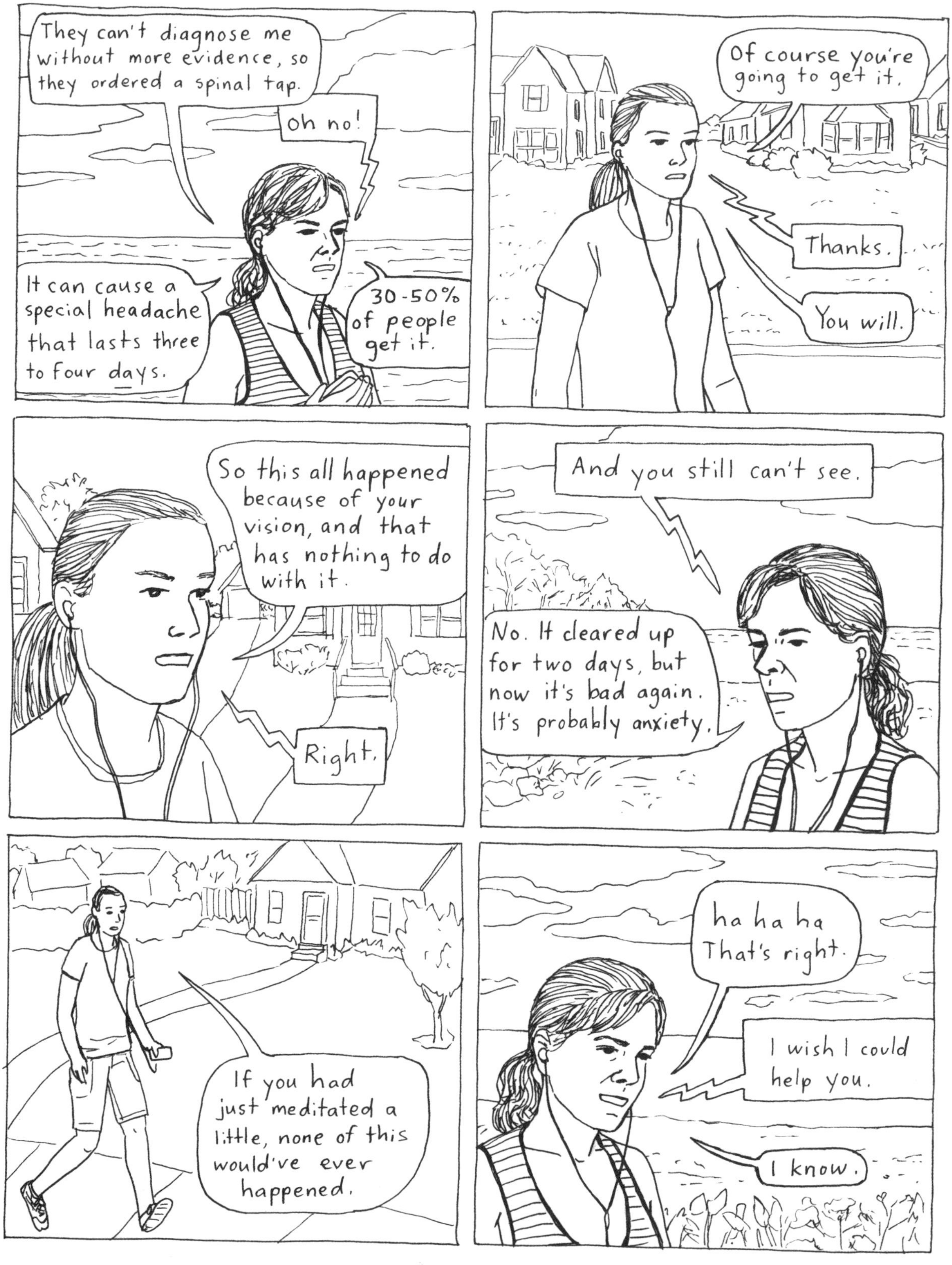

They can't diagnose me without more evidence, so they ordered a spinal tap.
Oh no!
It can cause a special headache that lasts three to four days.
30-50% of people get it.
Of course you're going to get it.
Thanks.
You will.
So this all happened because of your vision, and that has nothing to do with it.
Right.
And you still can't see.
No. It cleared up for two days, but now it's bad again. It's probably anxiety.
If you had just meditated a little, none of this would've ever happened.
ha ha ha That's right.
I wish I could help you.
I know.

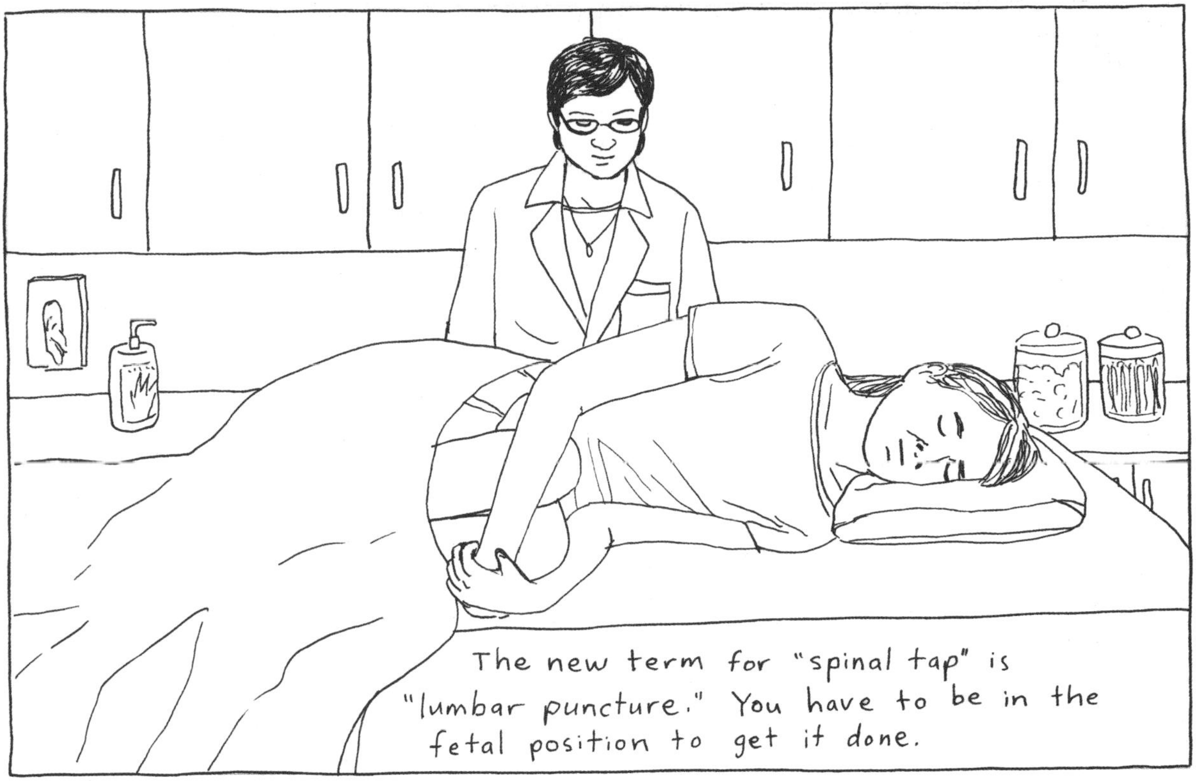
The new term for "spinal tap" is "lumbar puncture." You have to be in the fetal position to get it done.

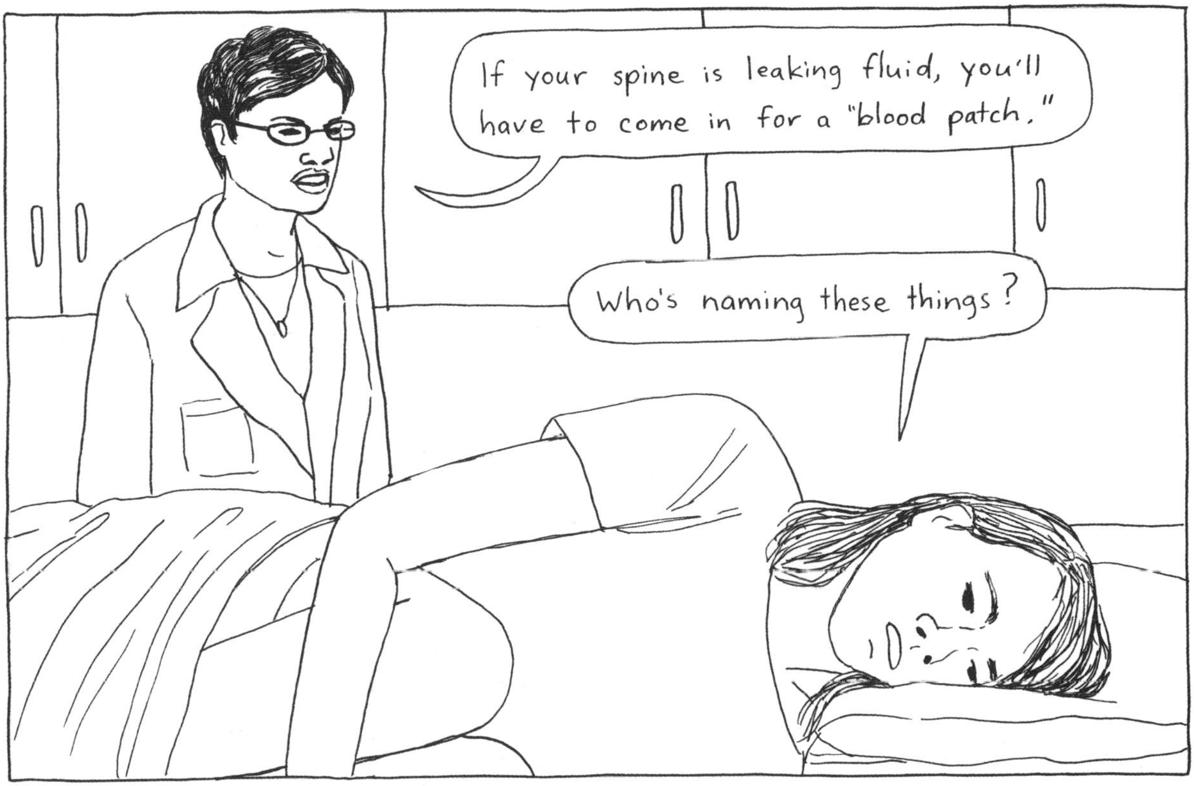
If your spine is leaking fluid, you'll have to come in for a "blood patch."
Who's naming these things?

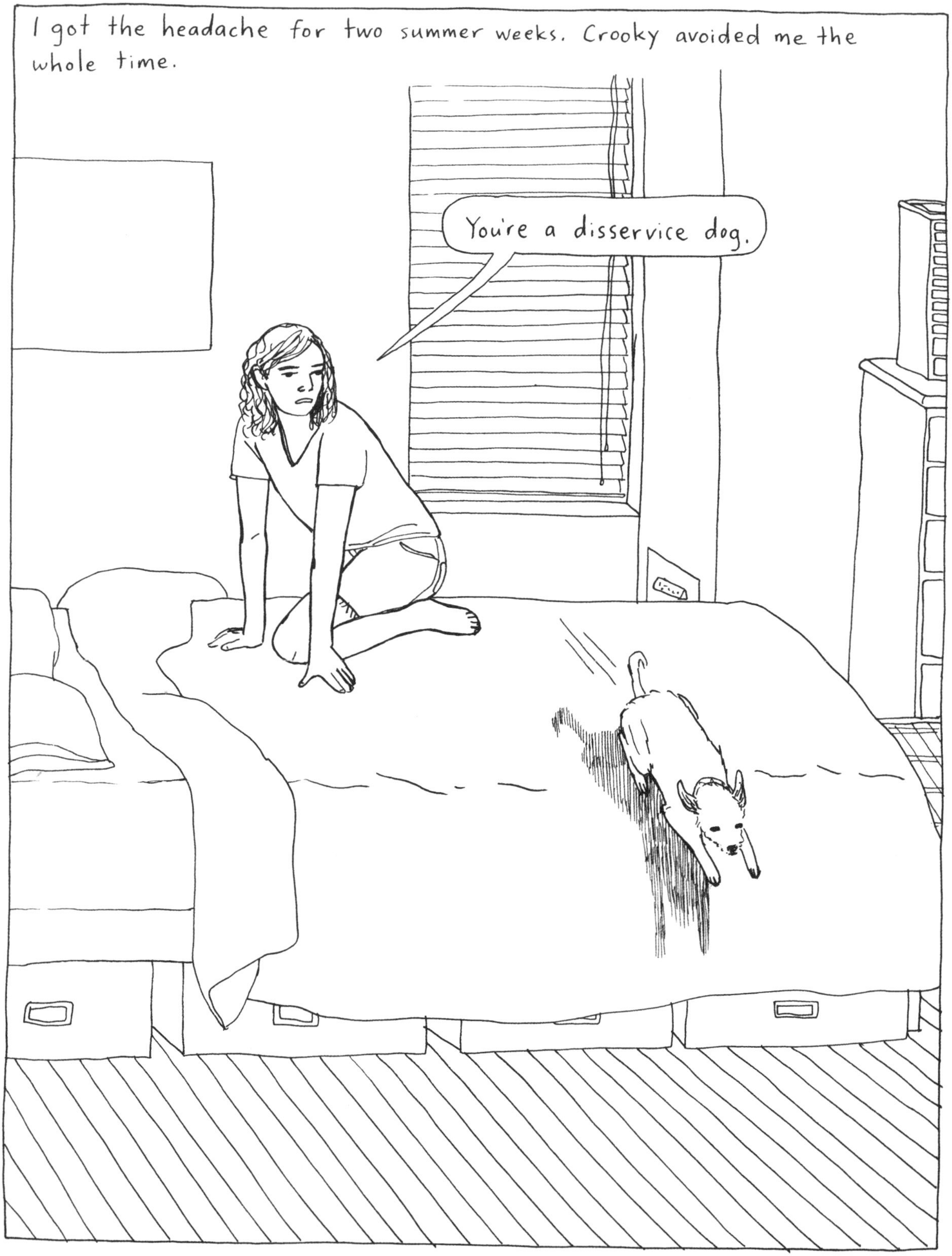
I got the headache for two summer weeks. Crooky avoided me the whole time.
You're a disservice dog.

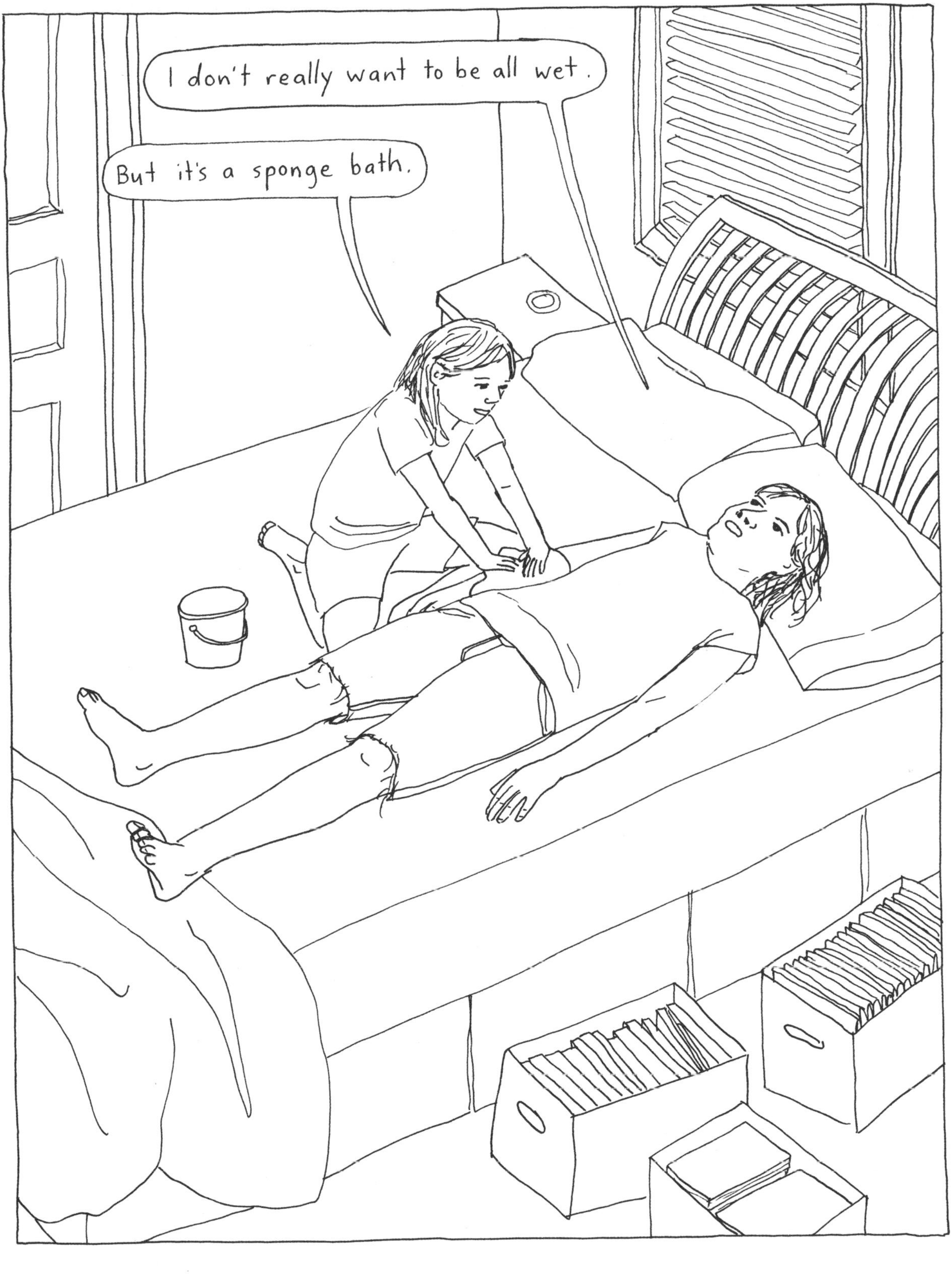
I don't really want to be all wet.
But it's a sponge bath.

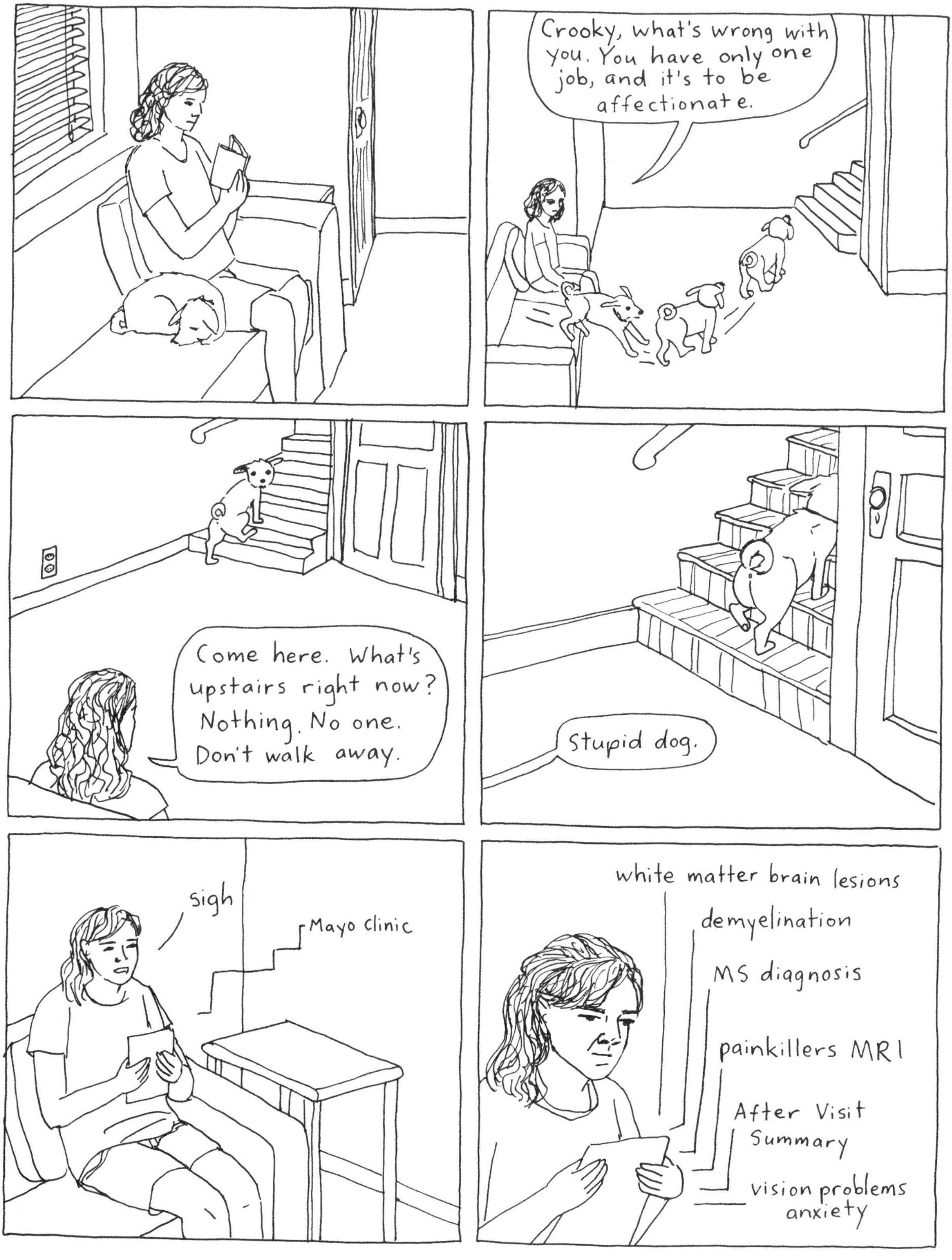
Crooky, what's wrong with you. You have only one job, and it's to be affectionate.
Come here. What's upstairs right now? Nothing. No one. Don't walk away.
Stupid dog.
sigh
Mayo Clinic
white matter brain lesions
demyelination
MS diagnosis
painkillers MRI
After Visit Summary
vision problems
anxiety

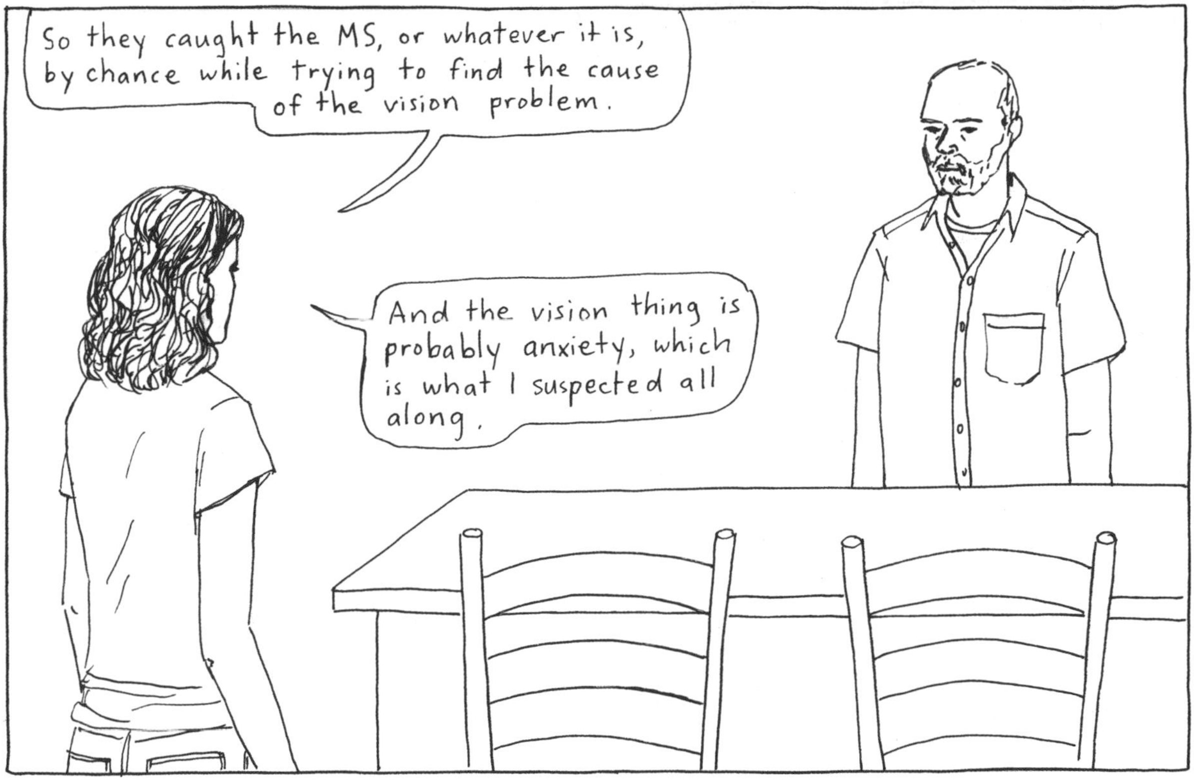
So they caught the MS, or whatever it is, by chance while trying to find the cause of the vision problem.
And the vision thing is probably anxiety, which is what I suspected all along.

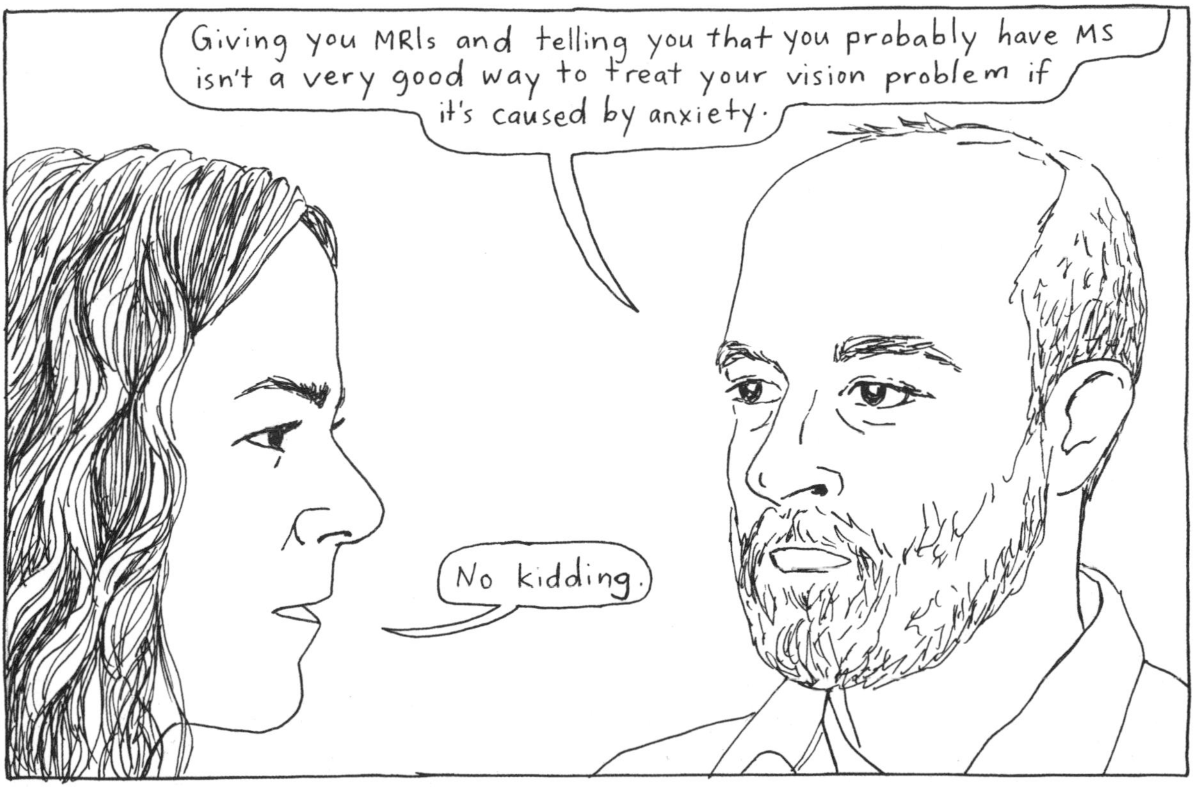
Giving you MRIs and telling you that you probably have MS isn't a very good way to treat your vision problem if it's caused by anxiety.
No kidding.

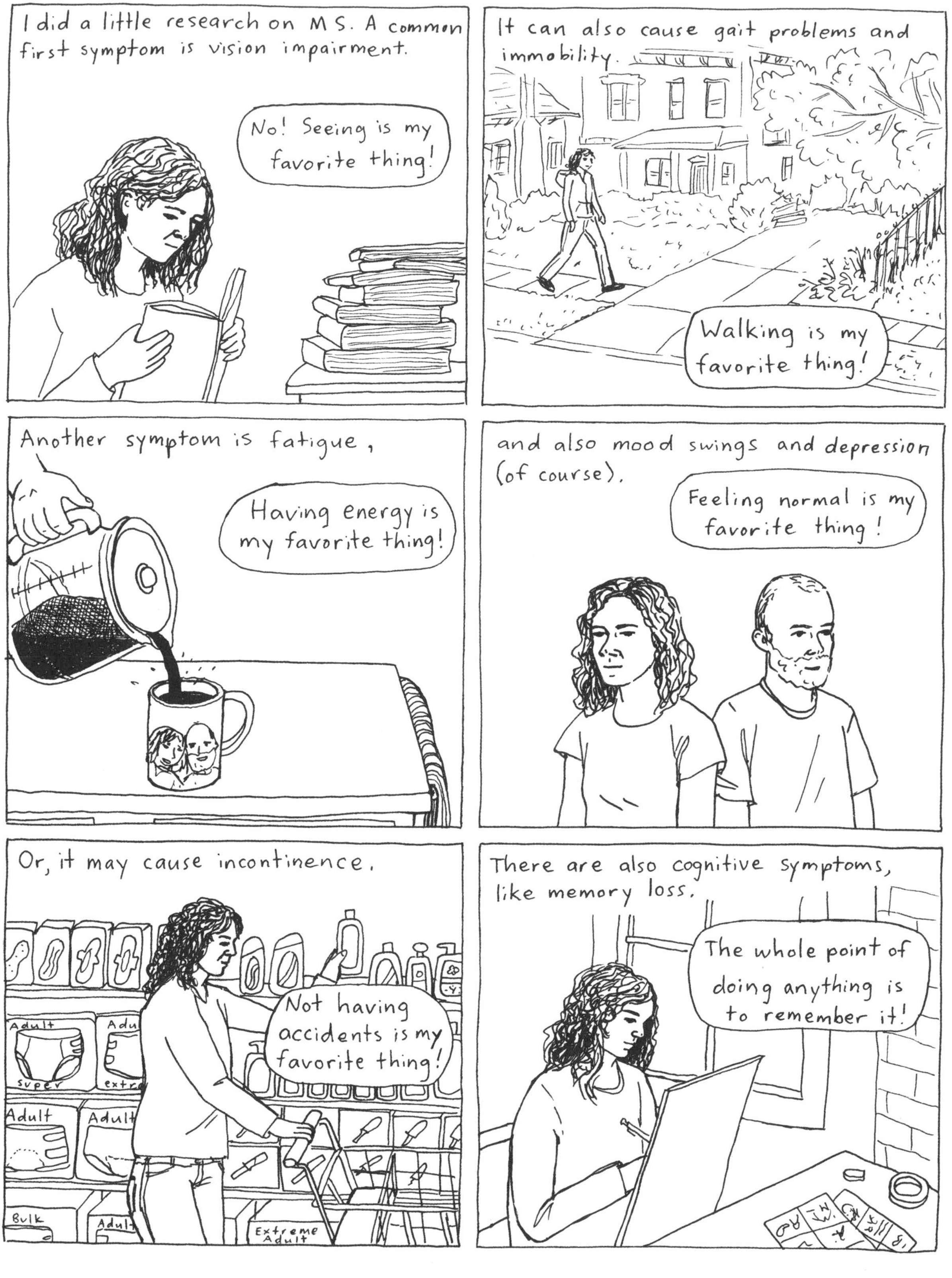
I did a little research on MS. A common first symptom is vision impairment.
No! Seeing is my favorite thing!
It can also cause gait problems and immobility.
Walking is my favorite thing!
Another symptom is fatigue,
Having energy is my favorite thing!
and also mood swings and depression (of course).
Feeling normal is my favorite thing!
Or, it may cause incontinence.
Adult
super
Adult
Adult
Bulk
Extreme Adult
Not having accidents is my favorite thing!
There are also cognitive symptoms, like memory loss.
The whole point of doing anything is to remember it!

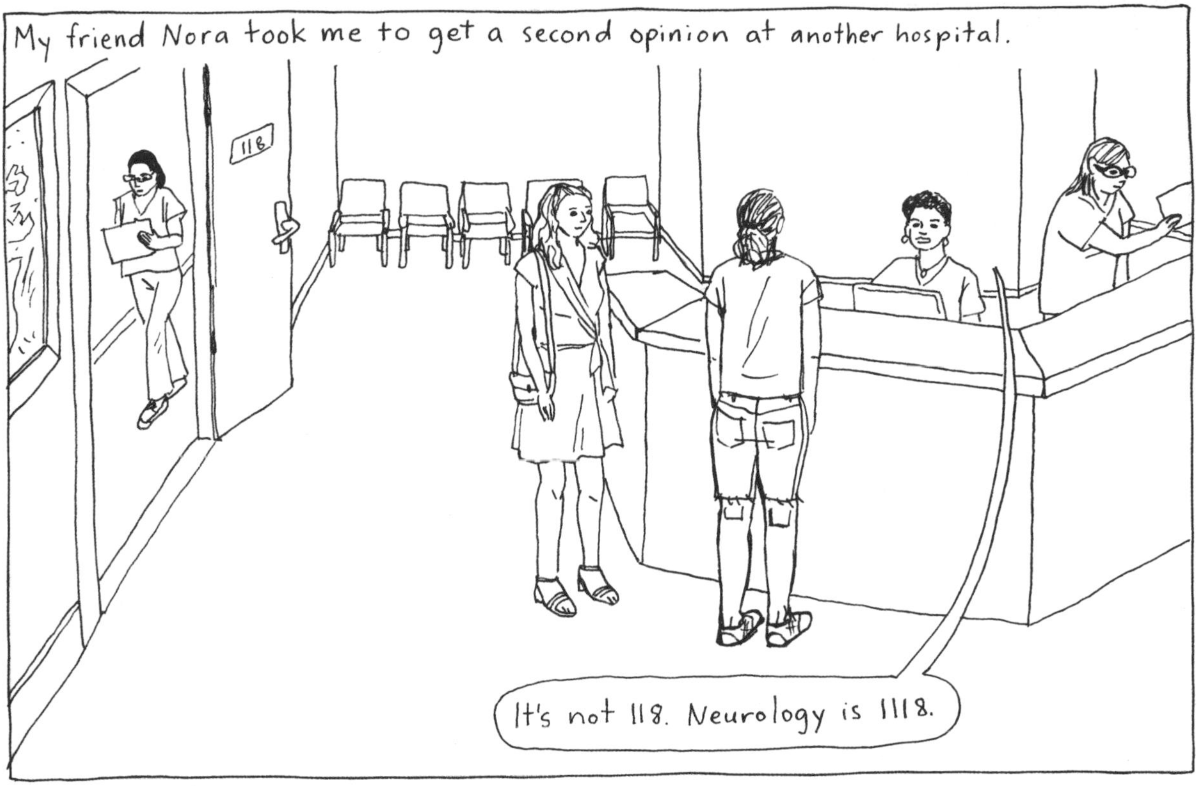
My friend Nora took me to get a second opinion at another hospital.
118
It's not 118. Neurology is 1118.

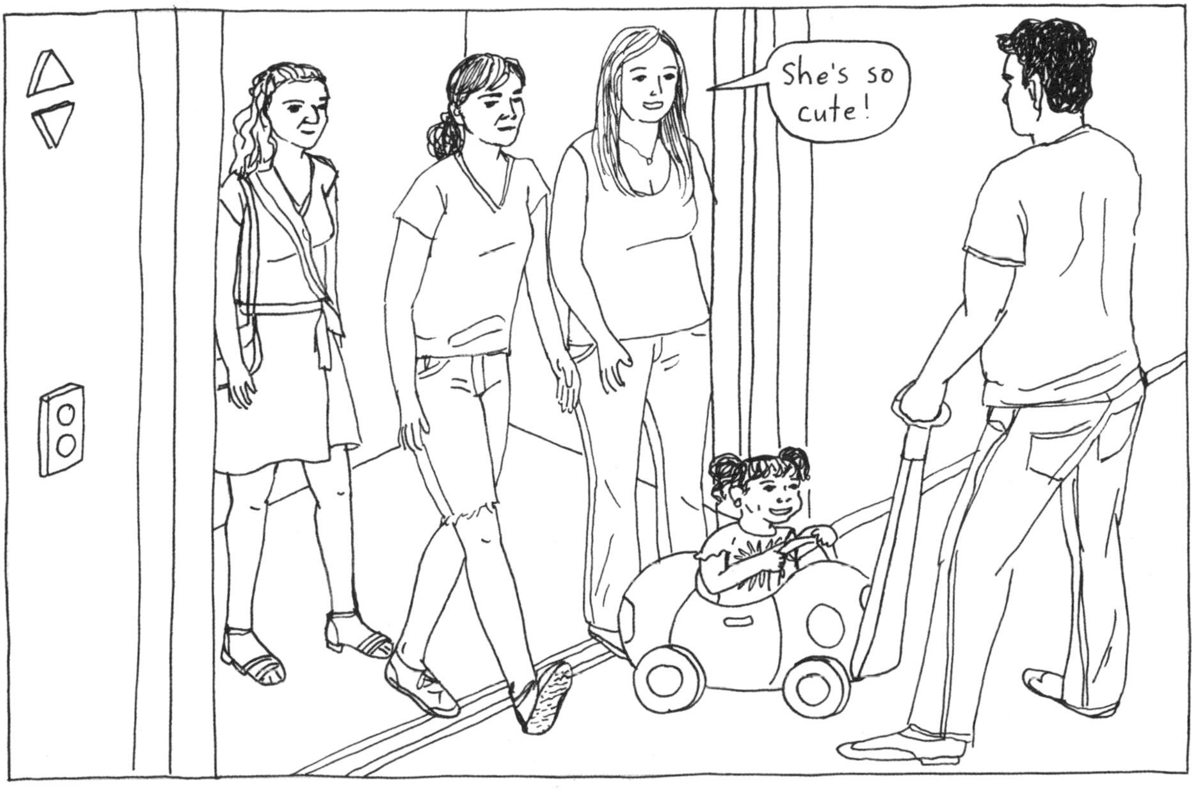
She's so cute!

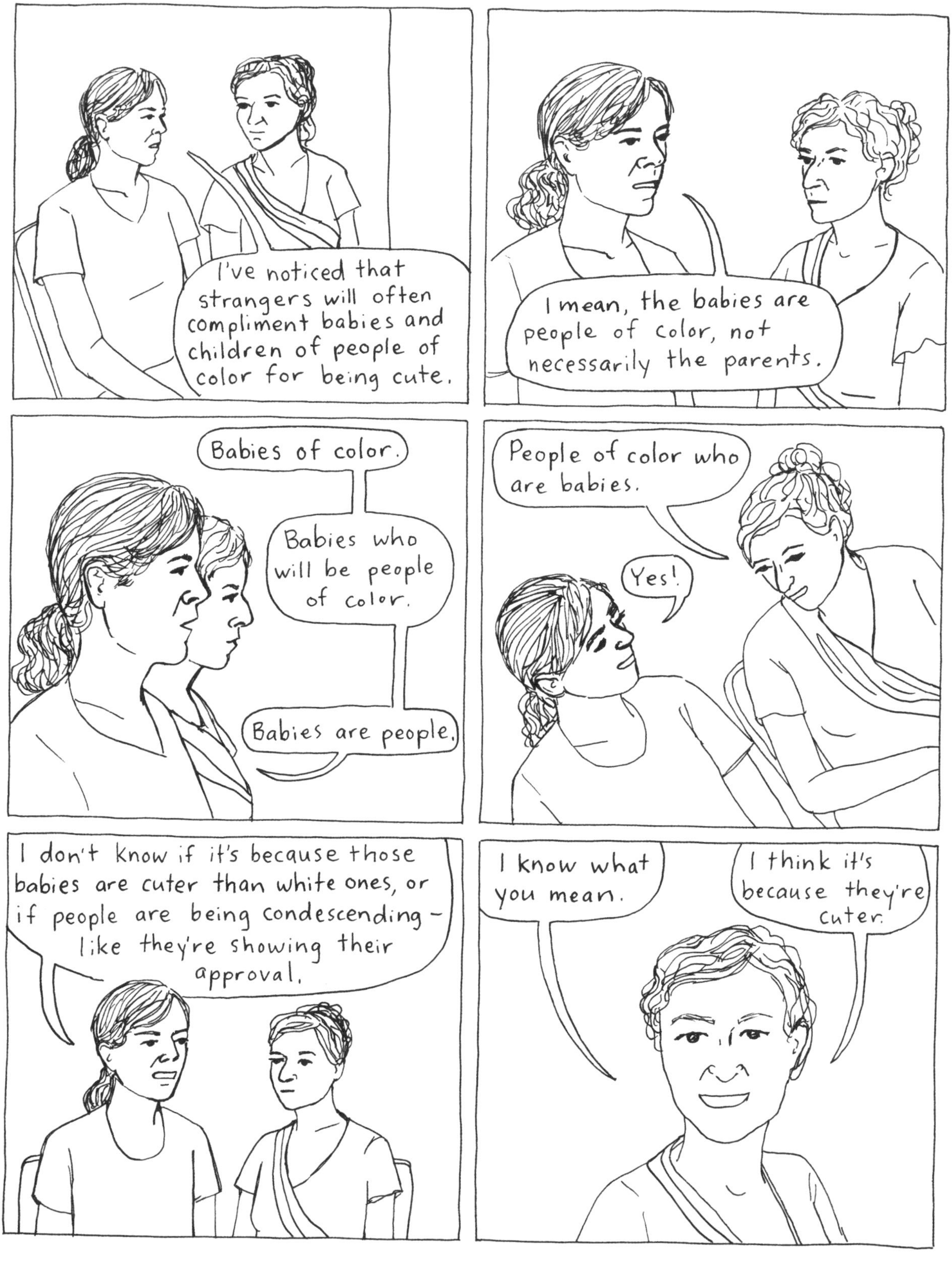
I've noticed that strangers will often compliment babies and children of people of color for being cute.
I mean, the babies are people of color, not necessarily the parents.
Babies of color.
Babies who will be people of color.
Babies are people.
People of color who are babies.
Yes!
I don't know if it's because those babies are cuter than white ones, or if people are being condescending – like they're showing their approval.
I know what you mean.
I think it's because they're cuter.

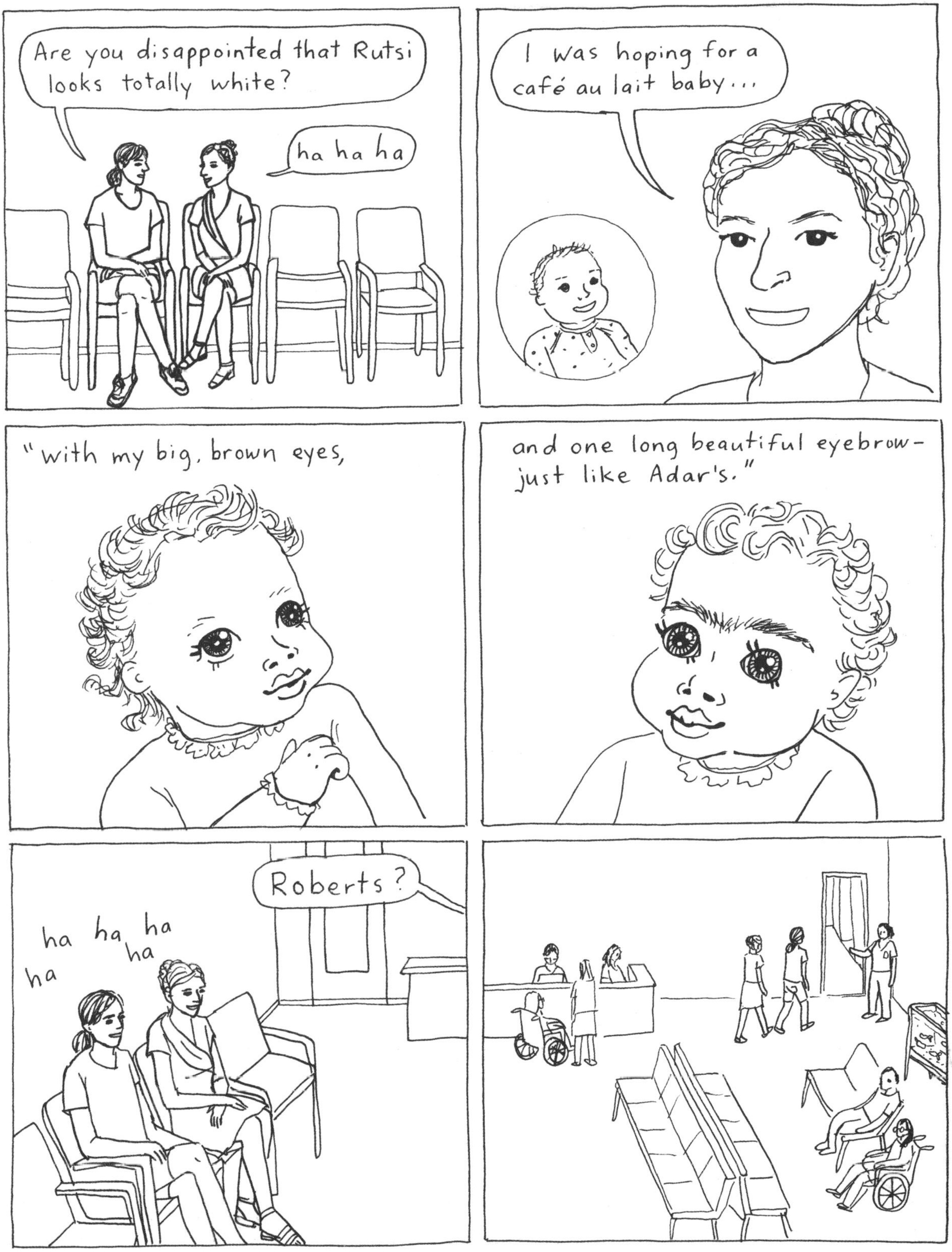
Are you disappointed that Rutsi looks totally white?
ha ha ha
I was hoping for a café au lait baby...
"with my big, brown eyes,
and one long beautiful eyebrow- just like Adar's."
Roberts?
ha ha ha ha ha

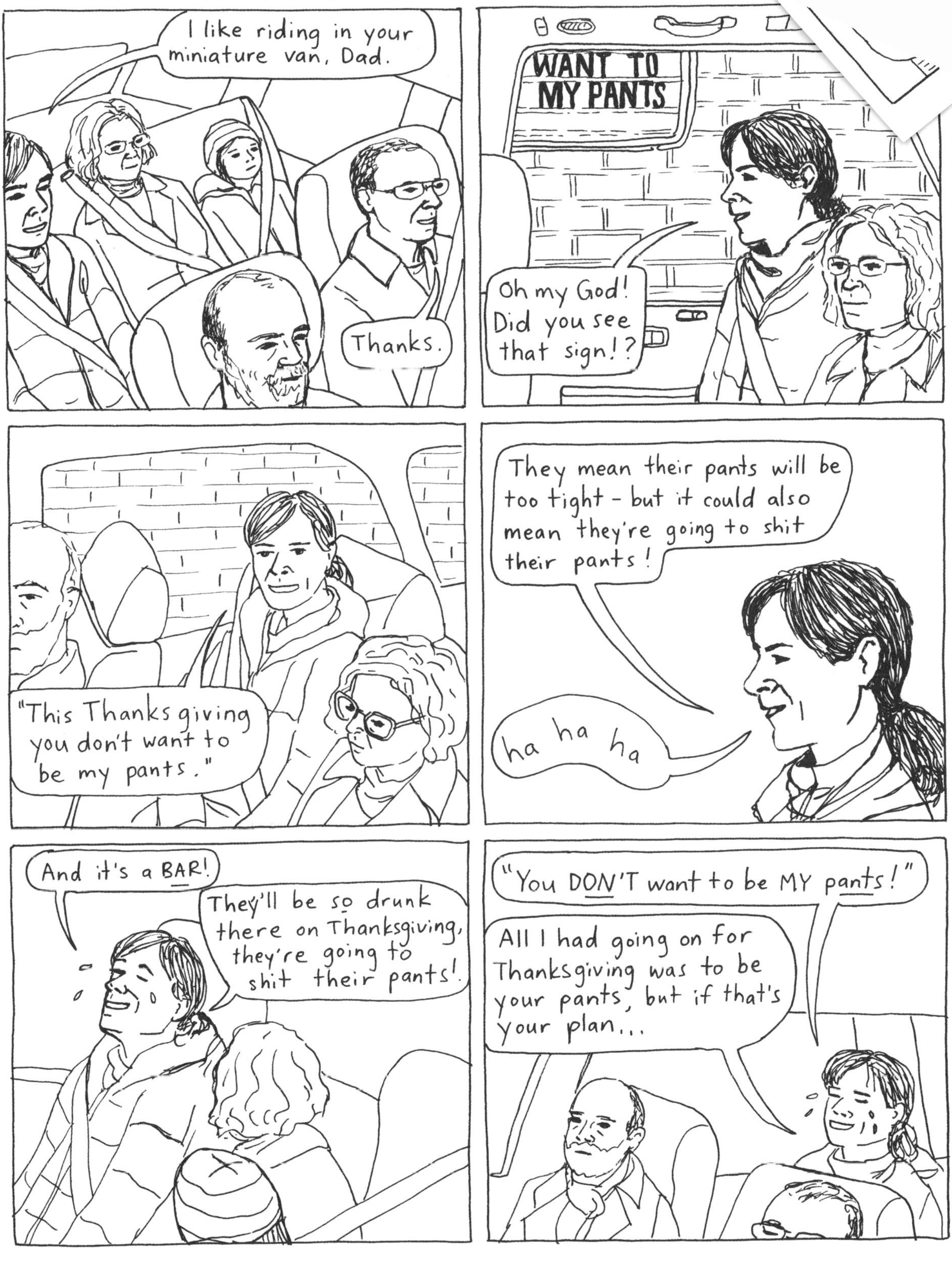

I like riding in your miniature van, Dad.
Thanks.
WANT TO MY PANTS
Oh my God! Did you see that sign!?
"This Thanksgiving you don't want to be my pants."
They mean their pants will be too tight - but it could also mean they're going to shit their pants!
ha ha ha
And it's a BAR!
They'll be so drunk there on Thanksgiving, they're going to shit their pants!
"You DON'T want to be MY pants!"
All I had going on for Thanksgiving was to be your pants, but if that's your plan...

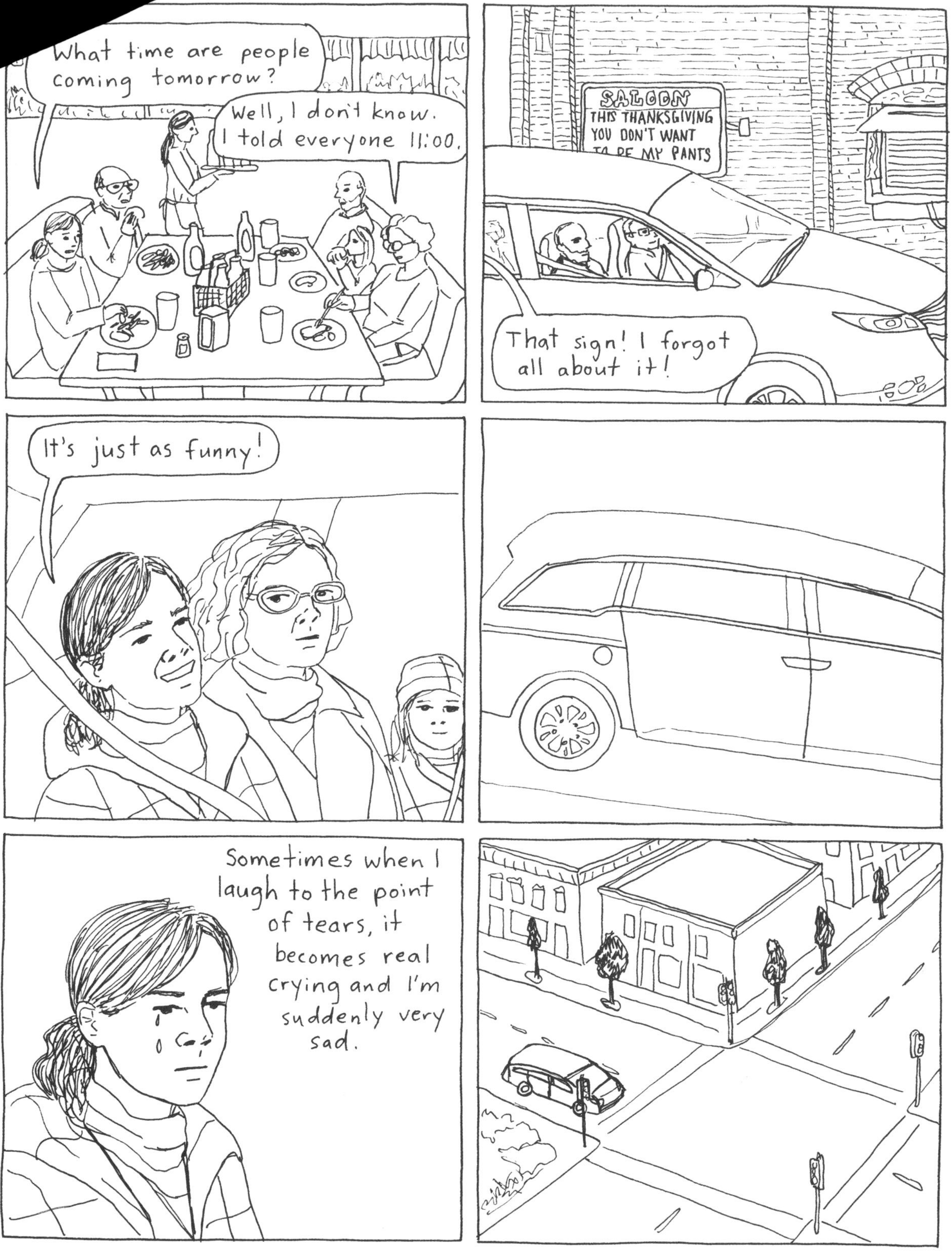

What time are people coming tomorrow?
Well, I don't know. I told everyone 11:00.
SALOON
THIS THANKSGIVING
YOU DON'T WANT
MY PANTS
That sign! I forgot all about it!
It's just as funny!
Sometimes when I laugh to the point of tears, it becomes real crying and I'm suddenly very sad.

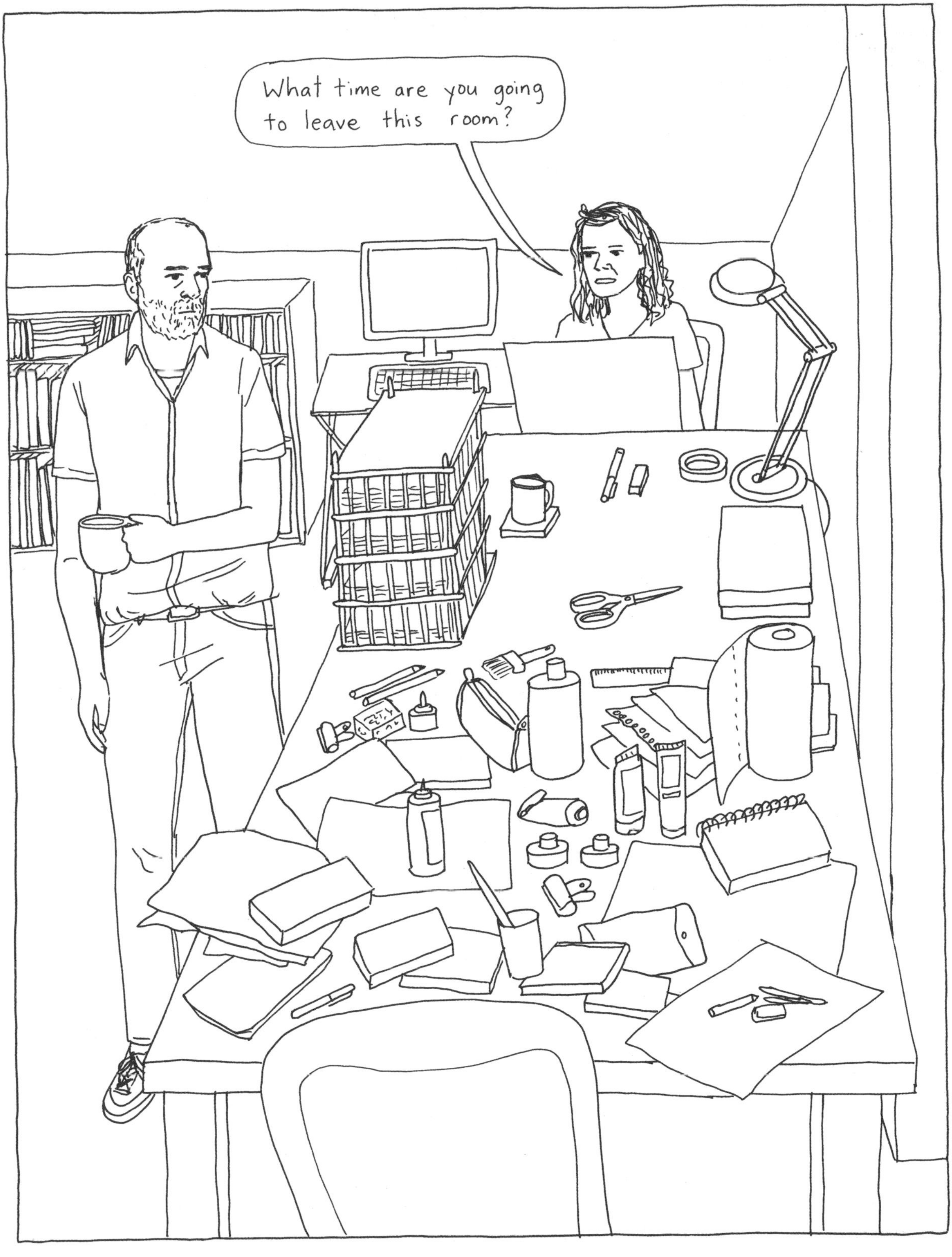
What time are you going to leave this room?

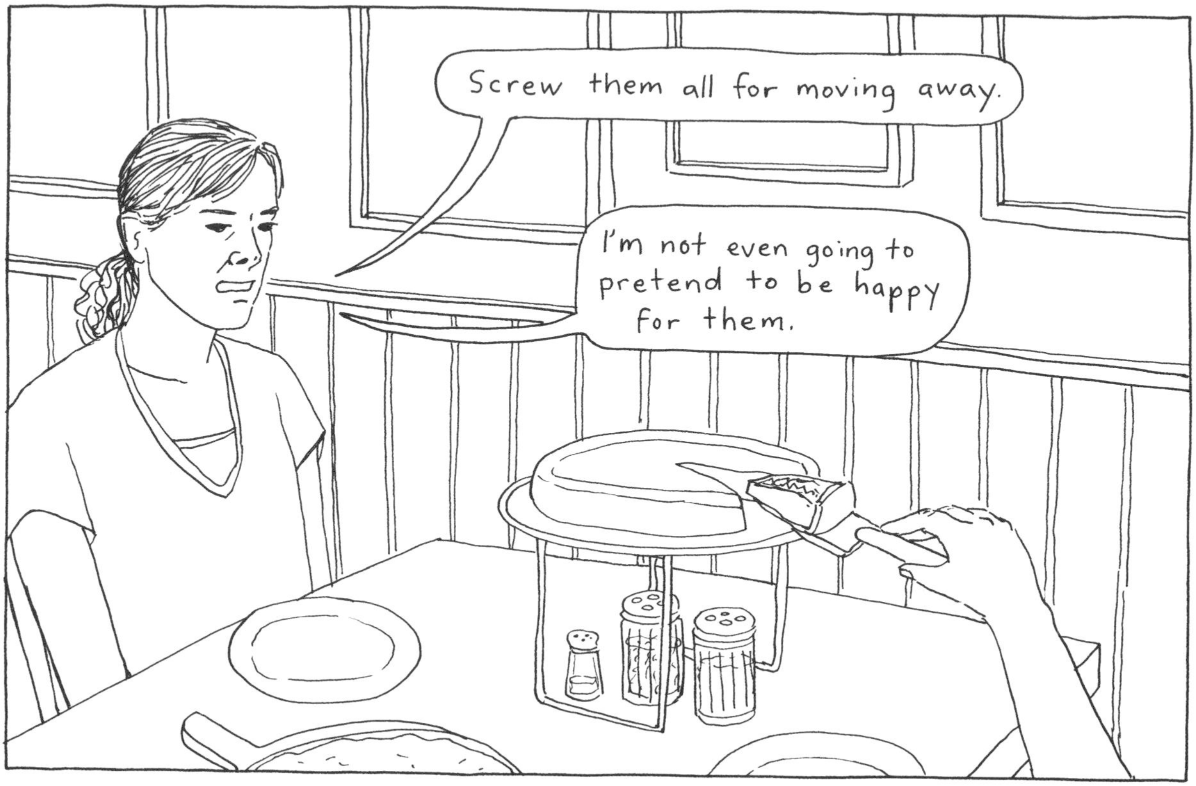
Screw them all for moving away.
I'm not even going to pretend to be happy for them.

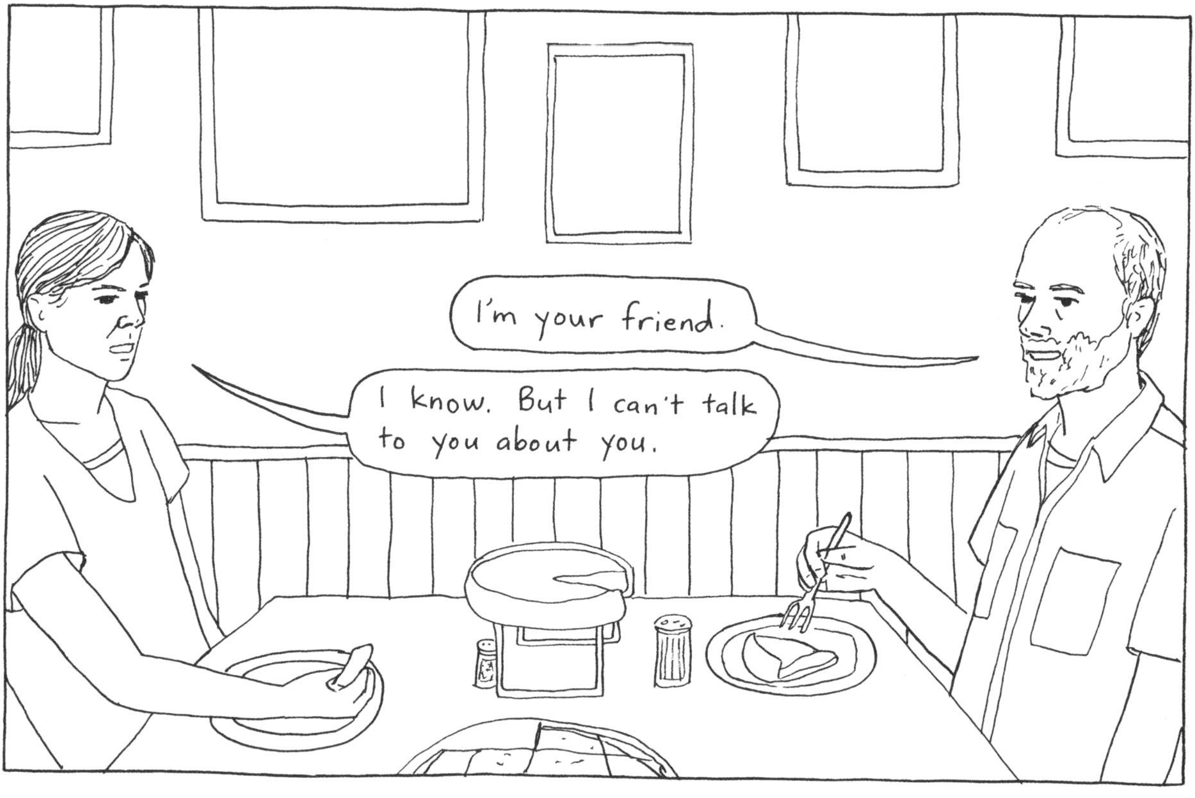
I'm your friend.
I know. But I can't talk to you about you.

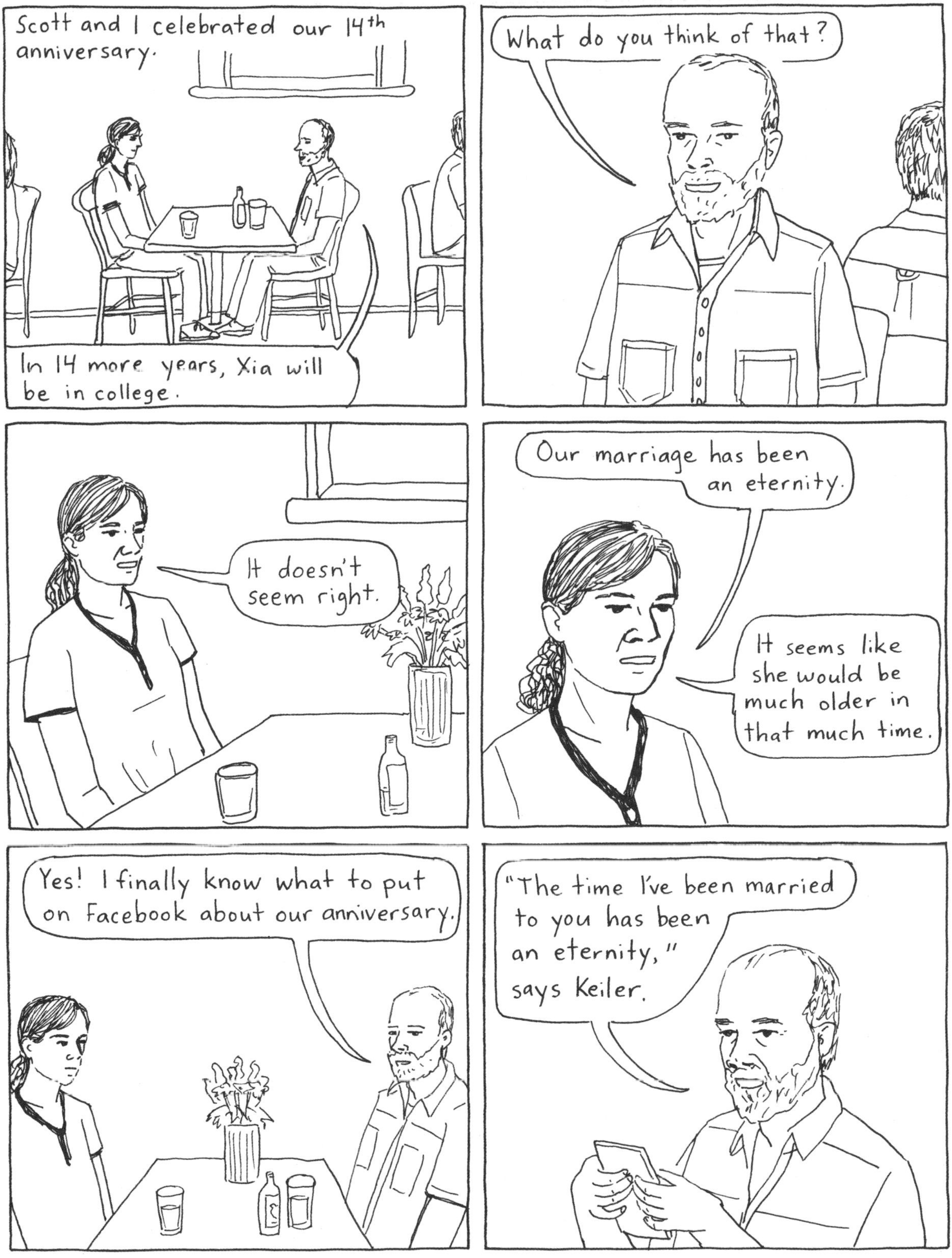
Scott and I celebrated our 14th anniversary.
In 14 more years, Xia will be in college.
What do you think of that?
It doesn't seem right.
Our marriage has been an eternity.
It seems like she would be much older in that much time.
Yes! I finally know what to put on Facebook about our anniversary.
"The time I've been married to you has been an eternity," says Keiler.

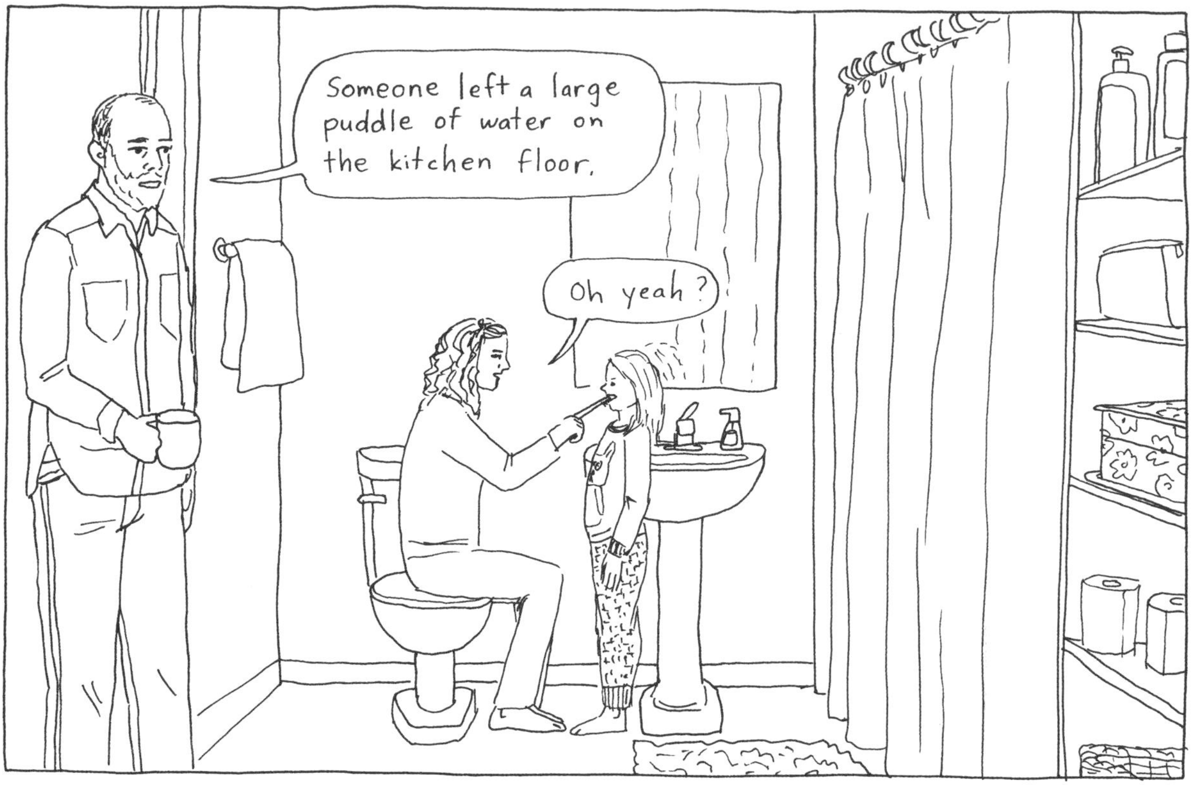
Someone left a large puddle of water on the kitchen floor.
Oh yeah?

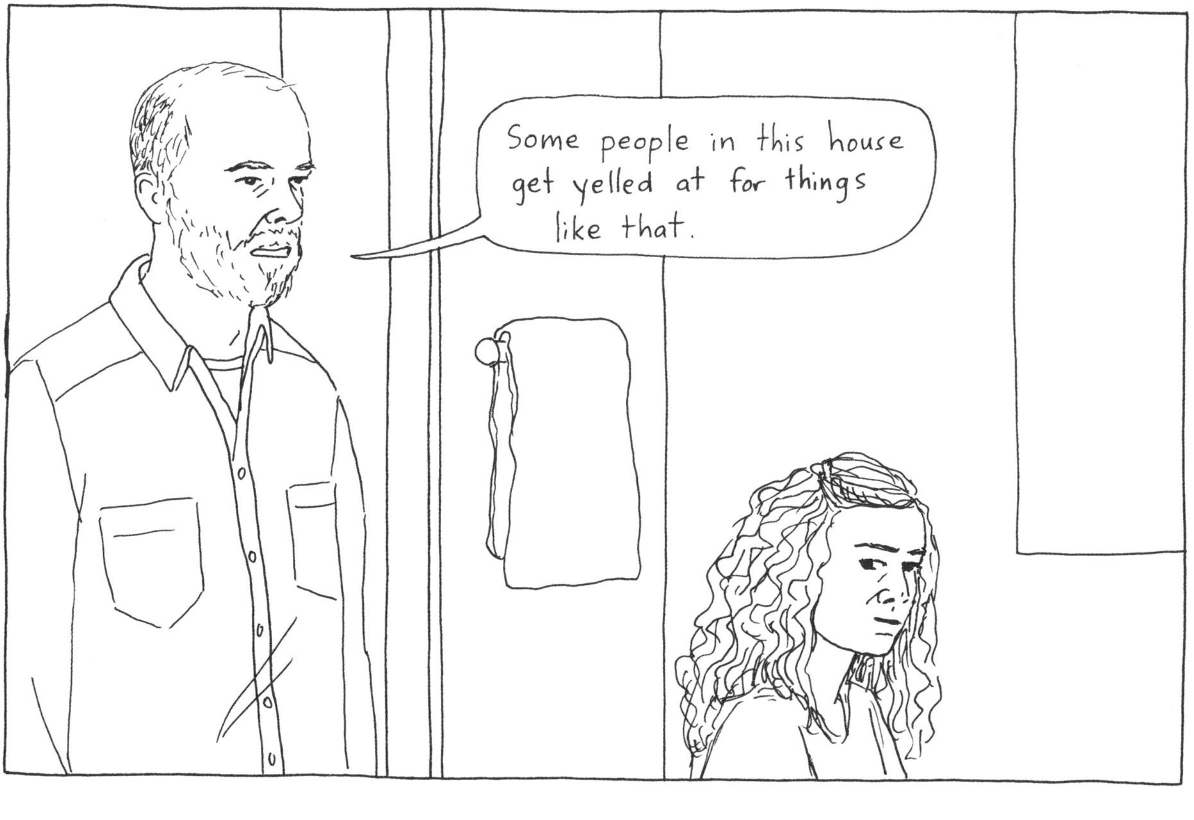
Some people in this house get yelled at for things like that.

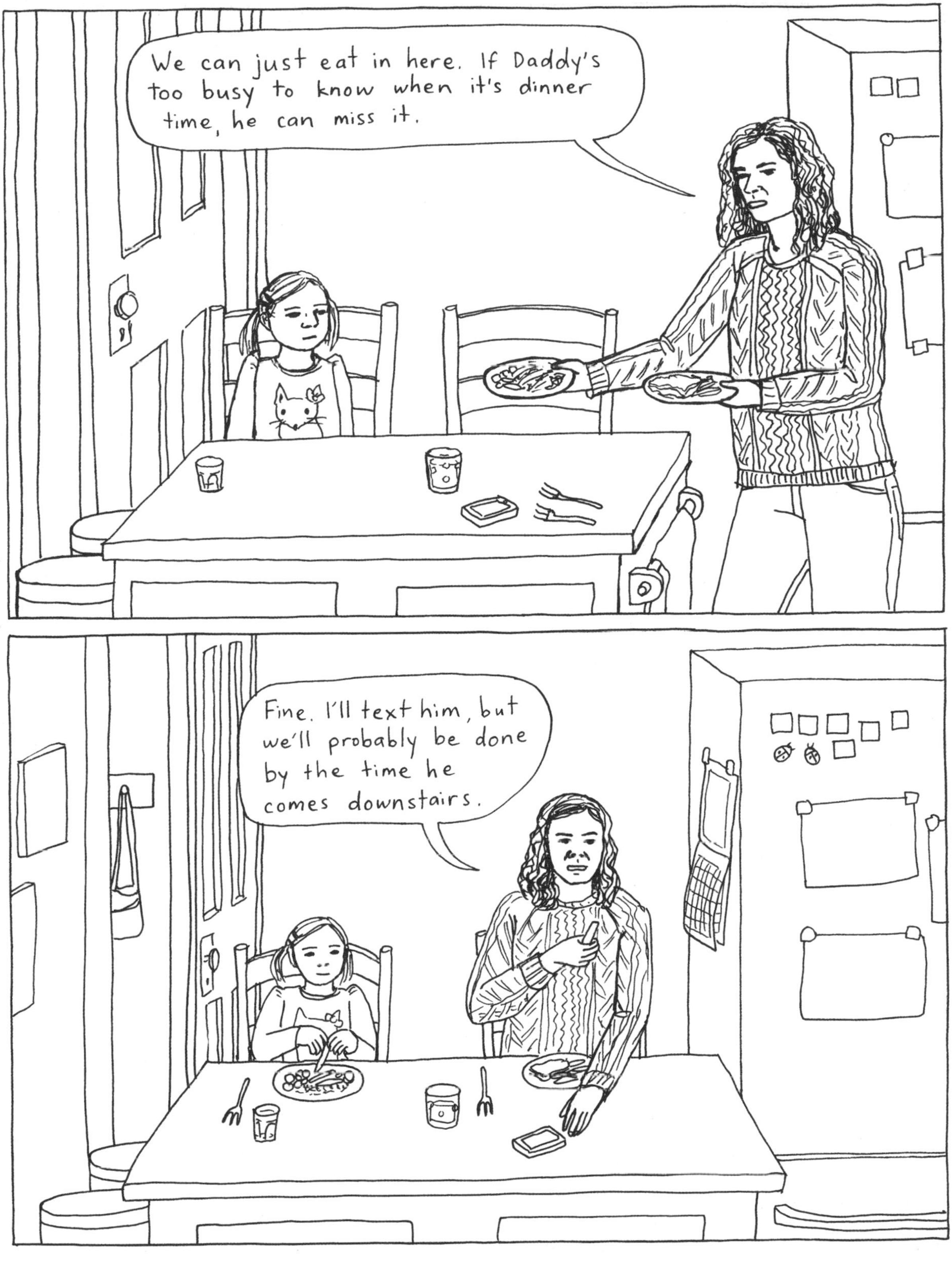
We can just eat in here. If Daddy's too busy to know when it's dinner time, he can miss it.
Fine. I'll text him, but we'll probably be done by the time he comes downstairs.

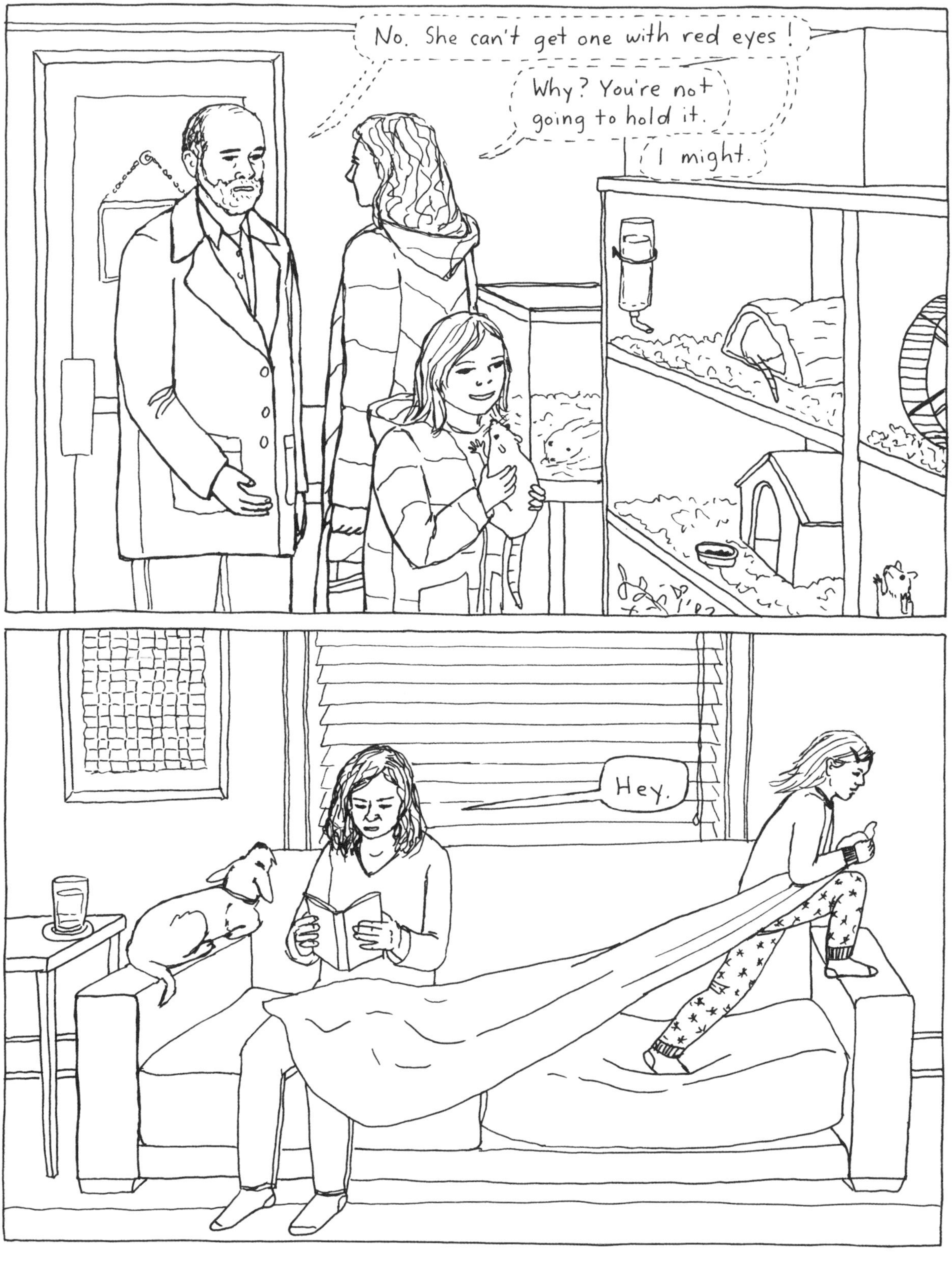
No. She can't get one with red eyes!
Why? You're not going to hold it.
I might.
Hey.

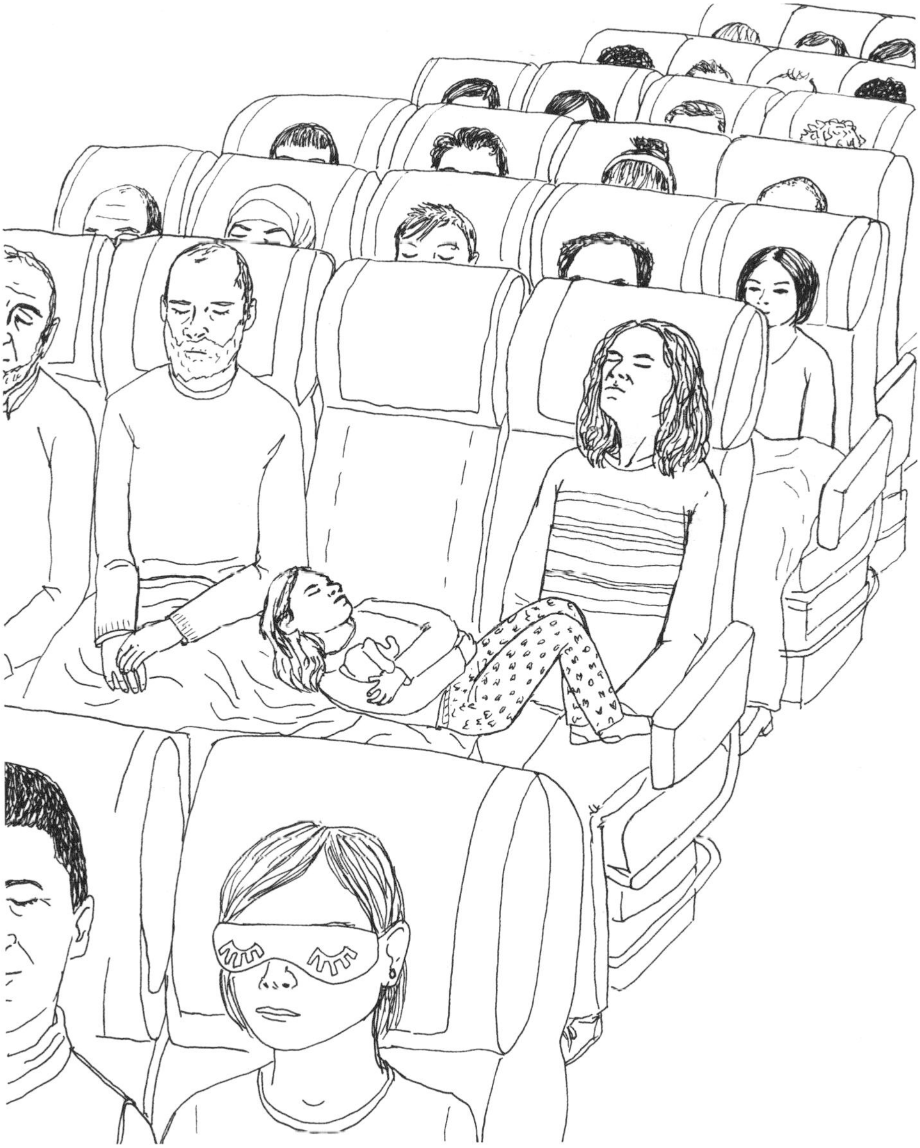

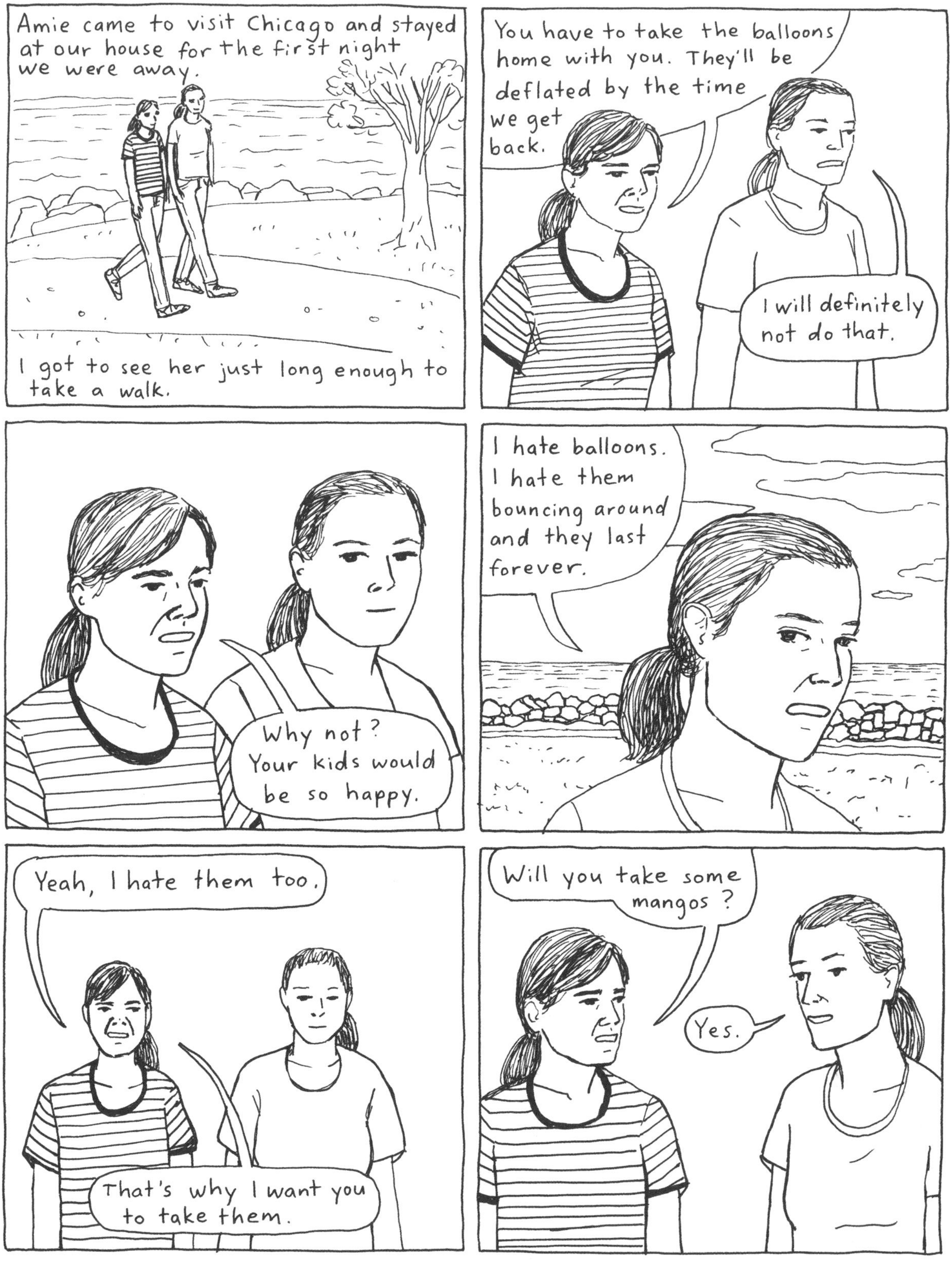
Amie came to visit Chicago and stayed at our house for the first night we were away.
I got to see her just long enough to take a walk.
You have to take the balloons home with you. They'll be deflated by the time we get back.
I will definitely not do that.
Why not? Your kids would be so happy.
I hate balloons. I hate them bouncing around and they last forever.
Yeah, I hate them too.
That's why I want you to take them.
Will you take some mangos?
Yes.

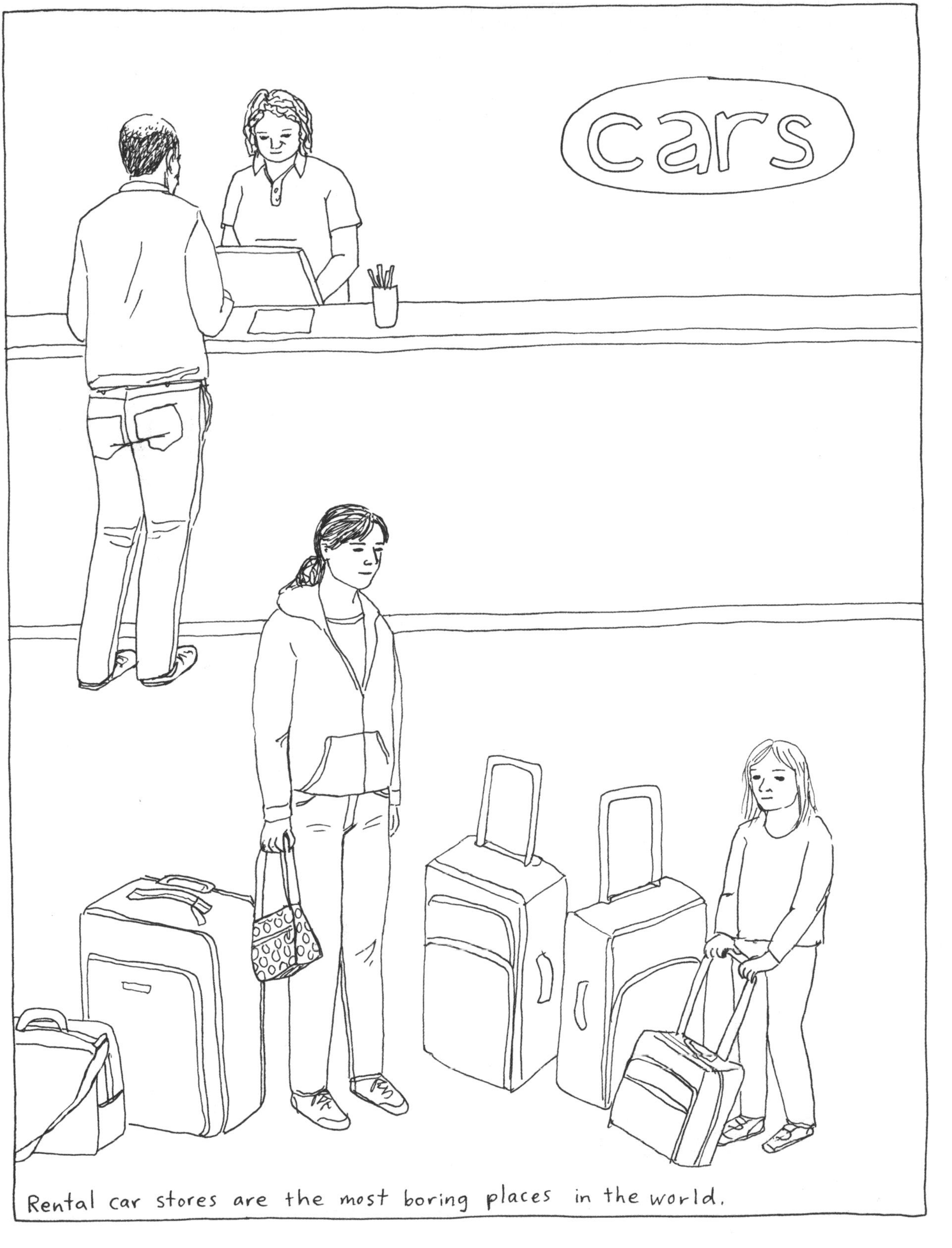
cars
Rental car stores are the most boring places in the world.

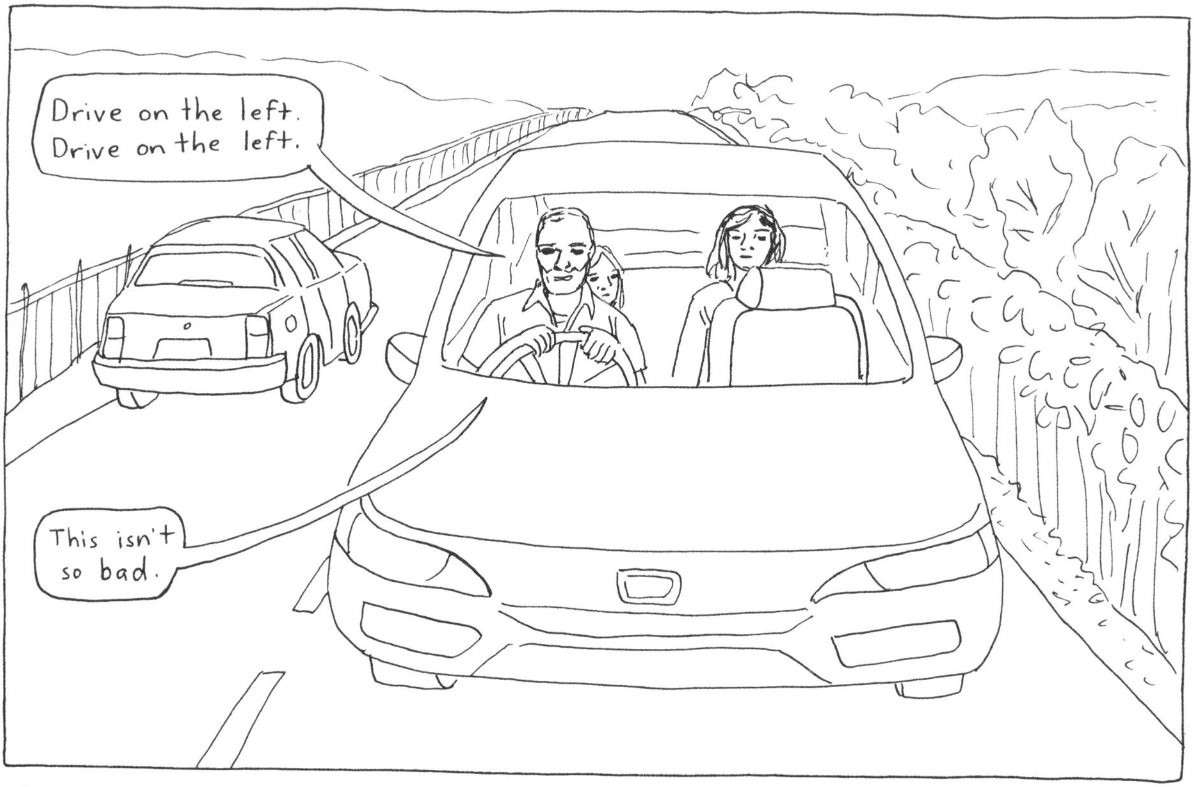
Drive on the left. Drive on the left.
This isn't so bad.

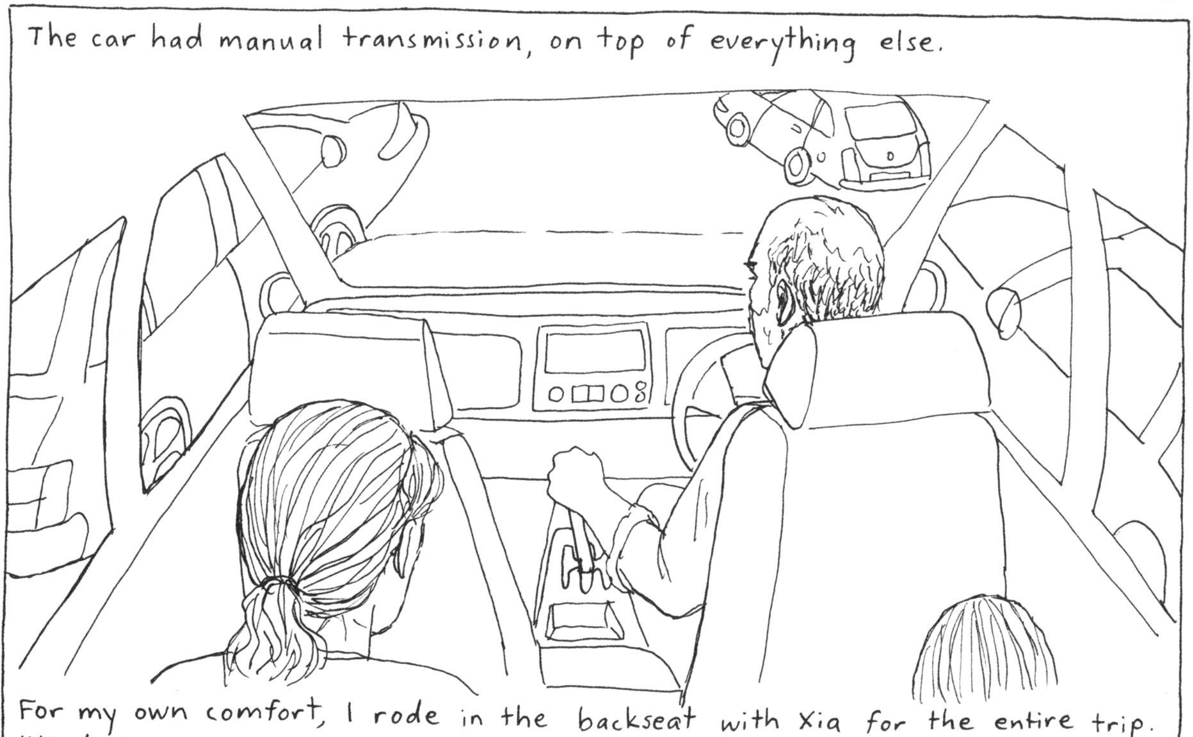
The car had manual transmission, on top of everything else.
For my own comfort, I rode in the backseat with Xia for the entire trip. It's less scary.

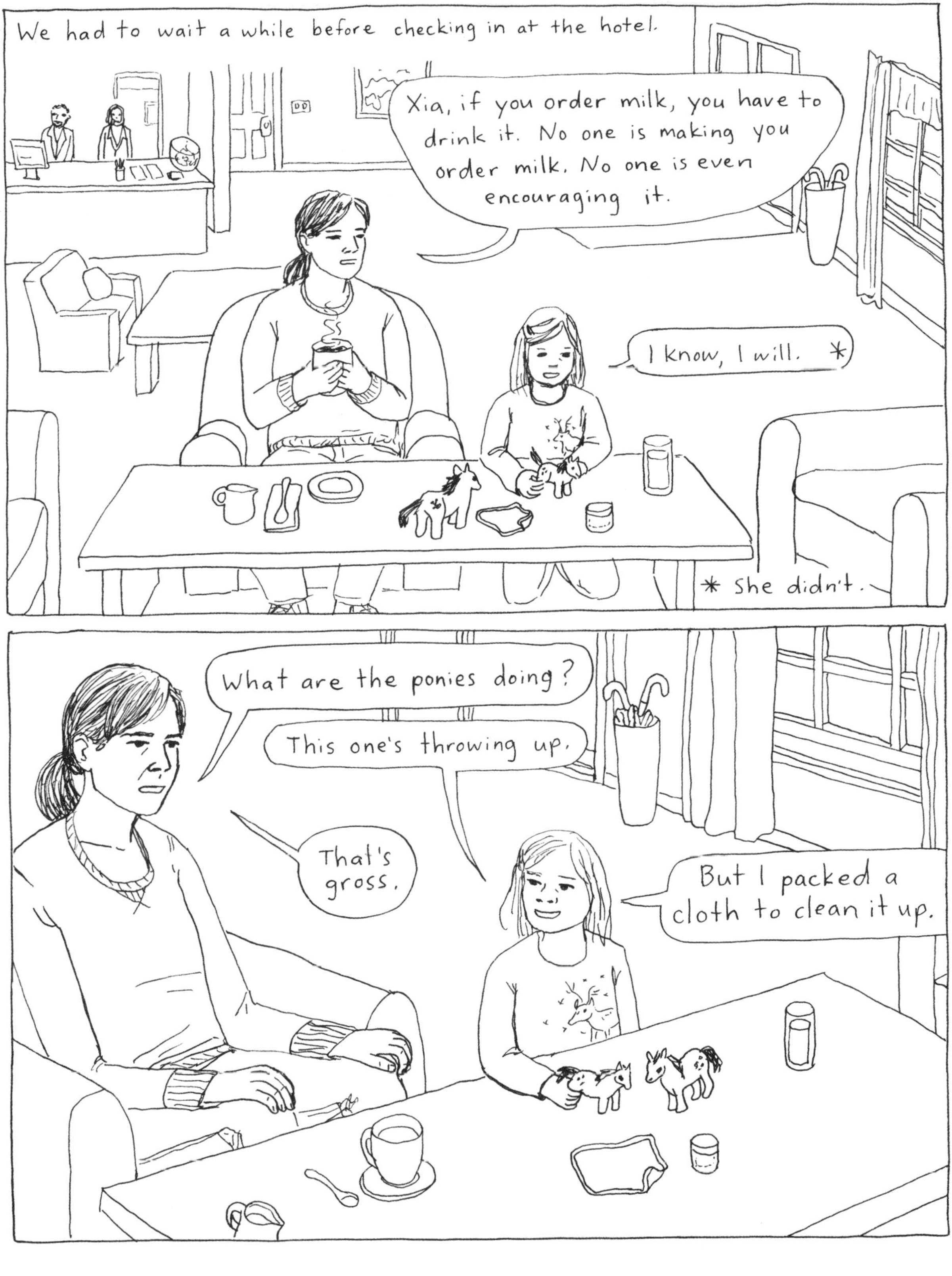

We had to wait a while before checking in at the hotel.
Xia, if you order milk, you have to drink it. No one is making you order milk. No one is even encouraging it.
I know, I will. *
* She didn't.
What are the ponies doing?
This one's throwing up.
That's gross.
But I packed a cloth to clean it up.

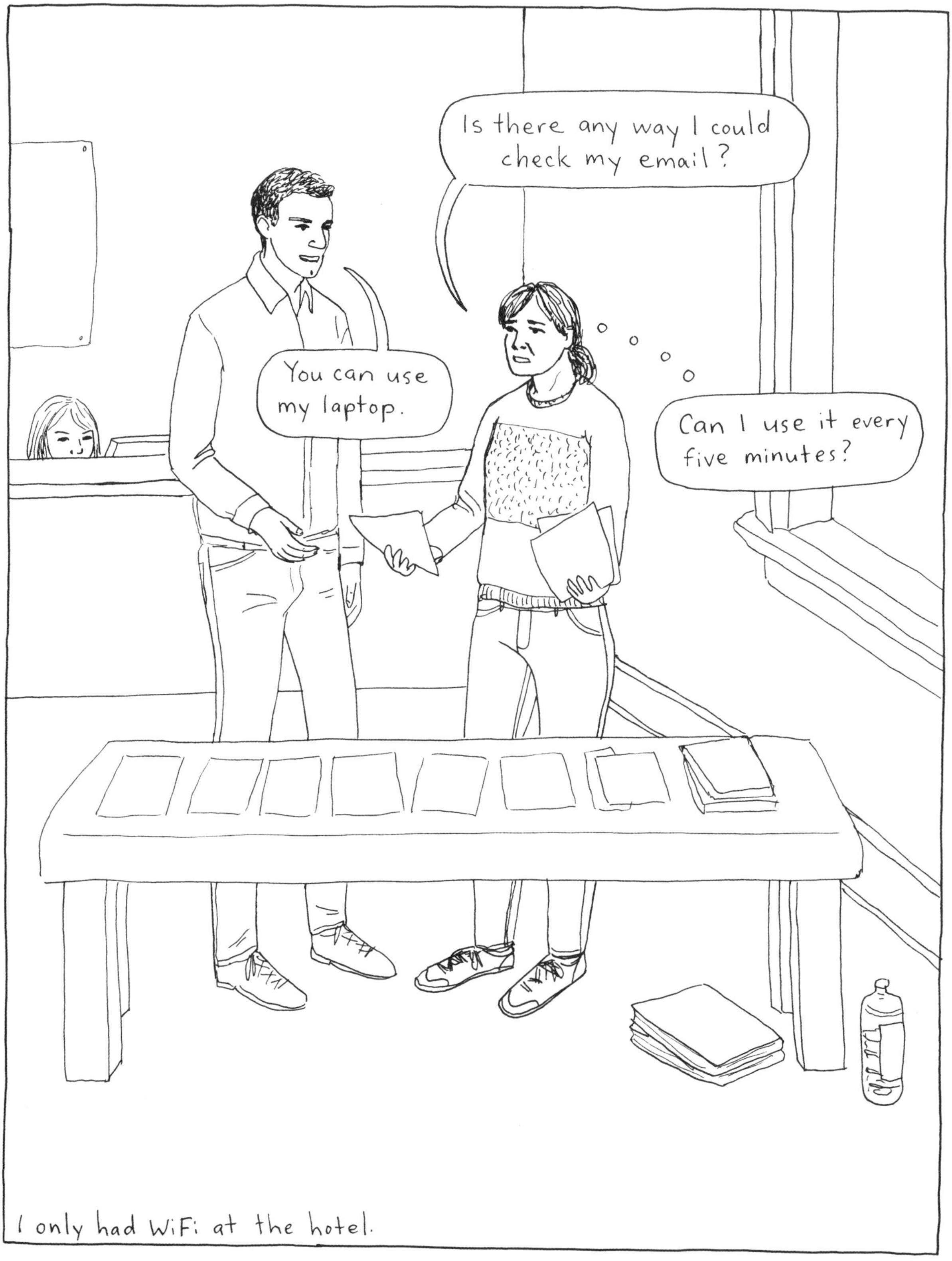
Is there any way I could check my email?
You can use my laptop.
Can I use it every five minutes?

I only had WiFi at the hotel.

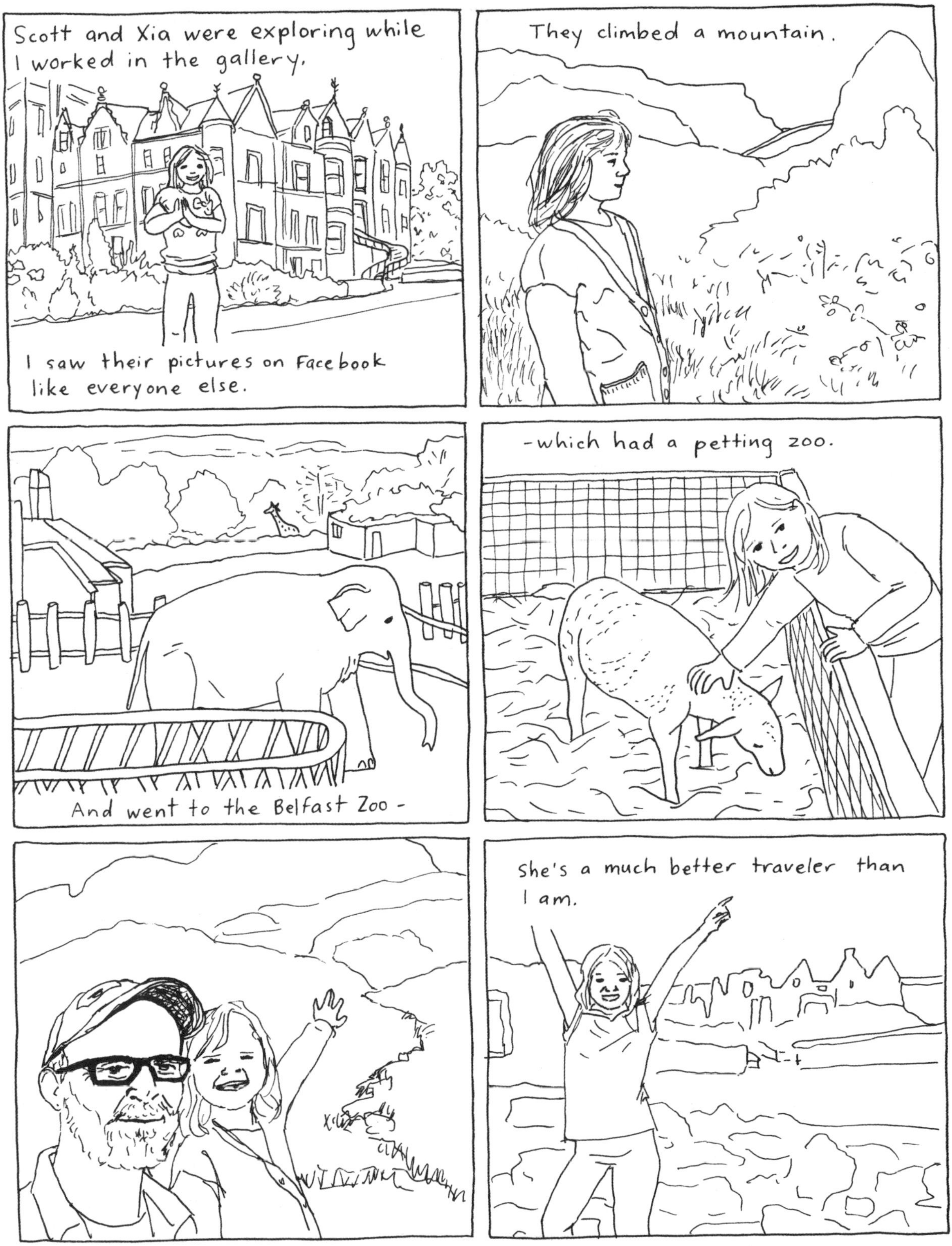
Scott and Xia were exploring while I worked in the gallery.
I saw their pictures on Facebook like everyone else.
They climbed a mountain.
And went to the Belfast Zoo -
-which had a petting zoo.
She's a much better traveler than I am.

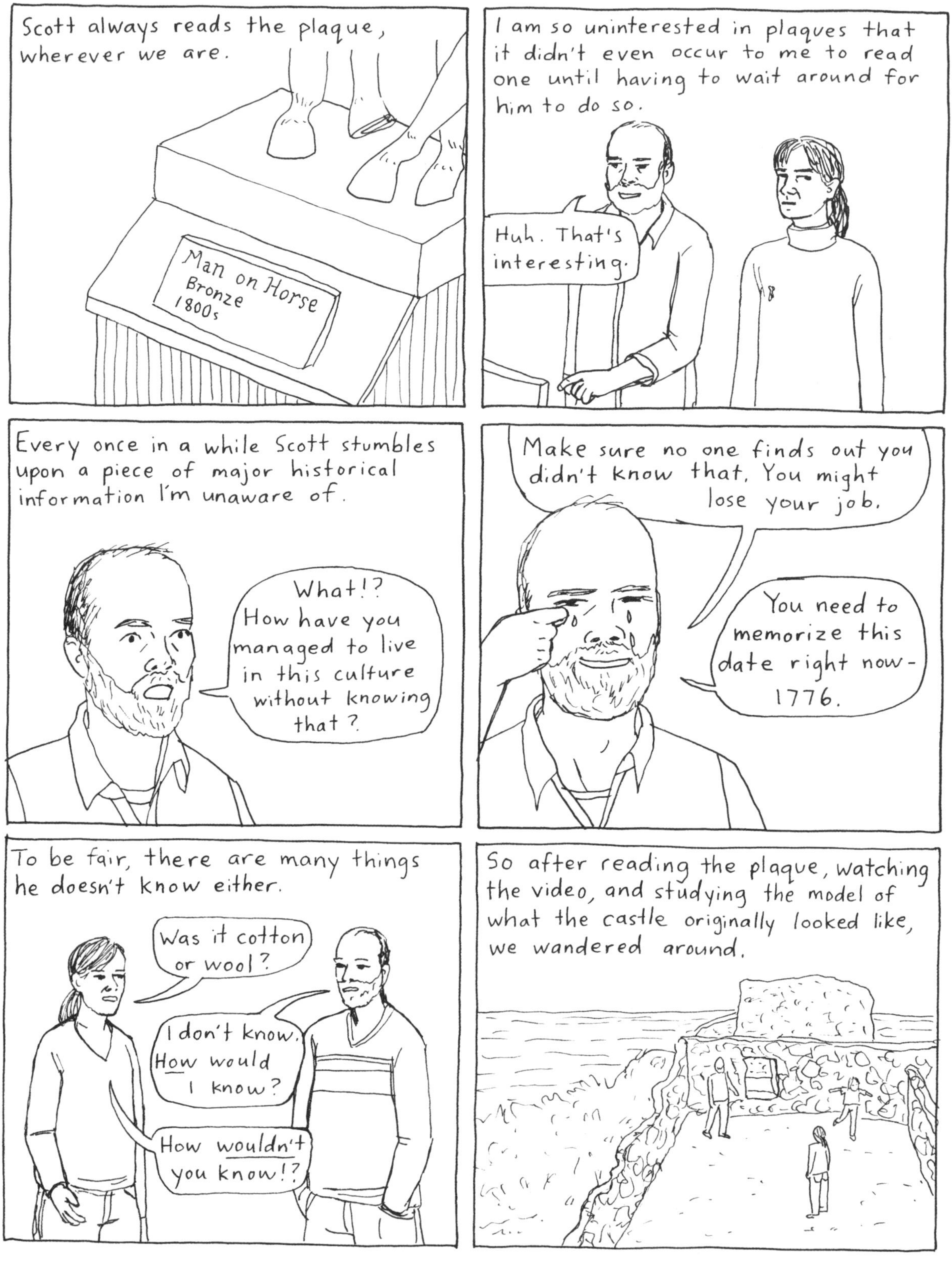
Scott always reads the plaque, wherever we are.
Man on Horse
Bronze
1800s
I am so uninterested in plaques that it didn't even occur to me to read one until having to wait around for him to do so.
Huh. That's interesting.
Every once in a while Scott stumbles upon a piece of major historical information I'm unaware of.
What!? How have you managed to live in this culture without knowing that?
Make sure no one finds out you didn't know that. You might lose your job.
You need to memorize this date right now - 1776.
To be fair, there are many things he doesn't know either.
Was it cotton or wool?
I don't know. How would I know?
How wouldn't you know!?
So after reading the plaque, watching the video, and studying the model of what the castle originally looked like, we wandered around.

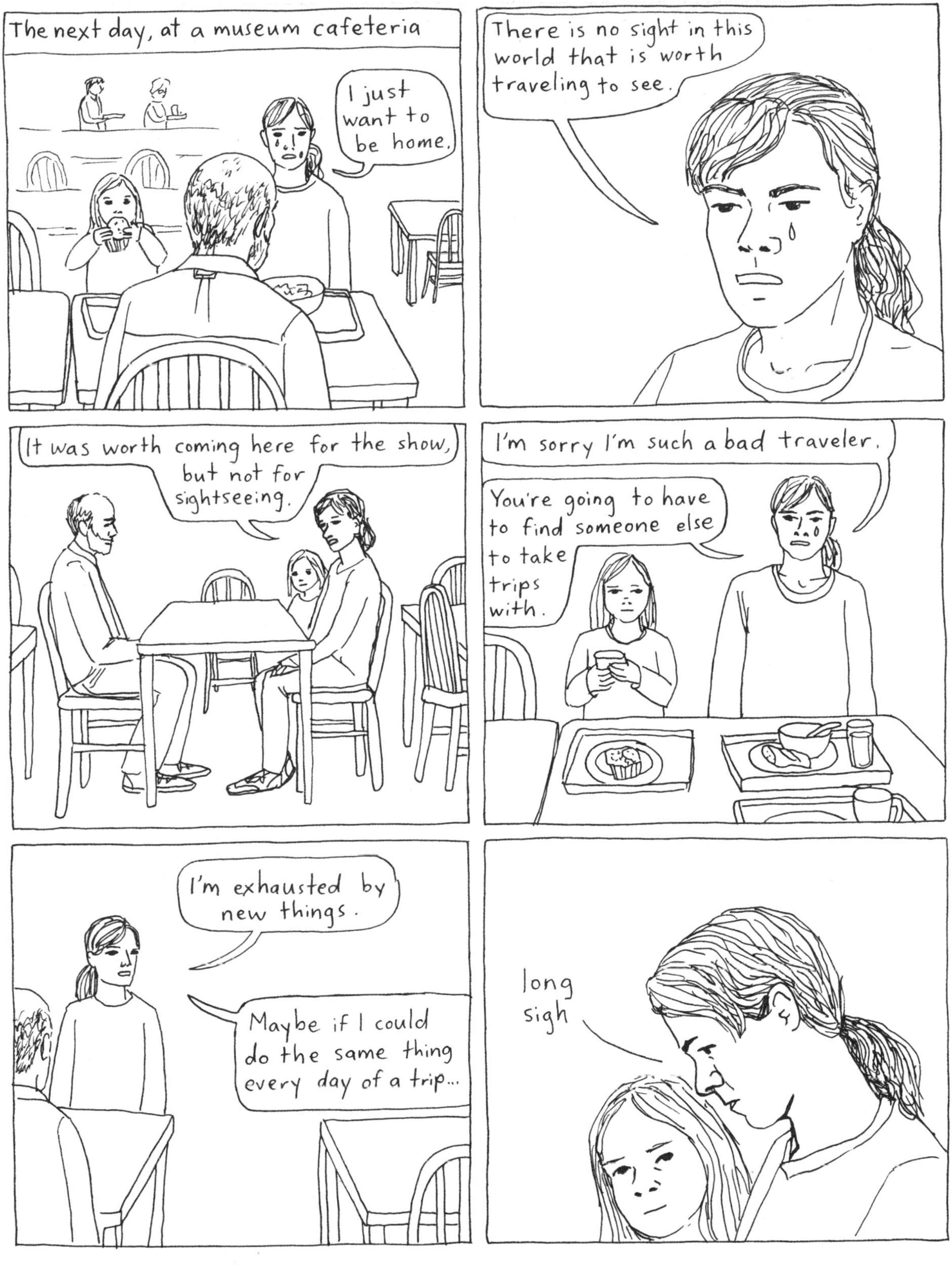
The next day, at a museum cafeteria
I just want to be home.
There is no sight in this world that is worth traveling to see.
It was worth coming here for the show, but not for sightseeing.
I'm sorry I'm such a bad traveler.
You're going to have to find someone else to take trips with.
I'm exhausted by new things.
Maybe if I could do the same thing every day of a trip...
long sigh

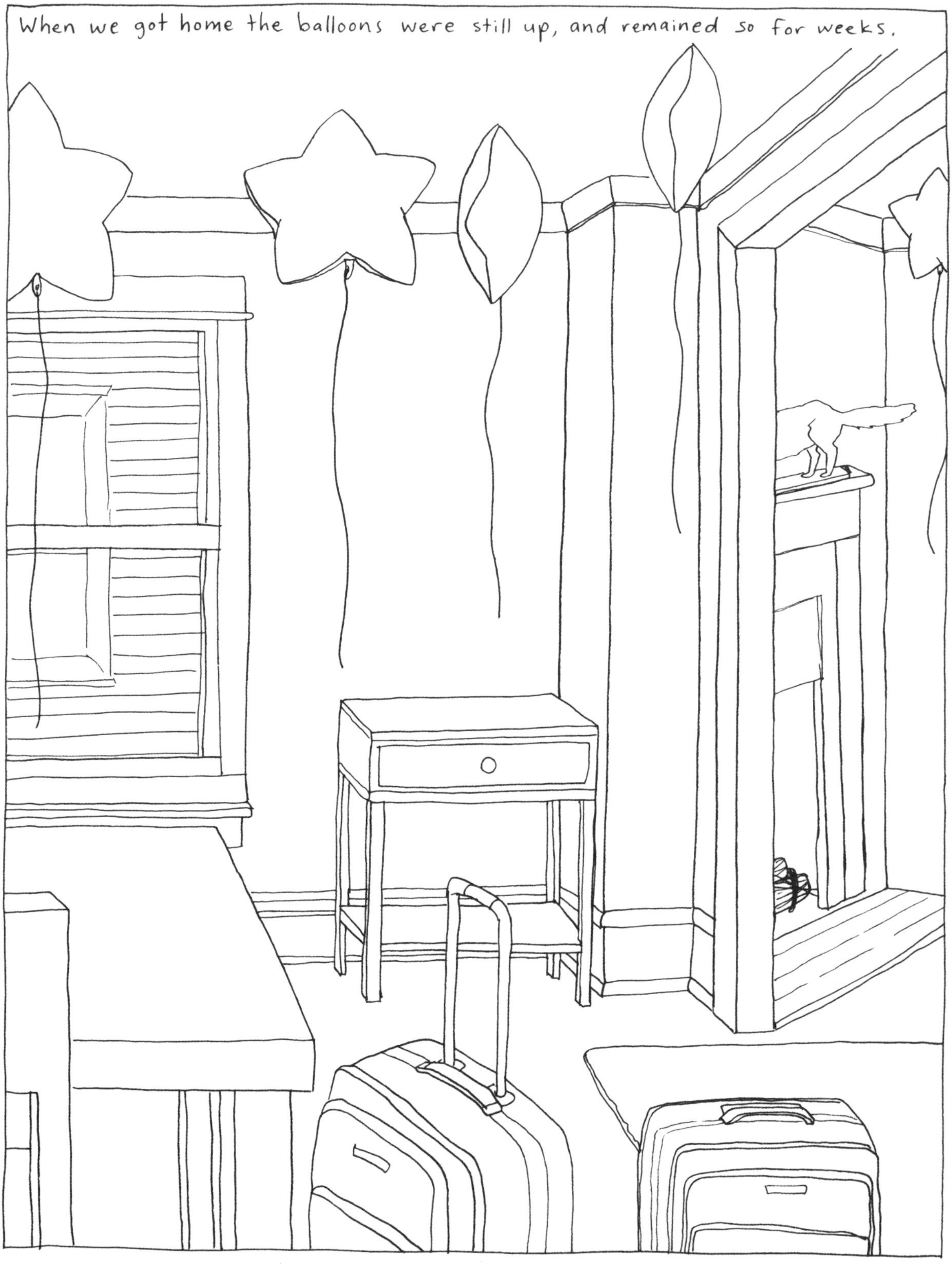
When we got home the balloons were still up, and remained so for weeks.

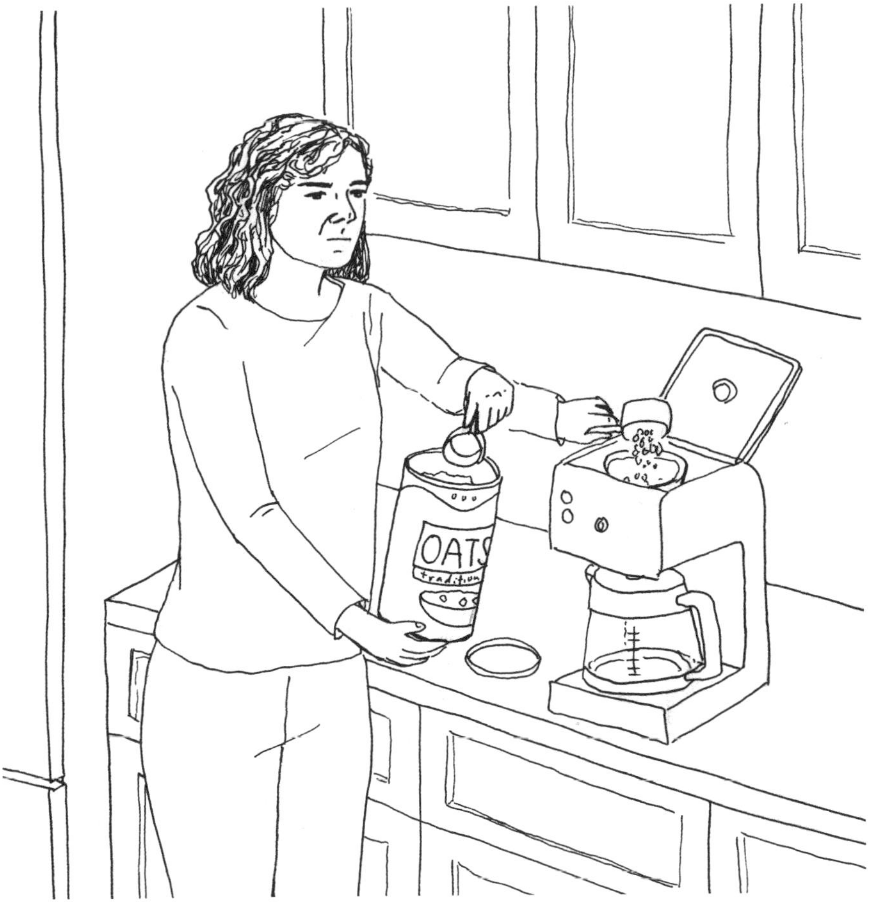
OATS

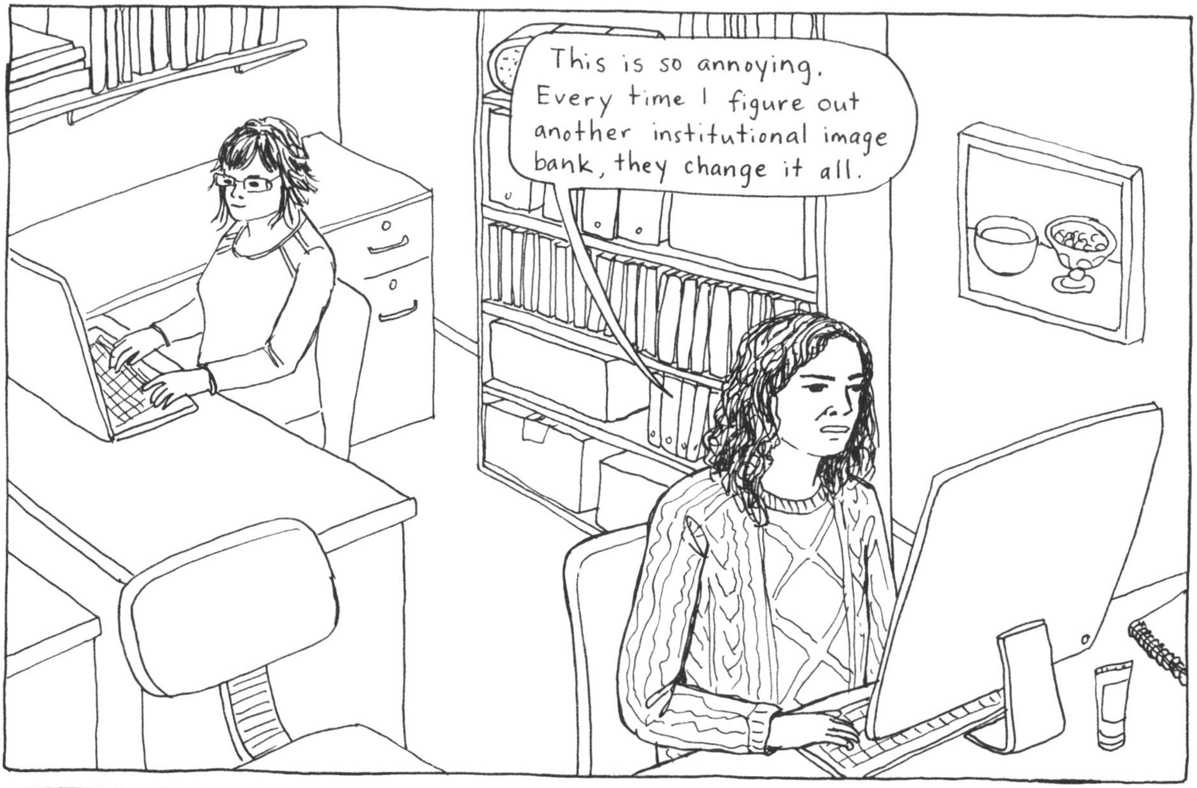
This is so annoying. Every time I figure out another institutional image bank, they change it all.

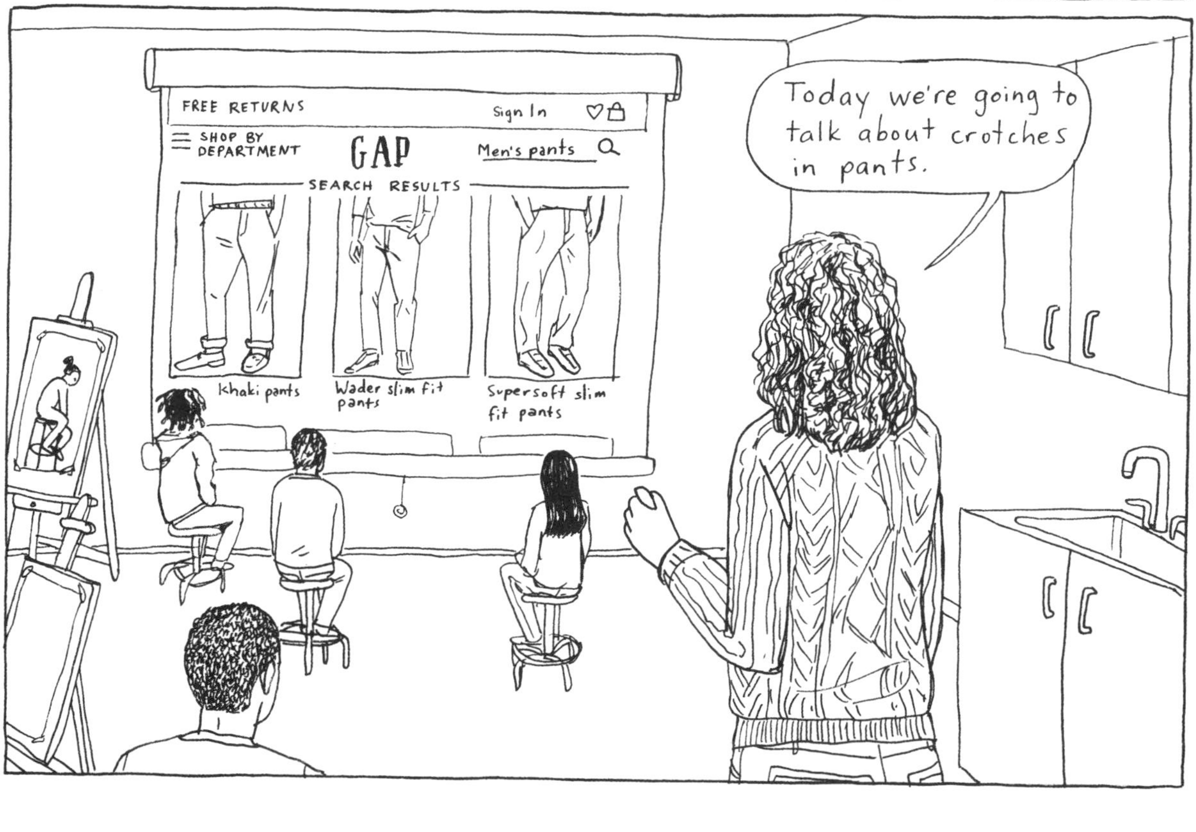
FREE RETURNS
Sign In
SHOP BY DEPARTMENT
GAP
Men's pants
SEARCH RESULTS
Khaki pants
Wader slim fit pants
Supersoft slim fit pants
Today we're going to talk about crotches in pants.

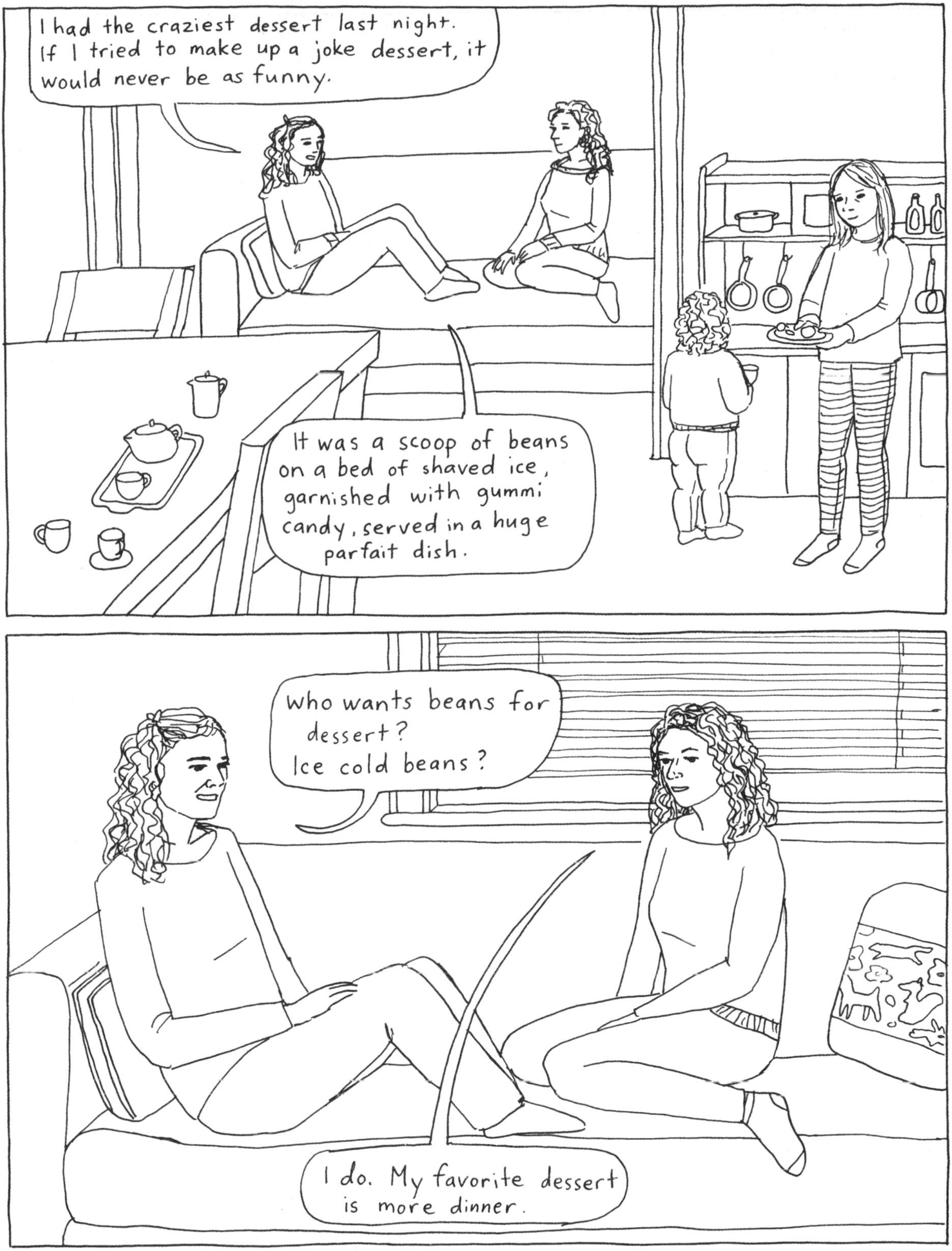
I had the craziest dessert last night. If I tried to make up a joke dessert, it would never be as funny.
It was a scoop of beans on a bed of shaved ice, garnished with gummi candy, served in a huge parfait dish.
Who wants beans for dessert? Ice cold beans?
I do. My favorite dessert is more dinner.

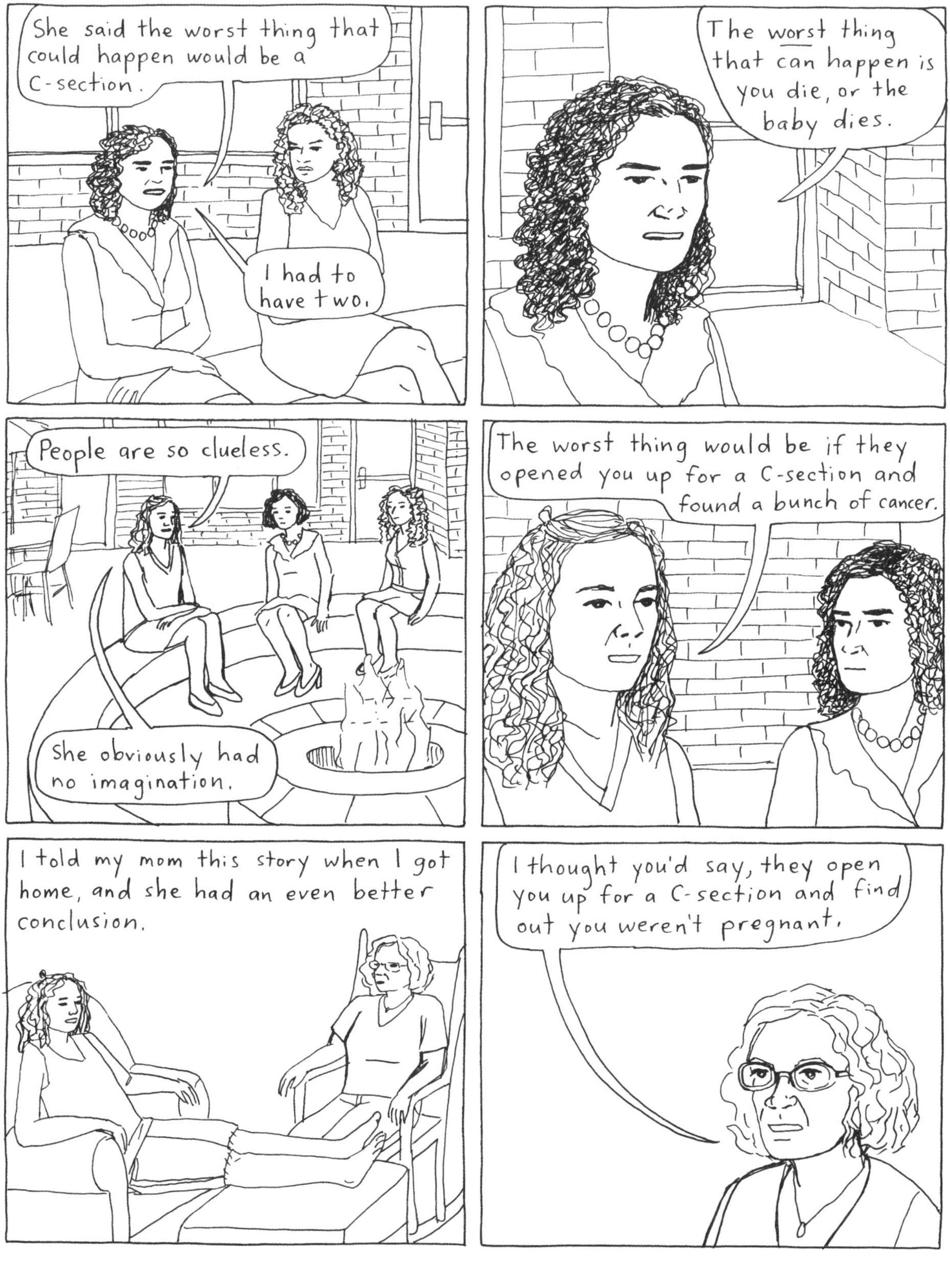

She said the worst thing that could happen would be a C-section.
I had to have two.
The worst thing that can happen is you die, or the baby dies.
People are so clueless.
She obviously had no imagination.
The worst thing would be if they opened you up for a C-section and found a bunch of cancer.
I told my mom this story when I got home, and she had an even better conclusion.
I thought you'd say, they open you up for a C-section and find out you weren't pregnant.

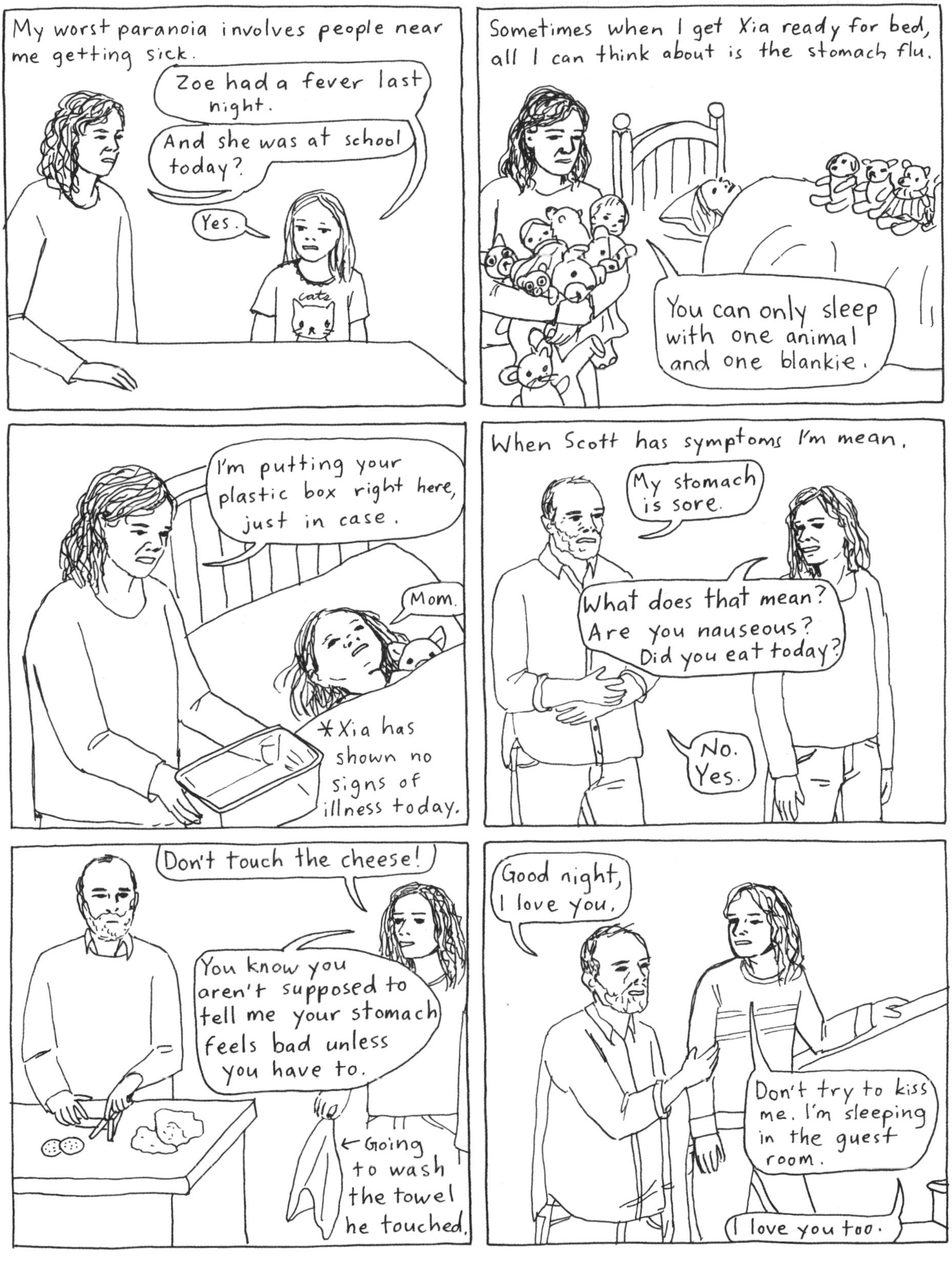
My worst paranoia involves people near me getting sick.
Zoe had a fever last night.
And she was at school today?
Yes.
cats
Sometimes when I get Xia ready for bed, all I can think about is the stomach flu.
You can only sleep with one animal and one blankie.
I'm putting your plastic box right here, just in case.
Mom.
*Xia has shown no signs of illness today.
When Scott has symptoms I'm mean.
My stomach is sore.
What does that mean? Are you nauseous? Did you eat today?
No. Yes.
Don't touch the cheese!
You know you aren't supposed to tell me your stomach feels bad unless you have to.
← Going to wash the towel he touched.
Good night, I love you.
Don't try to kiss me. I'm sleeping in the guest room.
I love you too.

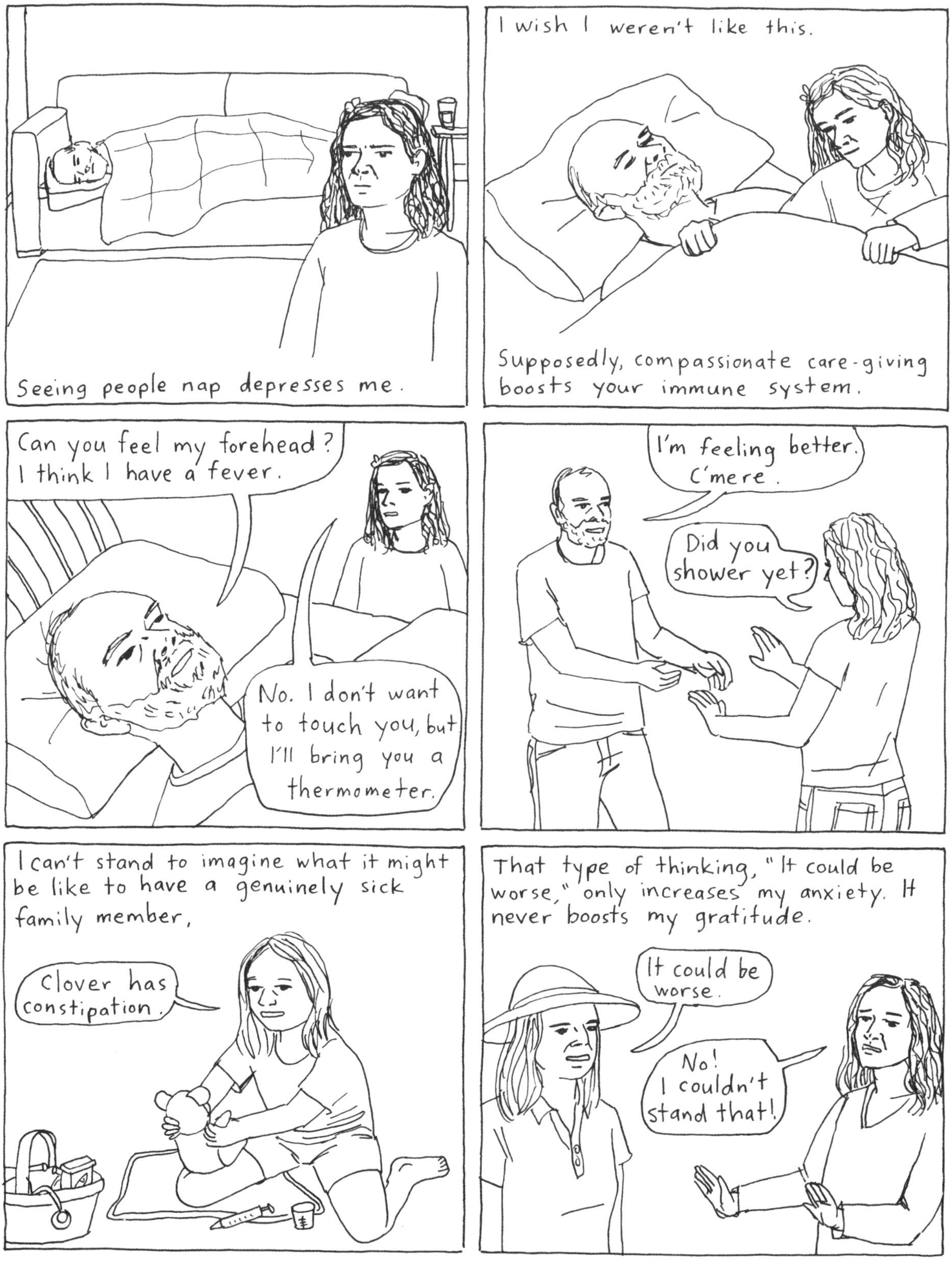
Seeing people nap depresses me.
I wish I weren't like this.
Supposedly, compassionate care-giving boosts your immune system.
Can you feel my forehead? I think I have a fever.
No. I don't want to touch you, but I'll bring you a thermometer.
I'm feeling better. C'mere.
Did you shower yet?
I can't stand to imagine what it might be like to have a genuinely sick family member,
Clover has constipation.
That type of thinking, "It could be worse," only increases my anxiety. It never boosts my gratitude.
It could be worse.
No! I couldn't stand that!

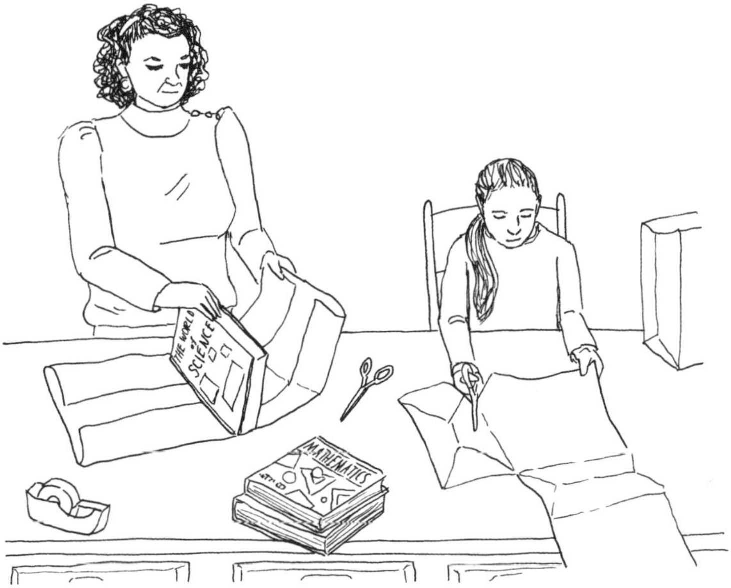
THE WORLD of SCIENCE
MATHEMATICS

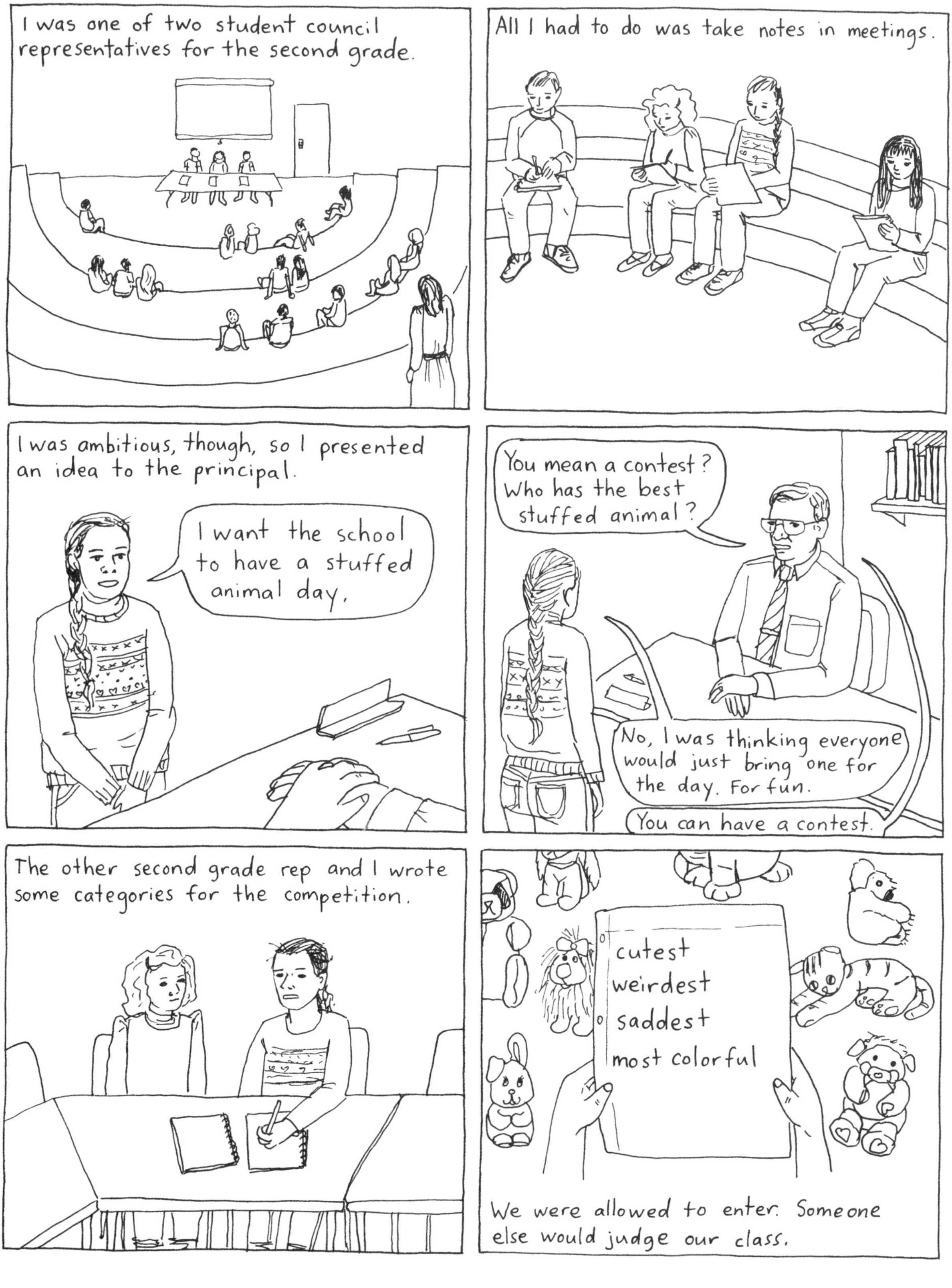
I was one of two student council representatives for the second grade.
All I had to do was take notes in meetings.
I was ambitious, though, so I presented an idea to the principal.
I want the school to have a stuffed animal day,
You mean a contest? Who has the best stuffed animal?
No, I was thinking everyone would just bring one for the day. For fun.
You can have a contest.
The other second grade rep and I wrote some categories for the competition.
cutest
weirdest
saddest
most colorful
We were allowed to enter. Someone else would judge our class.

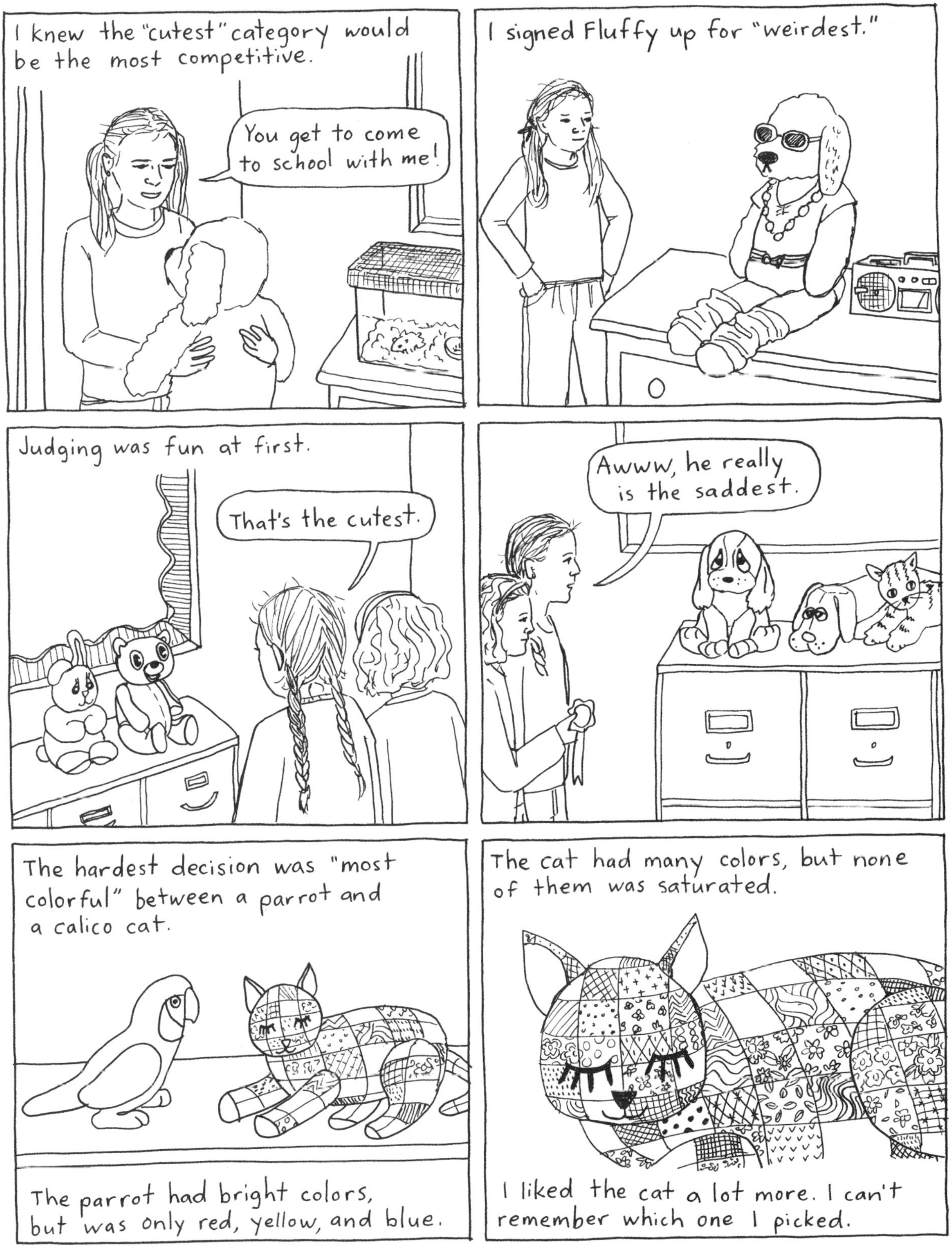
I knew the "cutest" category would be the most competitive.
You get to come to school with me!
I signed Fluffy up for "weirdest."
Judging was fun at first.
That's the cutest.
Awww, he really is the saddest.
The hardest decision was "most colorful" between a parrot and a calico cat.
The parrot had bright colors, but was only red, yellow, and blue.
The cat had many colors, but none of them was saturated.
I liked the cat a lot more. I can't remember which one I picked.

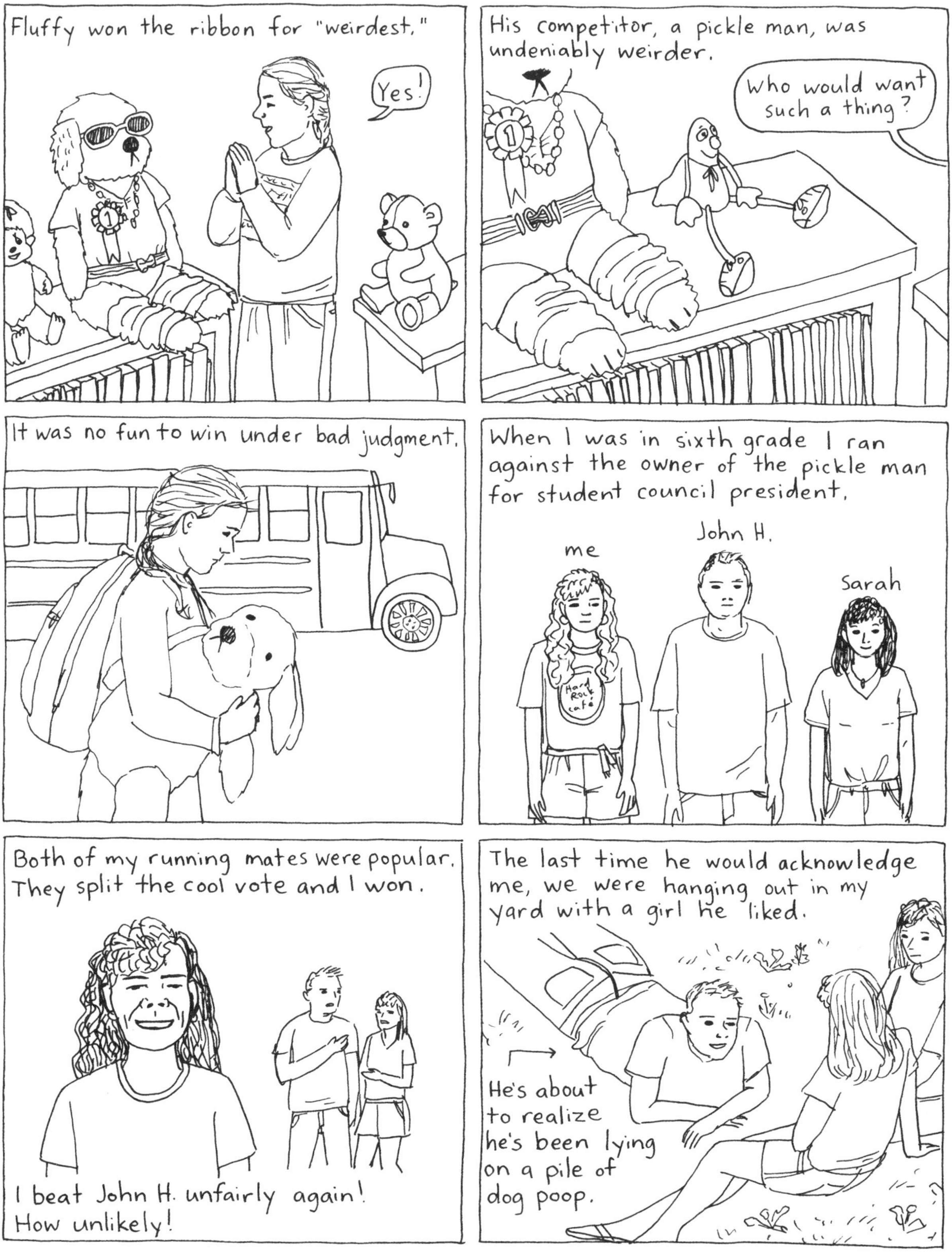
Fluffy won the ribbon for "weirdest."
Yes!
His competitor, a pickle man, was undeniably weirder.
Who would want such a thing?
It was no fun to win under bad judgment.
When I was in sixth grade I ran against the owner of the pickle man for student council president.
me
John H.
Sarah
Hard Rock café
Both of my running mates were popular. They split the cool vote and I won.
I beat John H. unfairly again! How unlikely!
The last time he would acknowledge me, we were hanging out in my yard with a girl he liked.
He's about to realize he's been lying on a pile of dog poop.

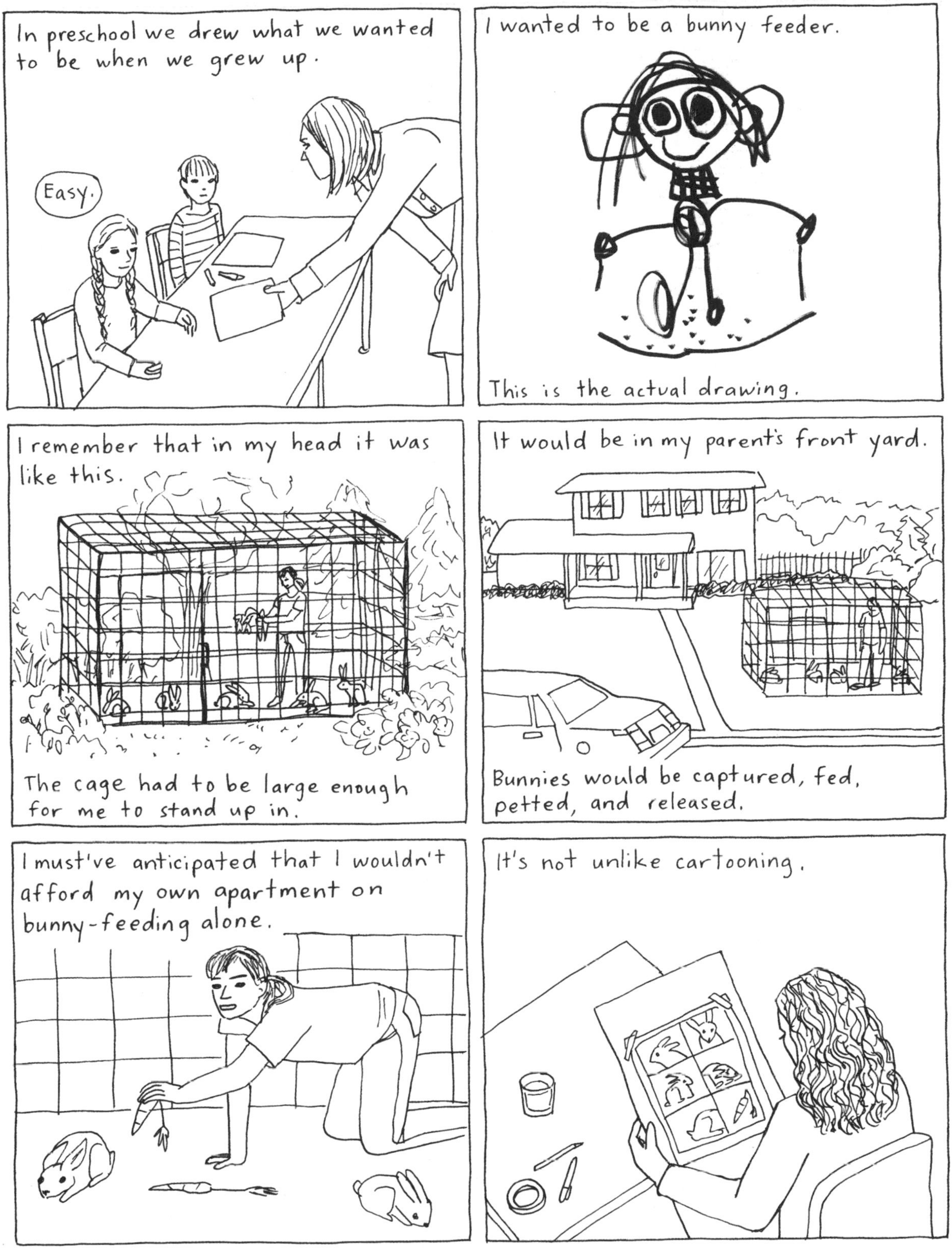
In preschool we drew what we wanted to be when we grew up.
Easy.
I wanted to be a bunny feeder.
This is the actual drawing.
I remember that in my head it was like this.
The cage had to be large enough for me to stand up in.
It would be in my parent's front yard.
Bunnies would be captured, fed, petted, and released.
I must've anticipated that I wouldn't afford my own apartment on bunny-feeding alone.
It's not unlike cartooning.

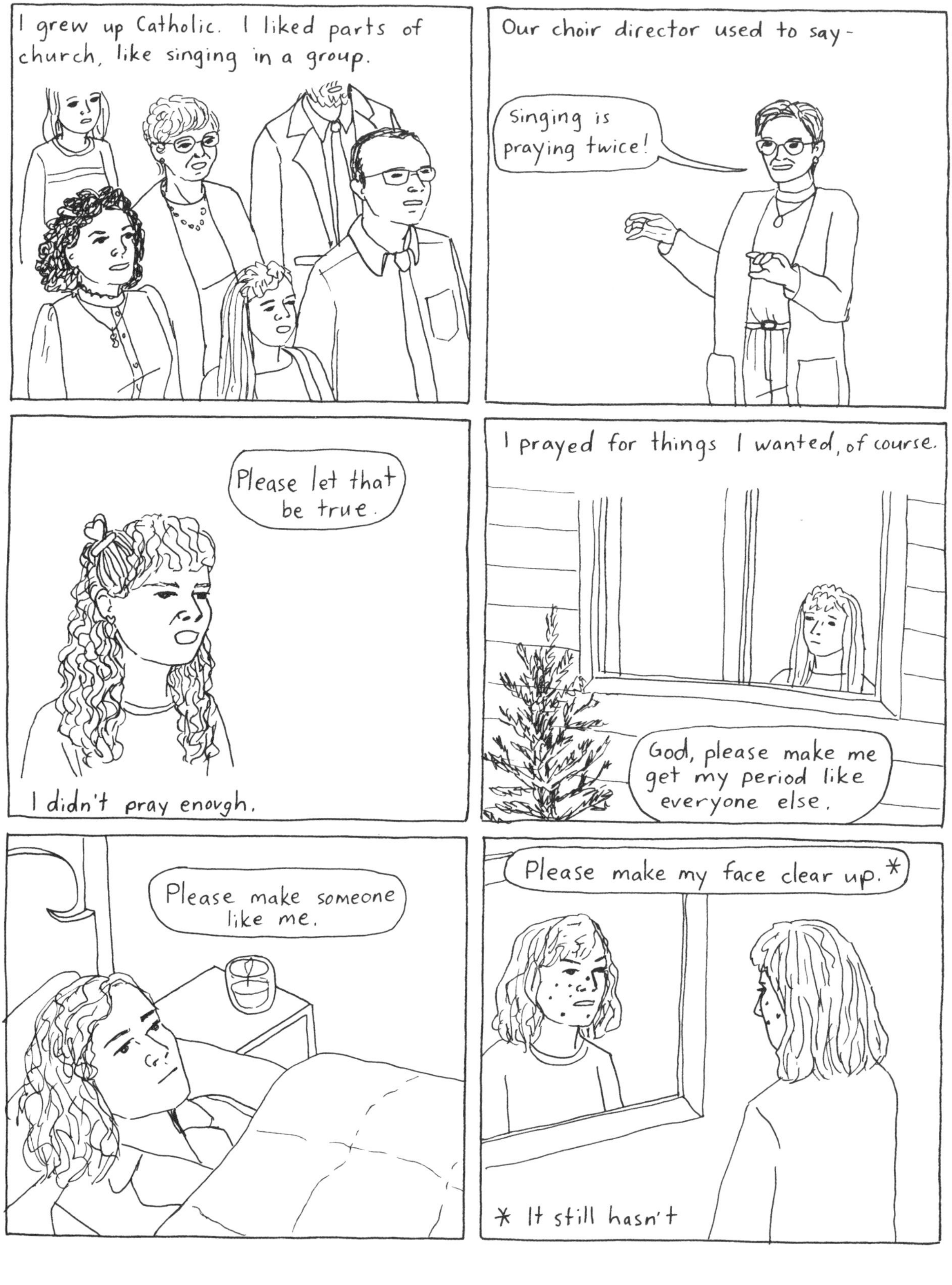

I grew up Catholic. I liked parts of church, like singing in a group.
Our choir director used to say-
Singing is praying twice!
Please let that be true.
I didn't pray enough.
I prayed for things I wanted, of course.
God, please make me get my period like everyone else.
Please make someone like me.
Please make my face clear up.*
* It still hasn't

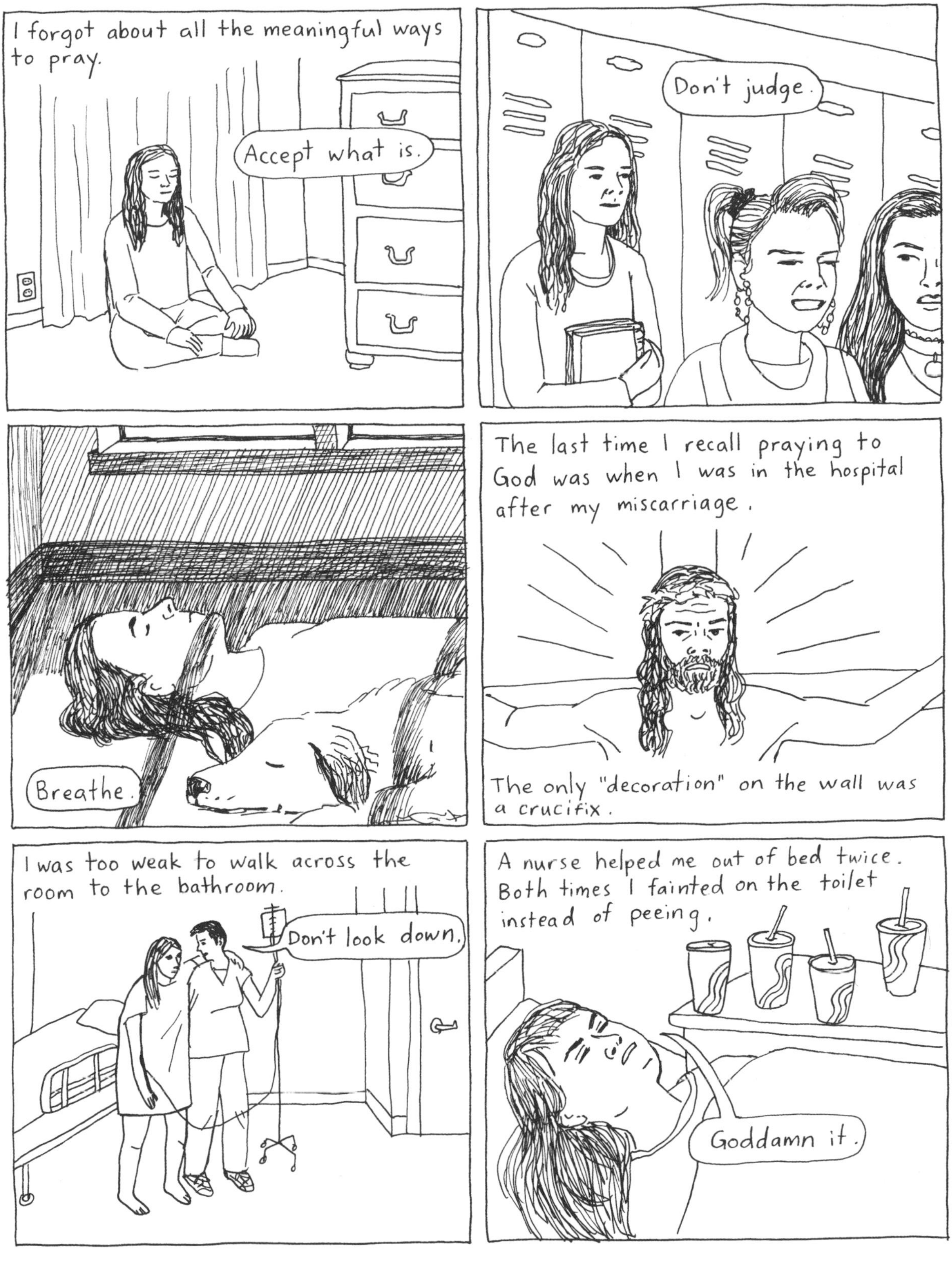
I forgot about all the meaningful ways to pray.
Accept what is.
Don't judge.
Breathe.
The last time I recall praying to God was when I was in the hospital after my miscarriage.
The only "decoration" on the wall was a crucifix.
I was too weak to walk across the room to the bathroom.
Don't look down.
A nurse helped me out of bed twice. Both times I fainted on the toilet instead of peeing.
Goddamn it.

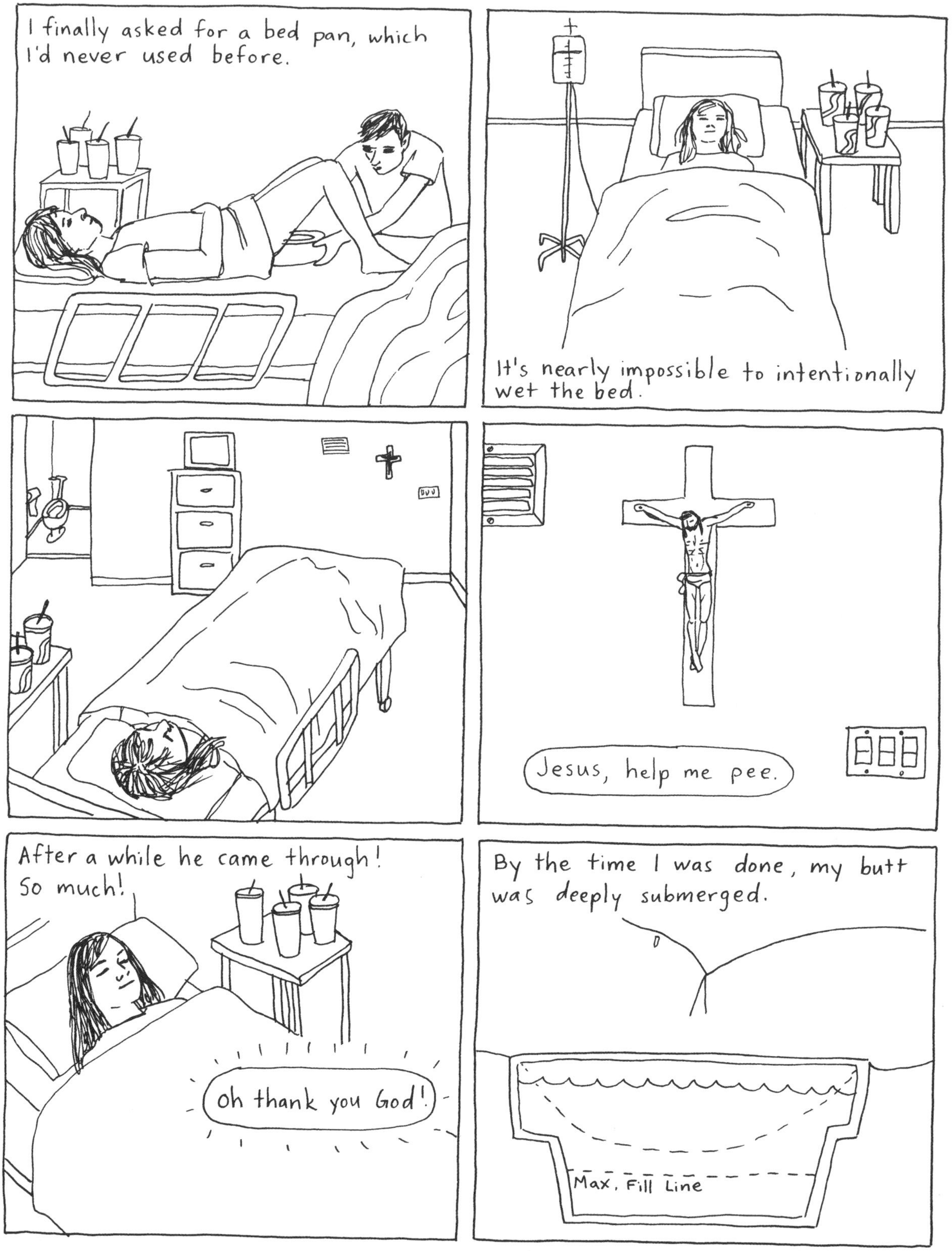
I finally asked for a bed pan, which I'd never used before.
It's nearly impossible to intentionally wet the bed.
Jesus, help me pee.
After a while he came through! So much!
Oh thank you God!
By the time I was done, my butt was deeply submerged.
Max. Fill Line

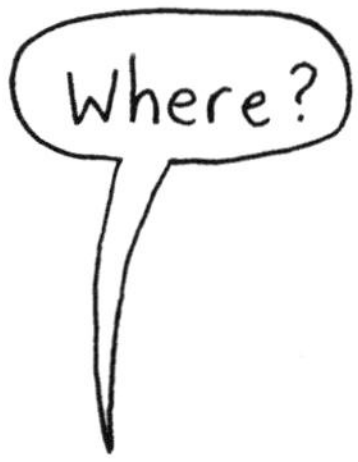
Where?

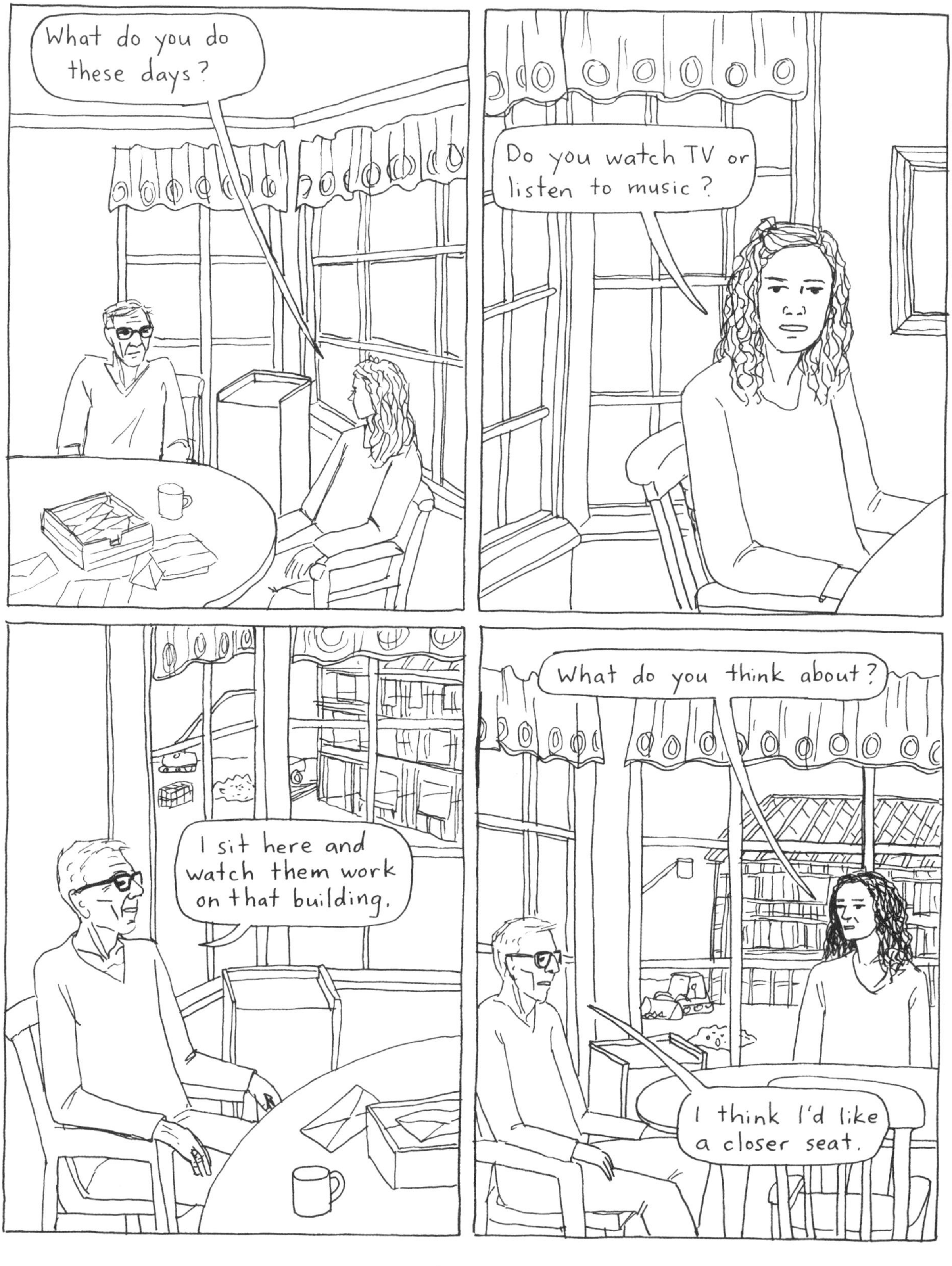
What do you do these days?
Do you watch TV or listen to music?
I sit here and watch them work on that building.
What do you think about?
I think I'd like a closer seat.

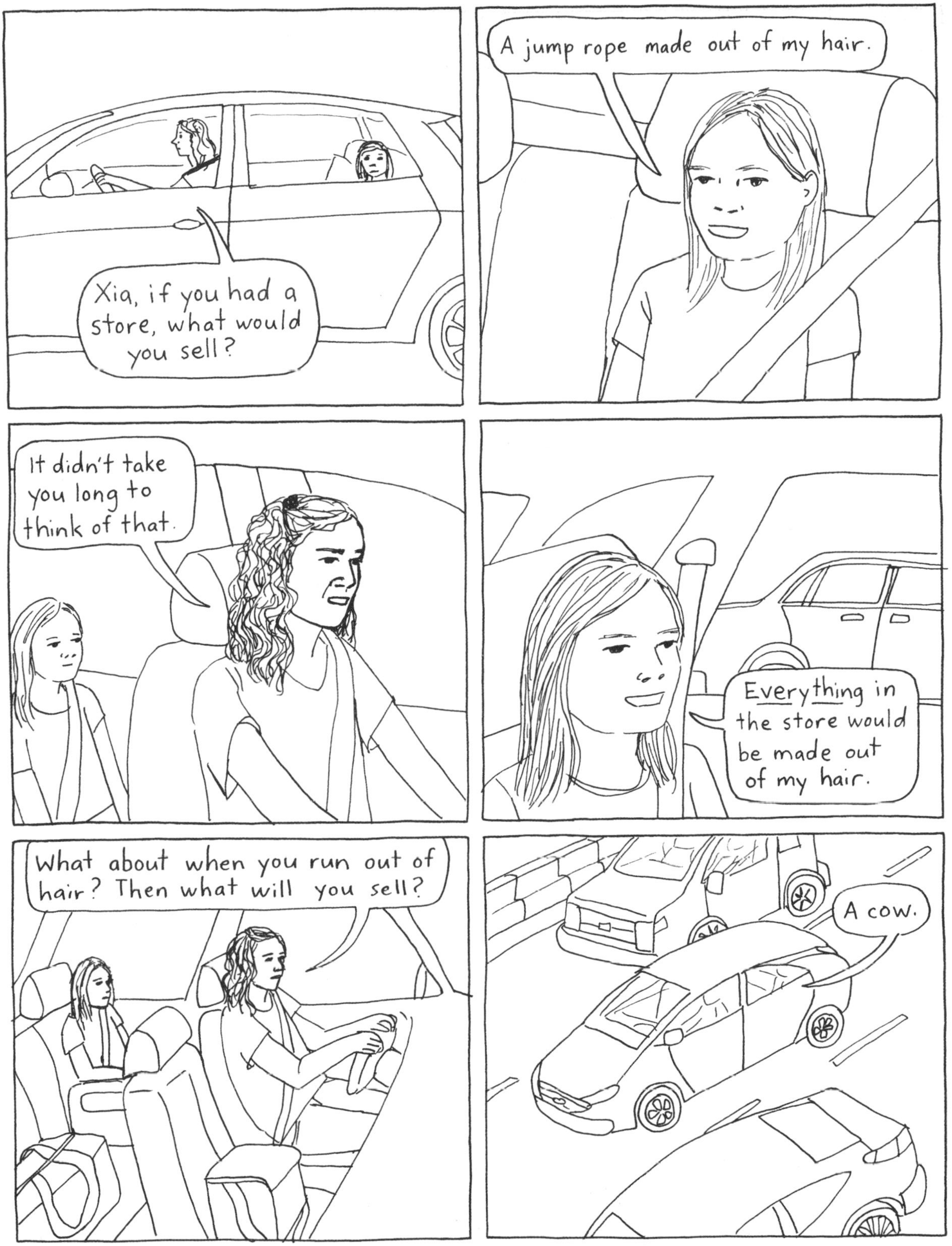
Xia, if you had a store, what would you sell?
A jump rope made out of my hair.
It didn't take you long to think of that.
Everything in the store would be made out of my hair.
What about when you run out of hair? Then what will you sell?
A cow.

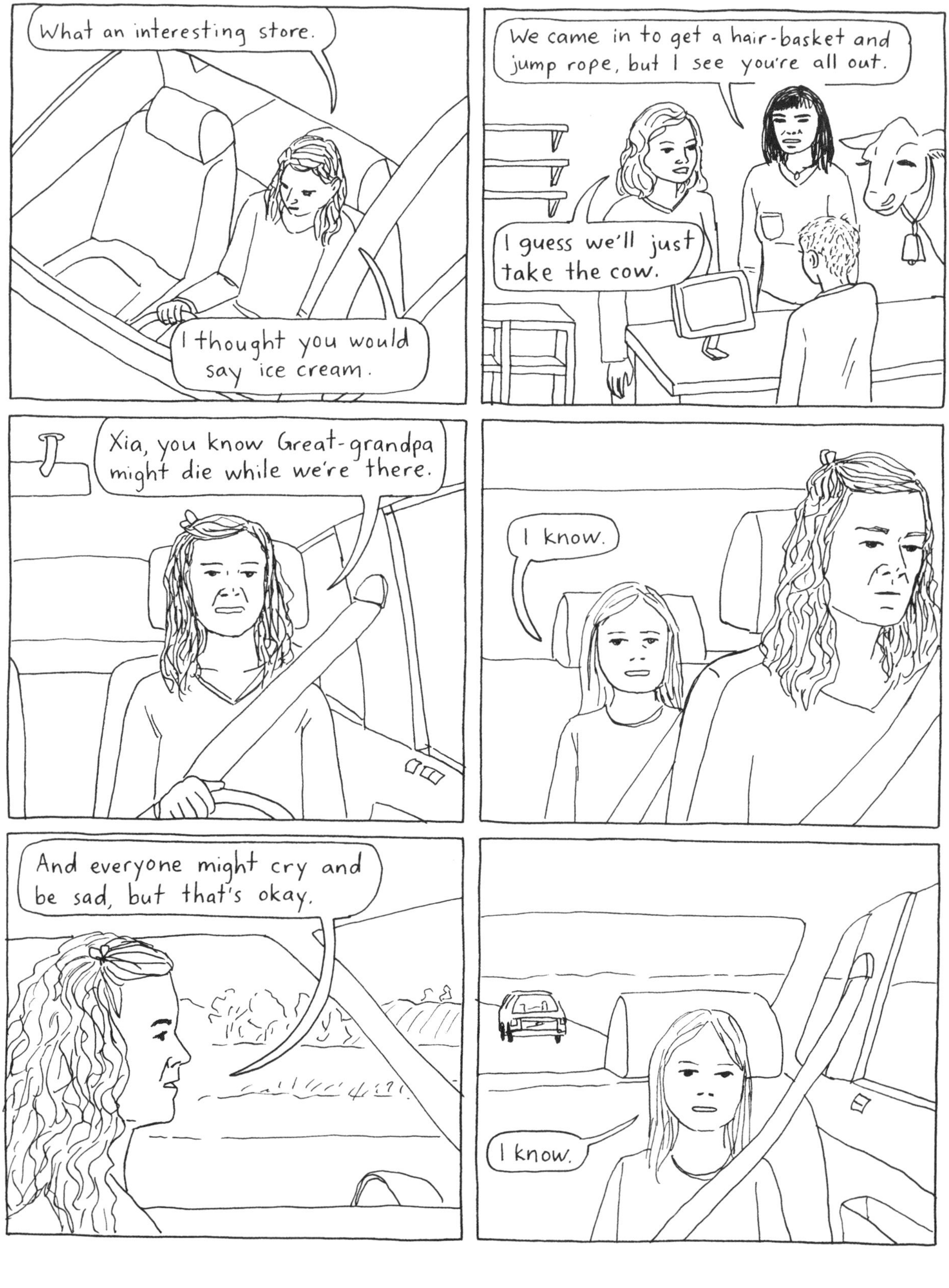
What an interesting store.
I thought you would say ice cream.
We came in to get a hair-basket and jump rope, but I see you're all out.
I guess we'll just take the cow.
Xia, you know Great-grandpa might die while we're there.
I know.
And everyone might cry and be sad, but that's okay.
I know.

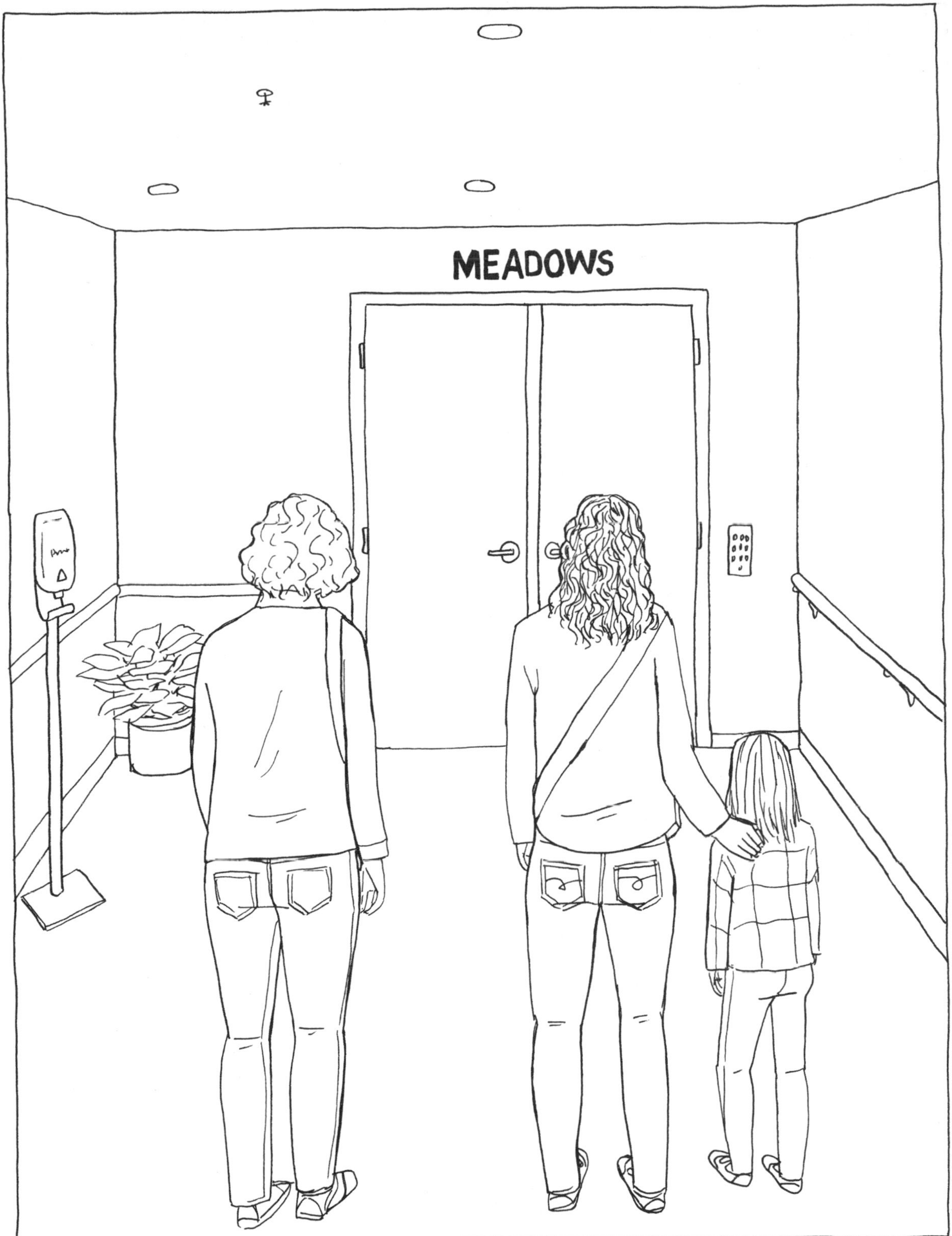
MEADOWS

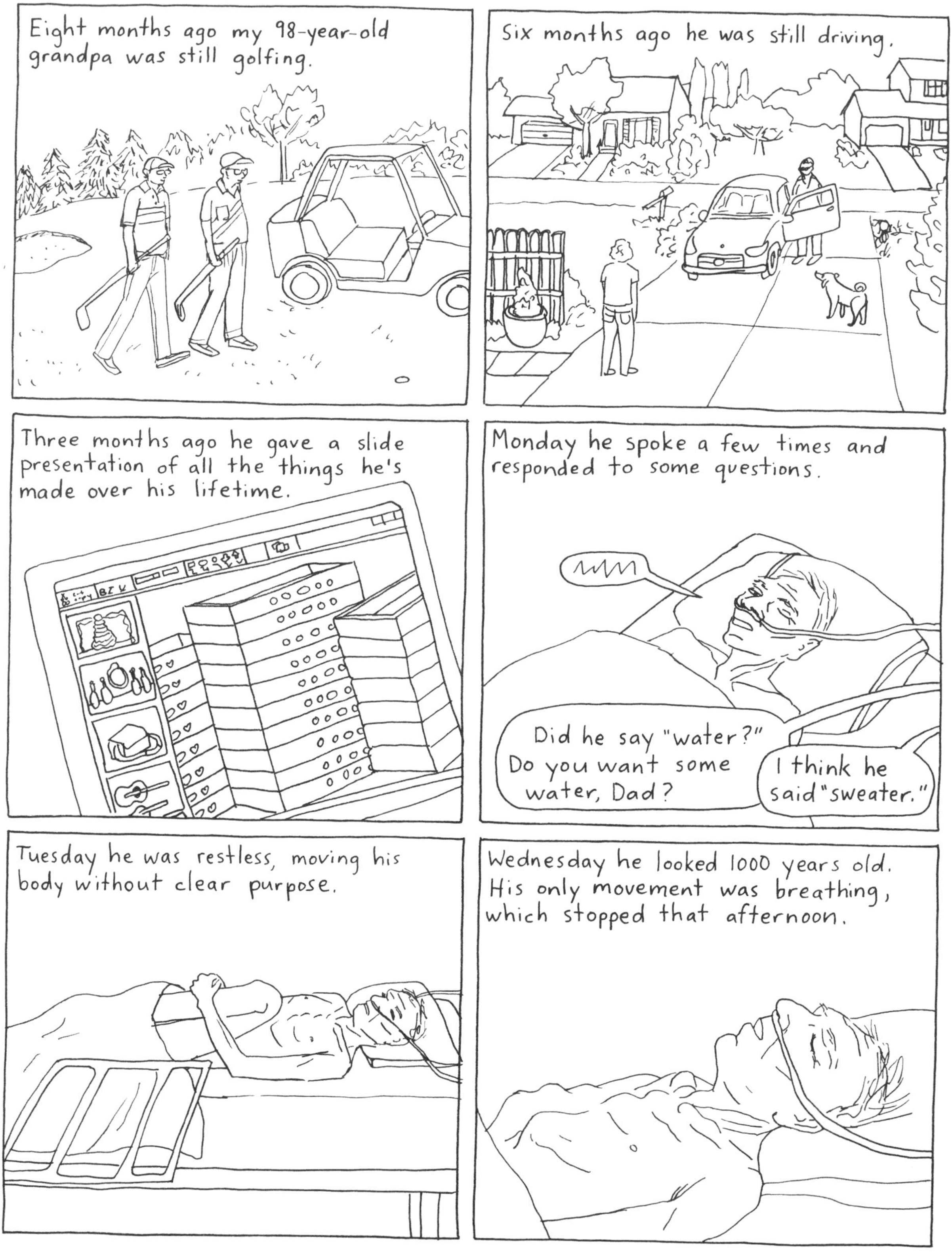
Eight months ago my 98-year-old grandpa was still golfing.
Six months ago he was still driving.
Three months ago he gave a slide presentation of all the things he's made over his lifetime.
Monday he spoke a few times and responded to some questions.
Did he say "water?" Do you want some water, Dad?
I think he said "sweater."
Tuesday he was restless, moving his body without clear purpose.
Wednesday he looked 1000 years old. His only movement was breathing, which stopped that afternoon.

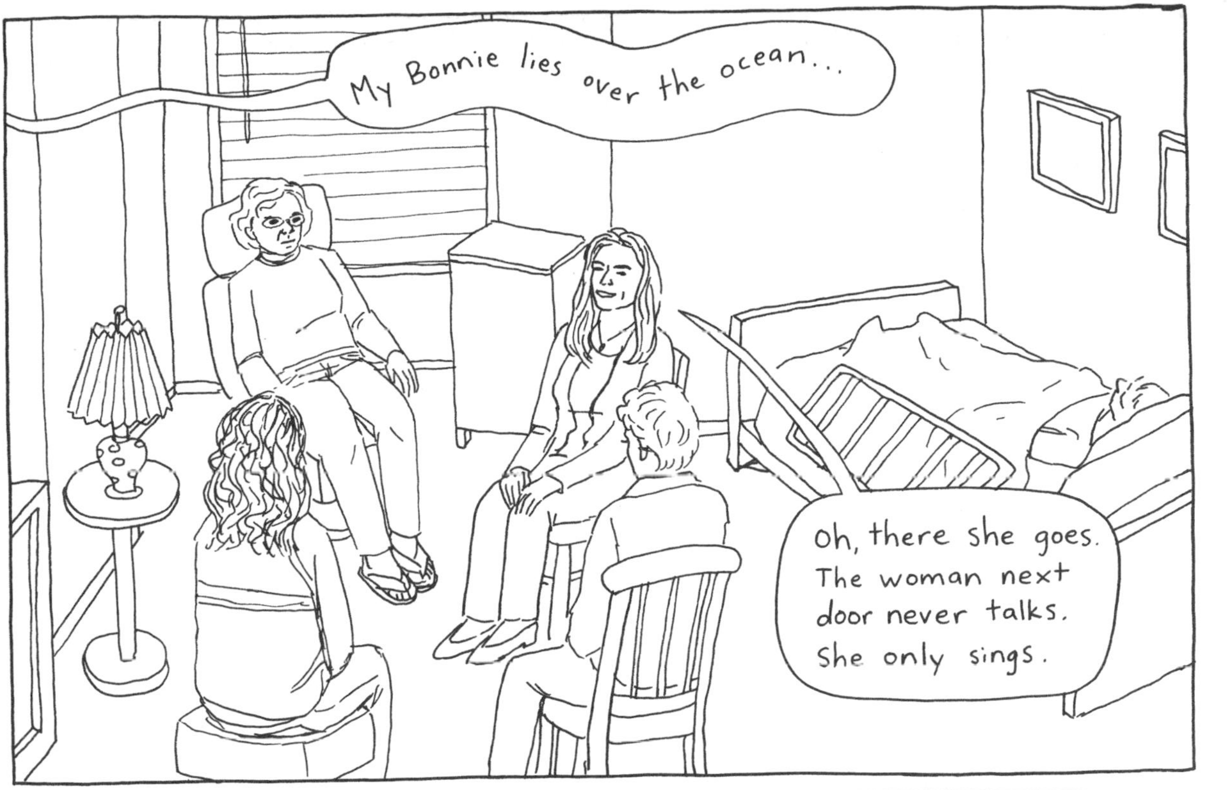
My Bonnie lies over the ocean...
Oh, there she goes. The woman next door never talks. She only sings.

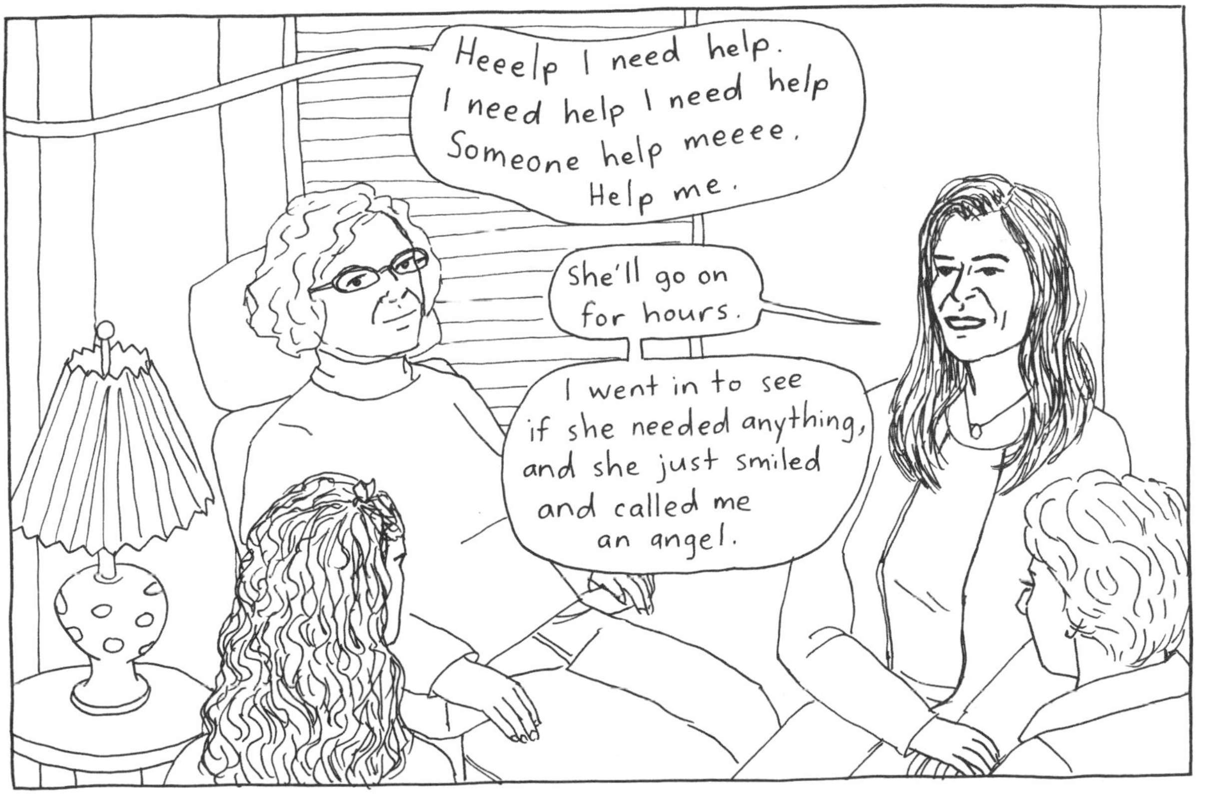
Heeelp I need help. I need help I need help Someone help meeee. Help me.
She'll go on for hours.
I went in to see if she needed anything, and she just smiled and called me an angel.

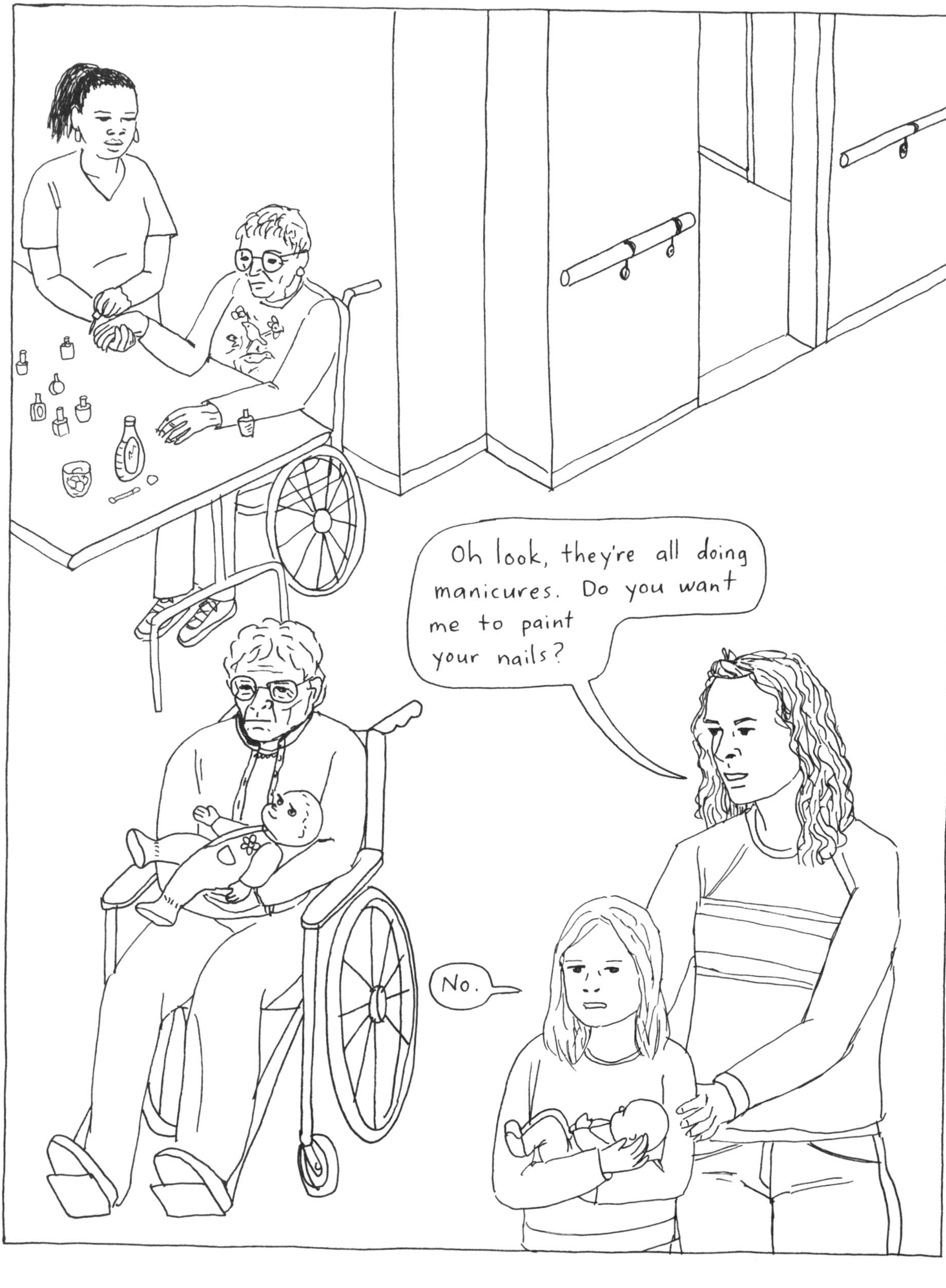
Oh look, they're all doing manicures. Do you want me to paint your nails?
No.

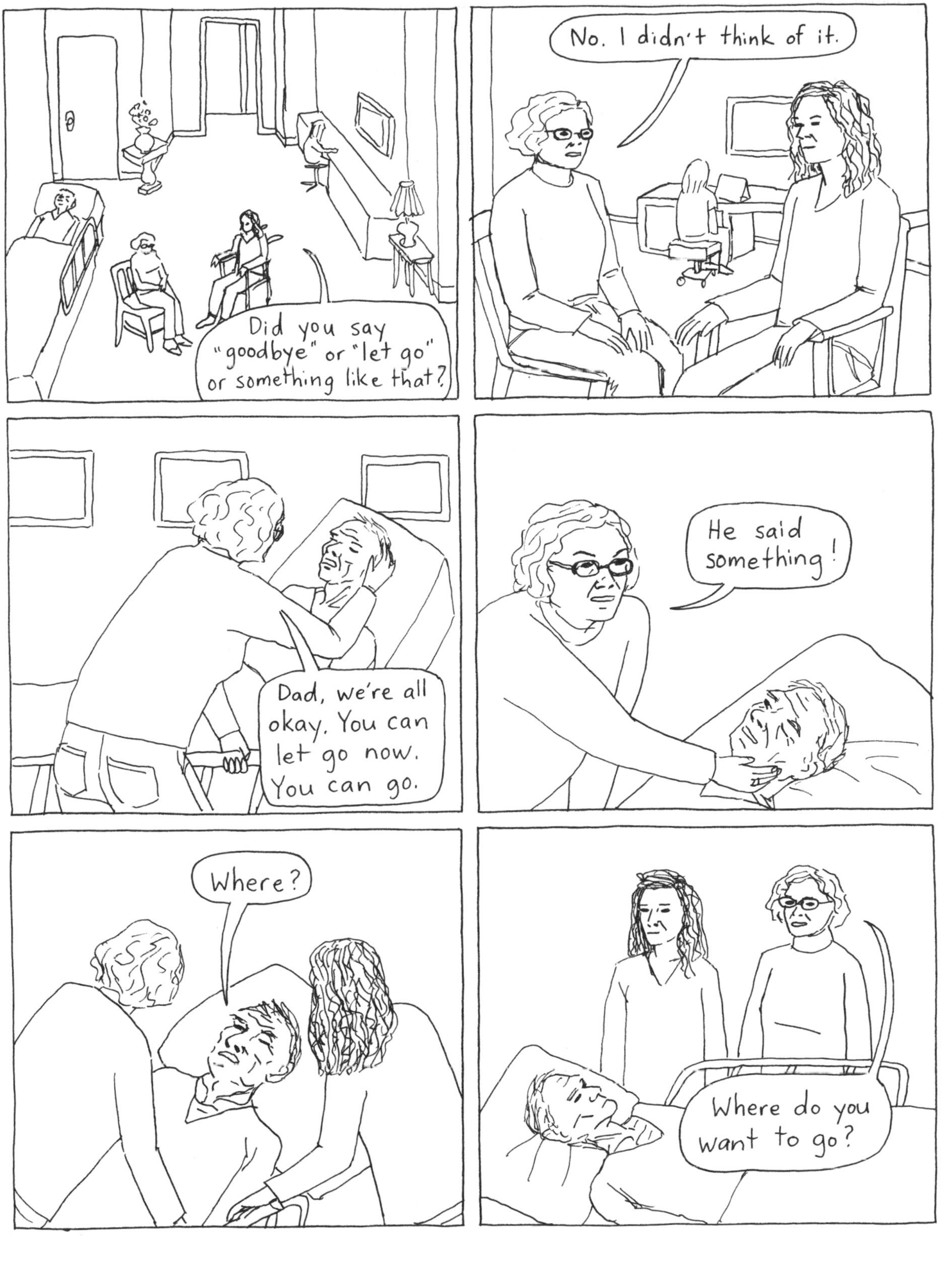
Did you say "goodbye" or "let go" or something like that?
No. I didn't think of it.
Dad, we're all okay. You can let go now. You can go.
He said something!
Where?
Where do you want to go?

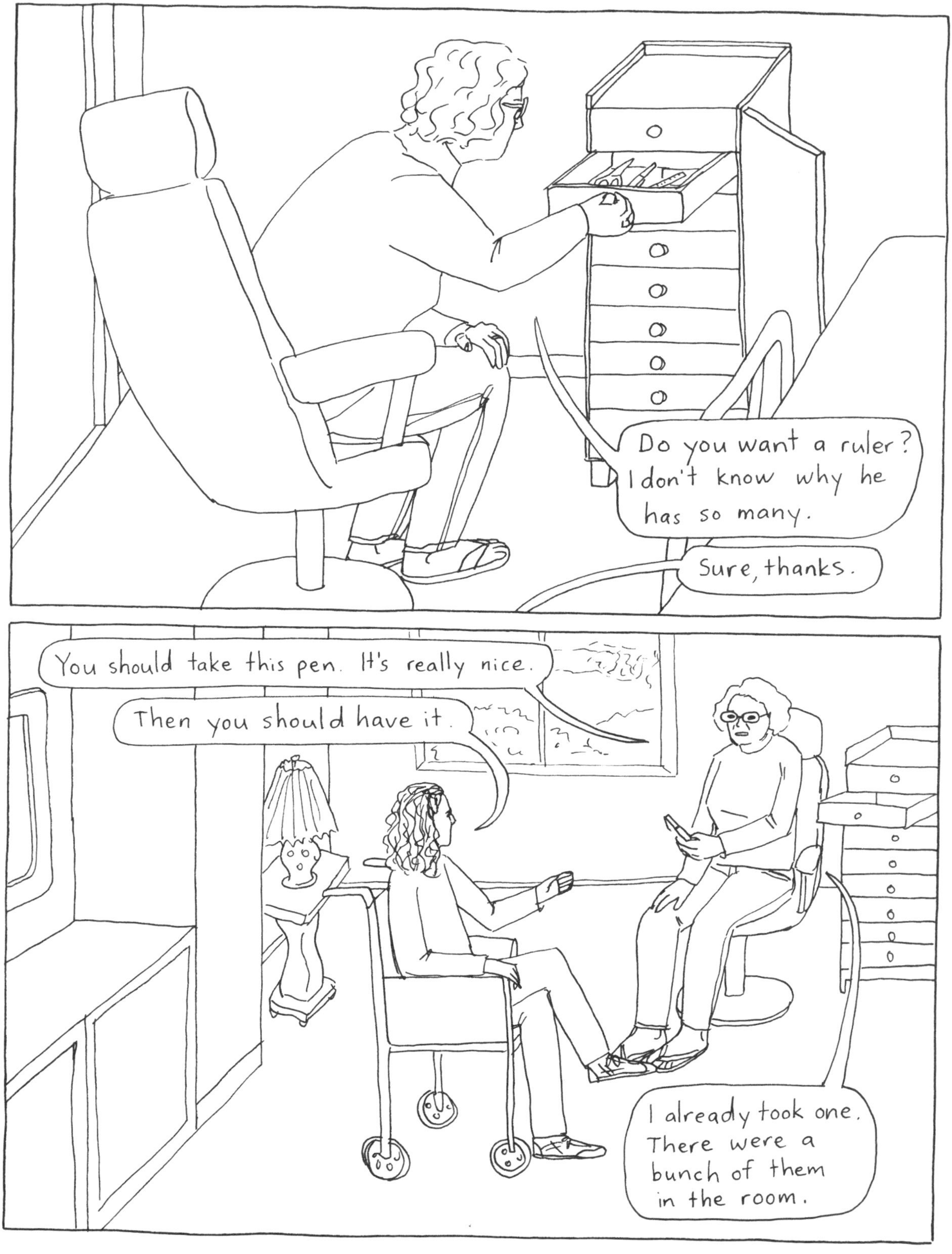
Do you want a ruler? I don't know why he has so many.
Sure, thanks.
You should take this pen. It's really nice.
Then you should have it.
I already took one. There were a bunch of them in the room.

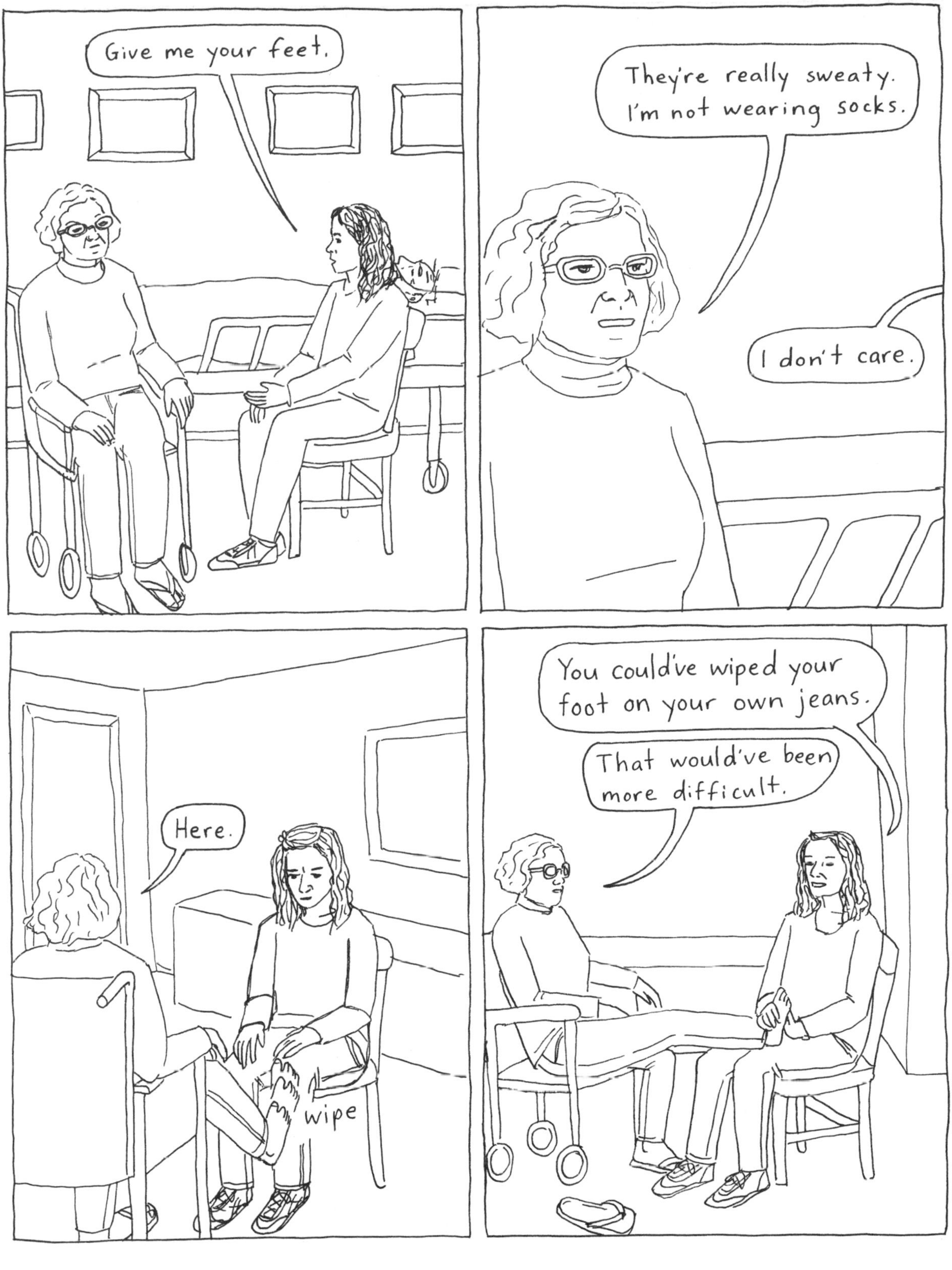
Give me your feet.
They're really sweaty. I'm not wearing socks.
I don't care.
Here.
wipe
You could've wiped your foot on your own jeans.
That would've been more difficult.

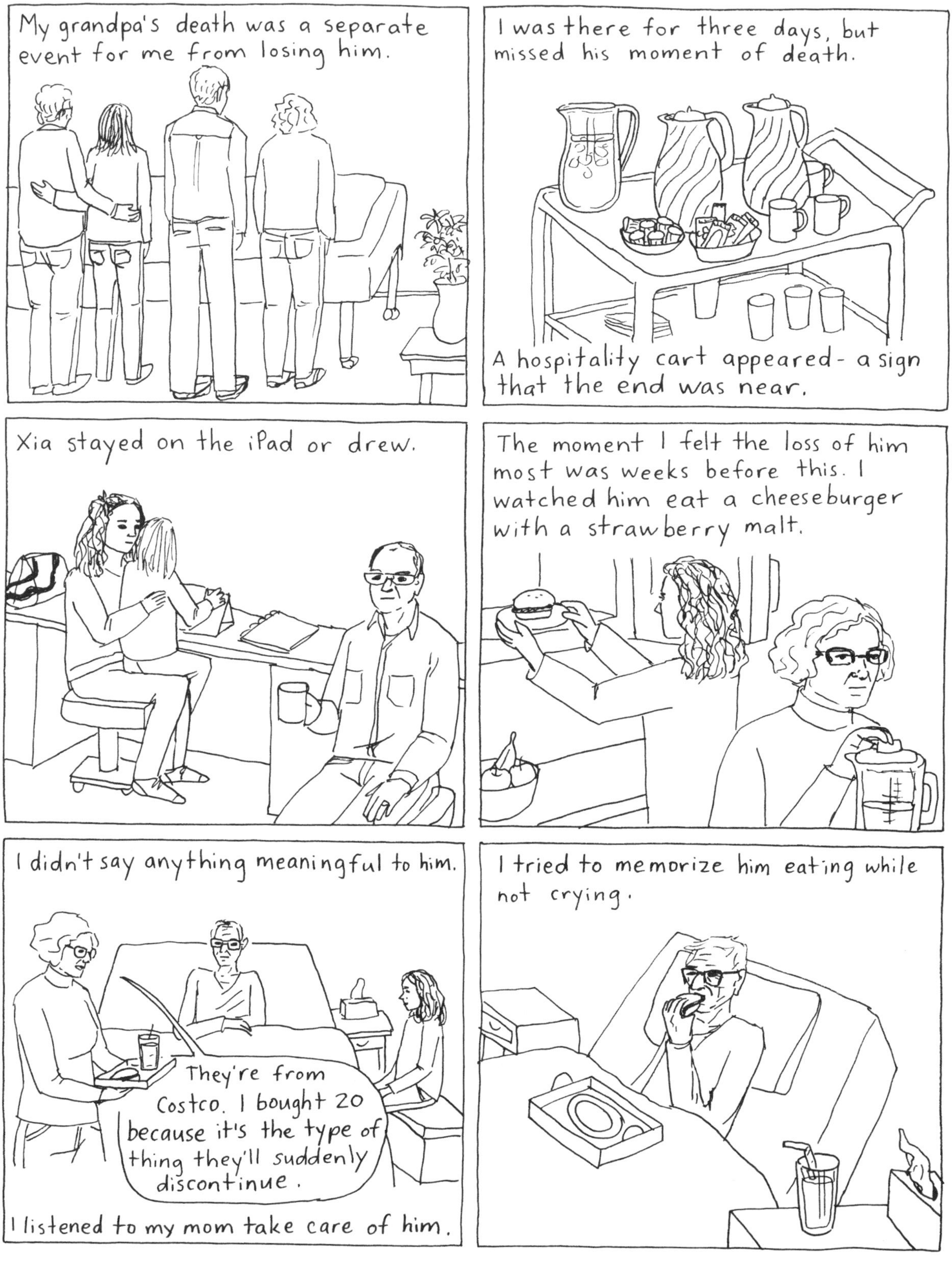
My grandpa's death was a separate event for me from losing him.
I was there for three days, but missed his moment of death.
A hospitality cart appeared - a sign that the end was near.
Xia stayed on the iPad or drew.
The moment I felt the loss of him most was weeks before this. I watched him eat a cheeseburger with a strawberry malt.
I didn't say anything meaningful to him.
They're from Costco. I bought 20 because it's the type of thing they'll suddenly discontinue.
I listened to my mom take care of him.
I tried to memorize him eating while not crying.

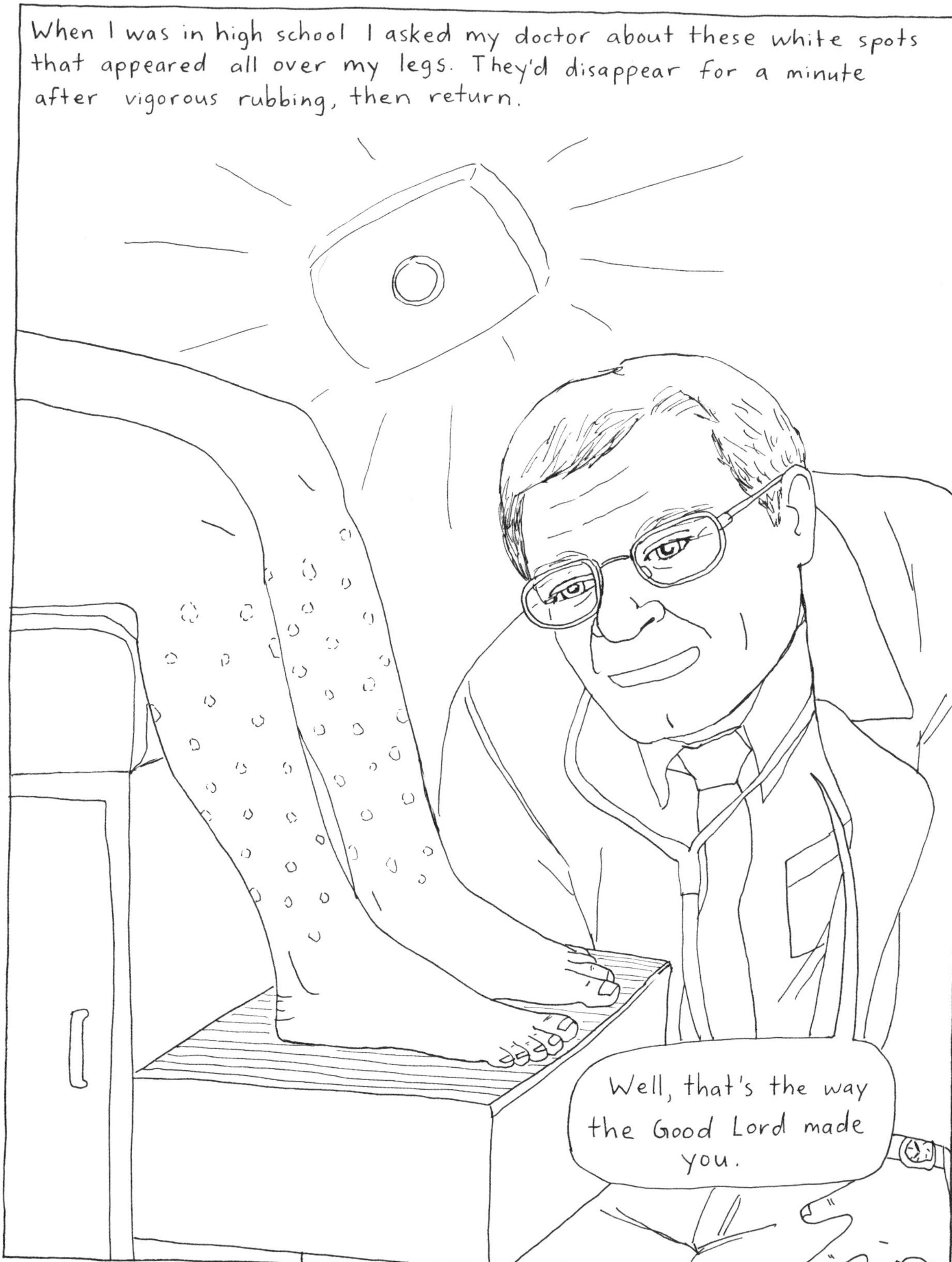
When I was in high school I asked my doctor about these white spots that appeared all over my legs. They'd disappear for a minute after vigorous rubbing, then return.
Well, that's the way the Good Lord made you.

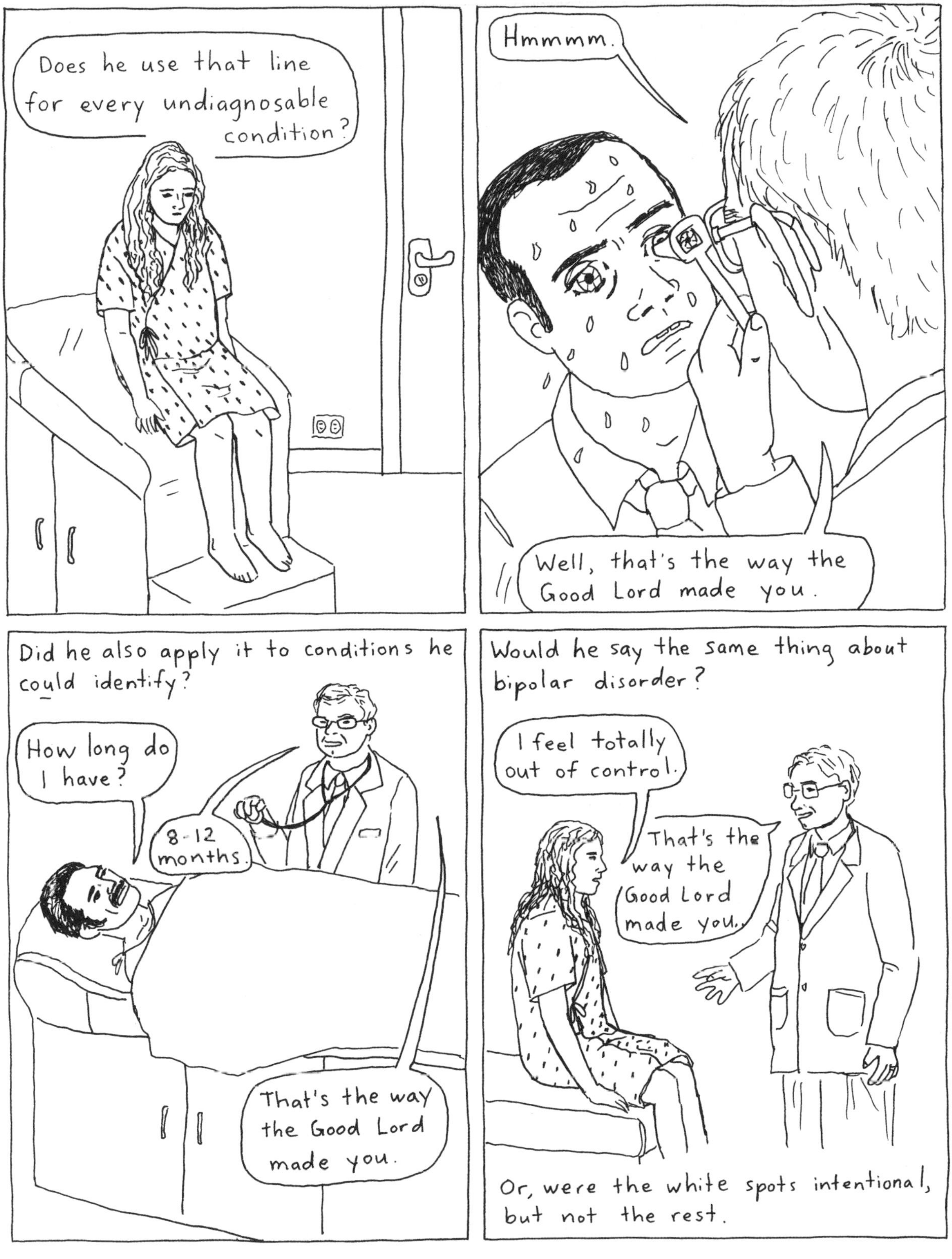
Does he use that line for every undiagnosable condition?
Hmmmm.
Well, that's the way the Good Lord made you.
Did he also apply it to conditions he could identify?
How long do I have?
8-12 months.
That's the way the Good Lord made you.
Would he say the same thing about bipolar disorder?
I feel totally out of control.
That's the way the Good Lord made you.
Or, were the white spots intentional, but not the rest.

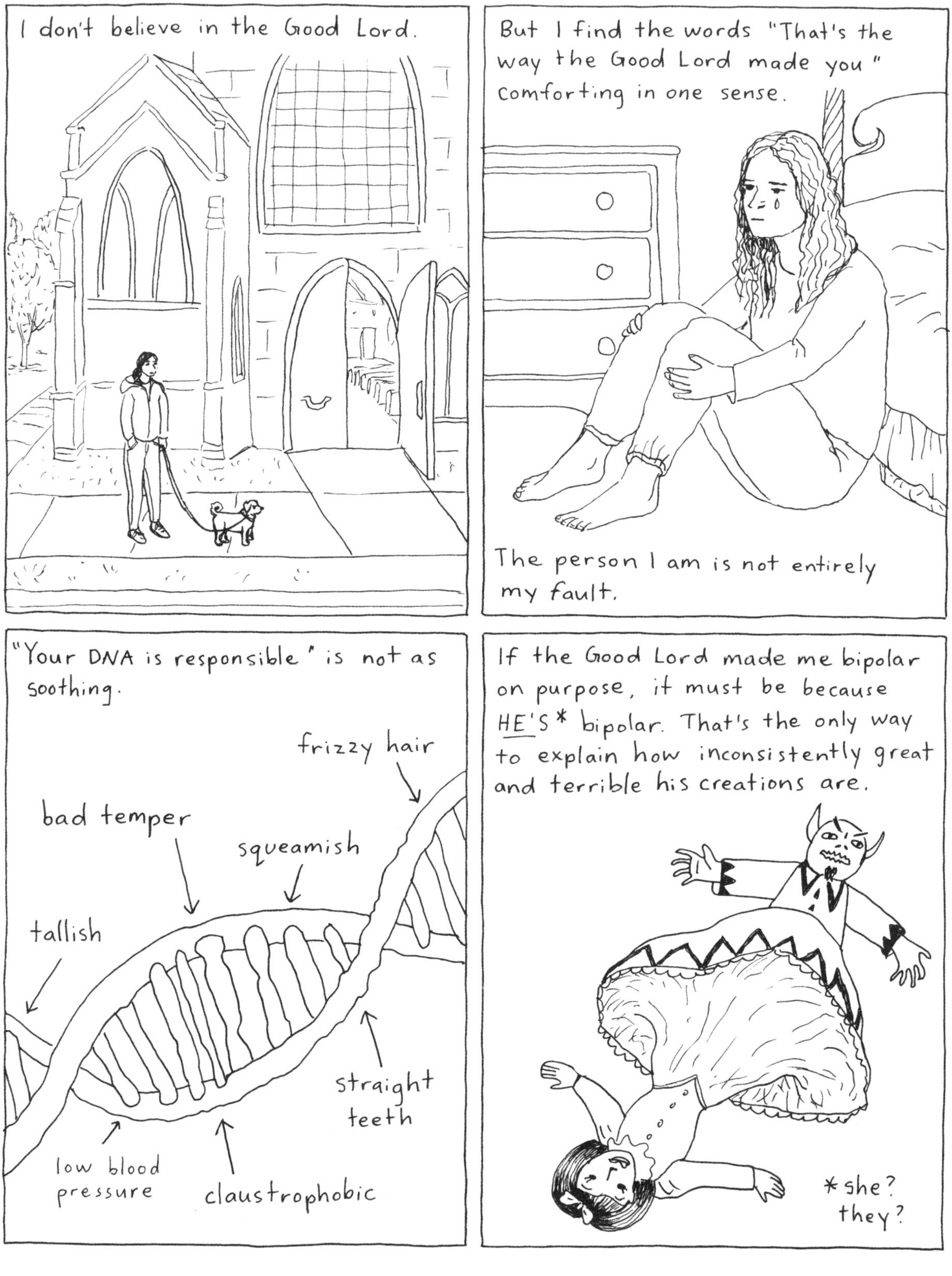
I don't believe in the Good Lord.
But I find the words "That's the way the Good Lord made you" comforting in one sense.
The person I am is not entirely my fault.
"Your DNA is responsible" is not as soothing.
frizzy hair
bad temper
squeamish
tallish
straight teeth
low blood pressure
claustrophobic
If the Good Lord made me bipolar on purpose, it must be because HE'S* bipolar. That's the only way to explain how inconsistently great and terrible his creations are.
*she? they?

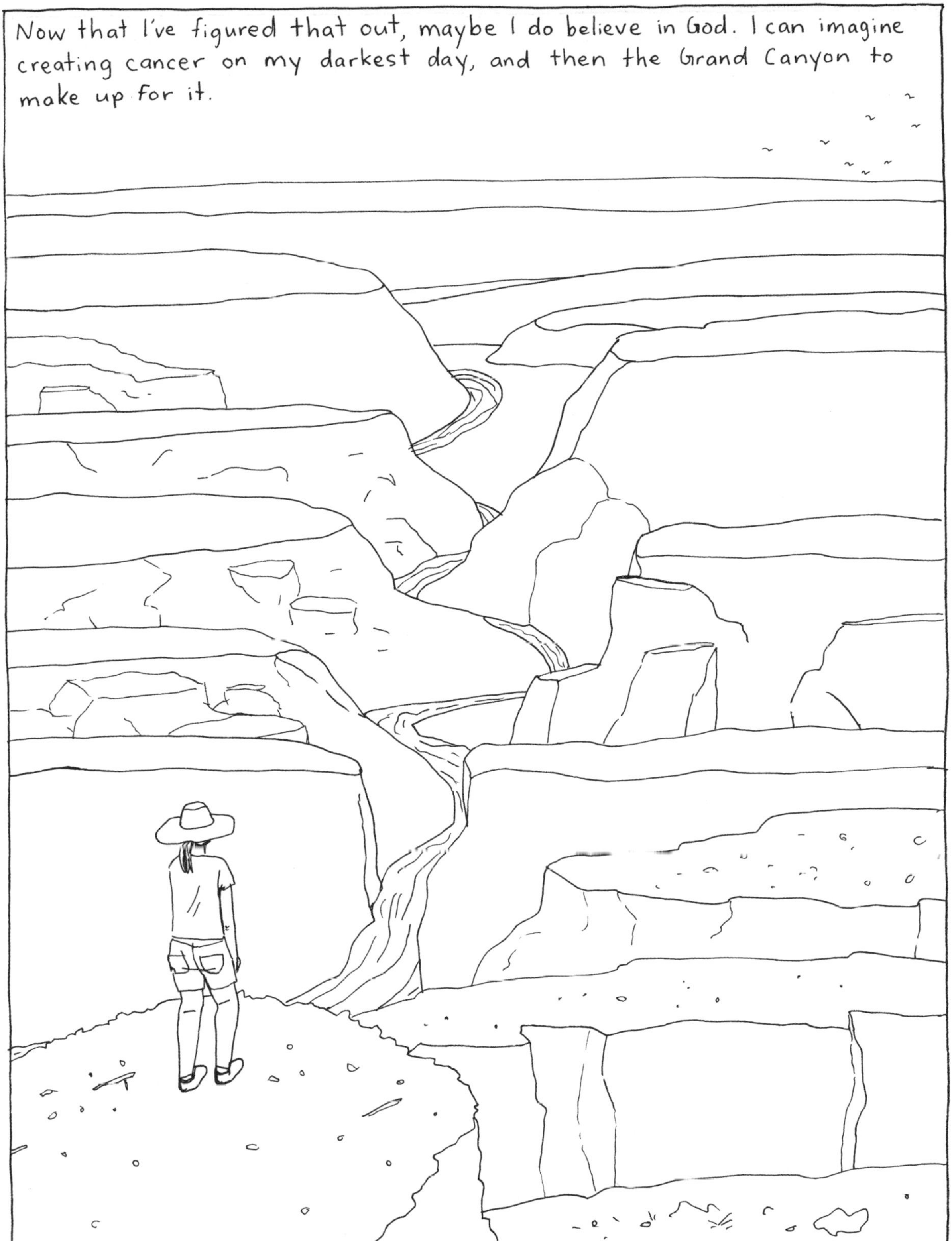
Now that I've figured that out, maybe I do believe in God. I can imagine creating cancer on my darkest day, and then the Grand Canyon to make up for it.

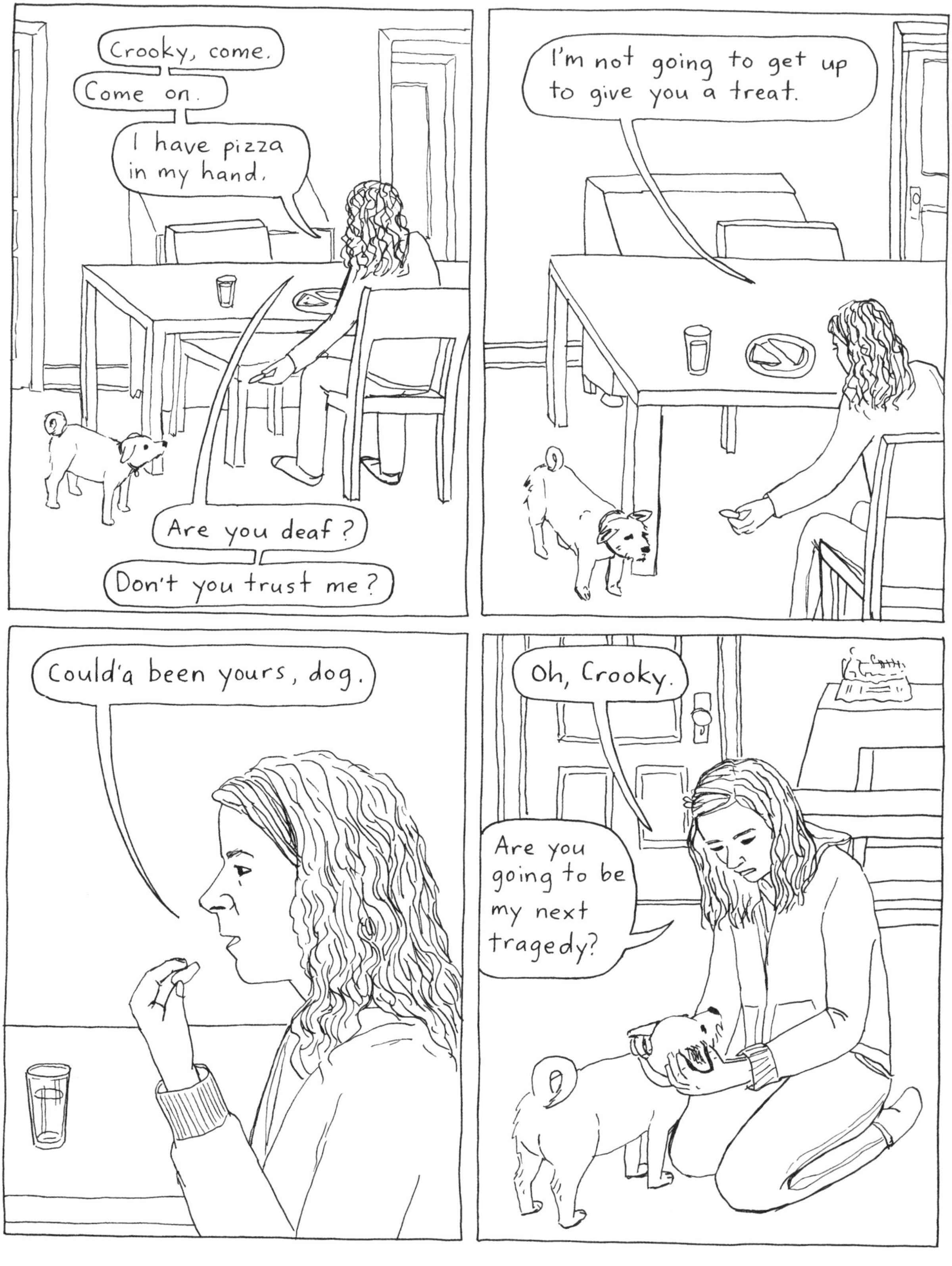
Crooky, come.
Come on.
I have pizza in my hand.
Are you deaf?
Don't you trust me?
I'm not going to get up to give you a treat.
Could'a been yours, dog.
Oh, Crooky.
Are you going to be my next tragedy?

Epilogue

S
EVANST
KEILE
1978 JU
Acc: M
Acq
AL

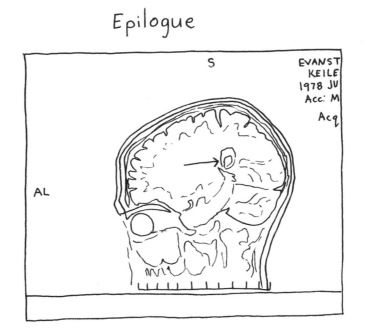

The MS was confirmed one year after the first MRI when a new lesion appeared.

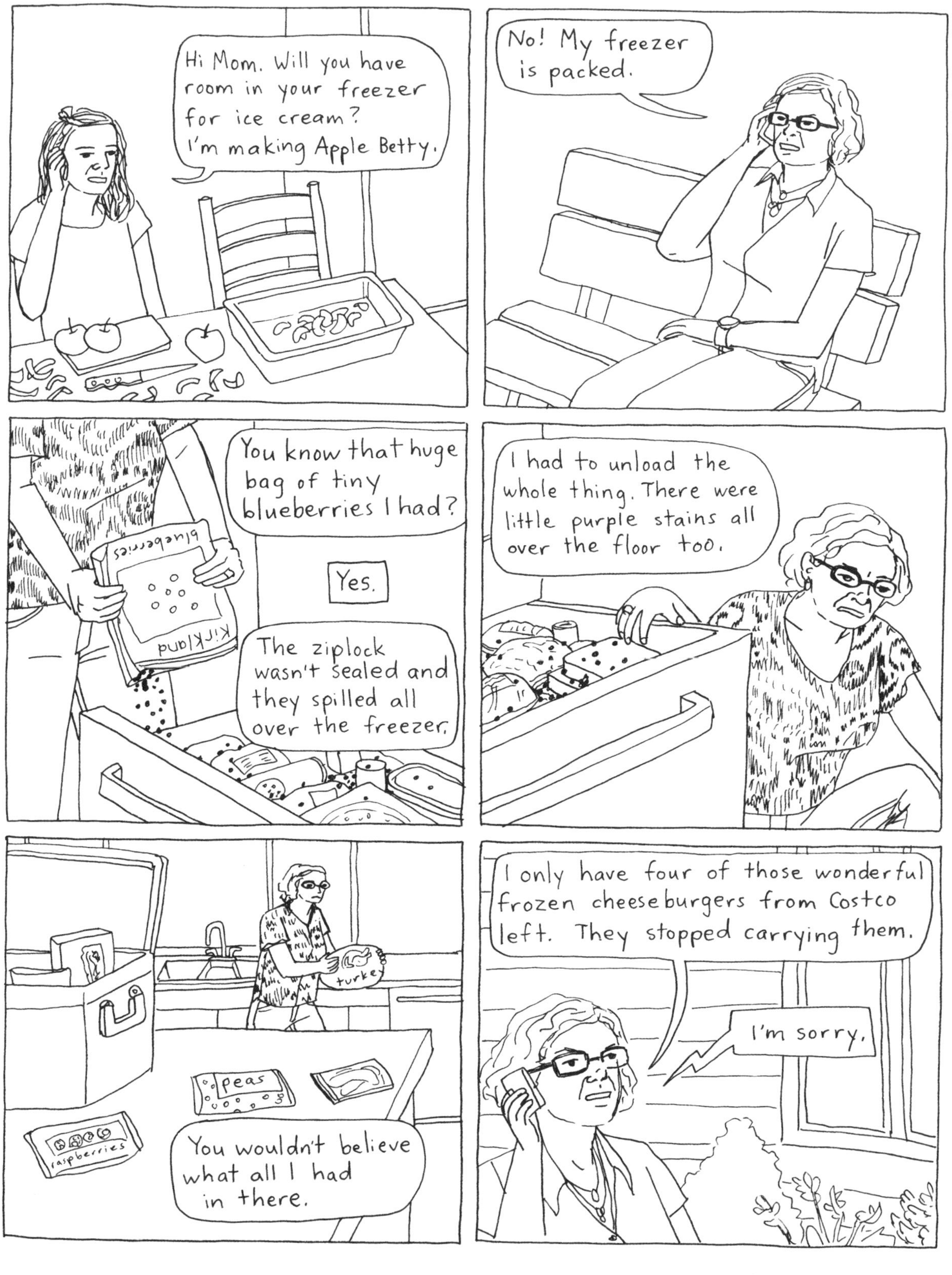
Hi Mom. Will you have room in your freezer for ice cream? I'm making Apple Betty.
No! My freezer is packed.
You know that huge bag of tiny blueberries I had?
blueberries
Kirkland
Yes.
The ziplock wasn't sealed and they spilled all over the freezer.
I had to unload the whole thing. There were little purple stains all over the floor too.
turkey
peas
raspberries
You wouldn't believe what all I had in there.
I only have four of those wonderful frozen cheeseburgers from Costco left. They stopped carrying them.
I'm sorry.

special thanks to the following people:

Scott & Xia Roberts, Annie Koyama, Ed Kanerva, Helen Koyama,
Daniel Nishio, Laura Legge, John Porcellino, Neil Brideau,
Rob Clough, Summer Pierre, Carta Monir, Robin McConnell,
Gil Roth, Kevin Budnik, Meg Lemke, Erik Kraft, Diana Sudyka, Jay
Ryan, Rebecca Dudley, Nissa Landman, Amie Larkin, Nora Fiffer,
Katie Shonk, Lisa Conforti, Ben Crothers, Rachel Brown, Emil Ferris,
Bill Kartalopoulos, Phoebe Gloeckner,
and Mom & Dad

thanks for nothing:

Crooky Roberts

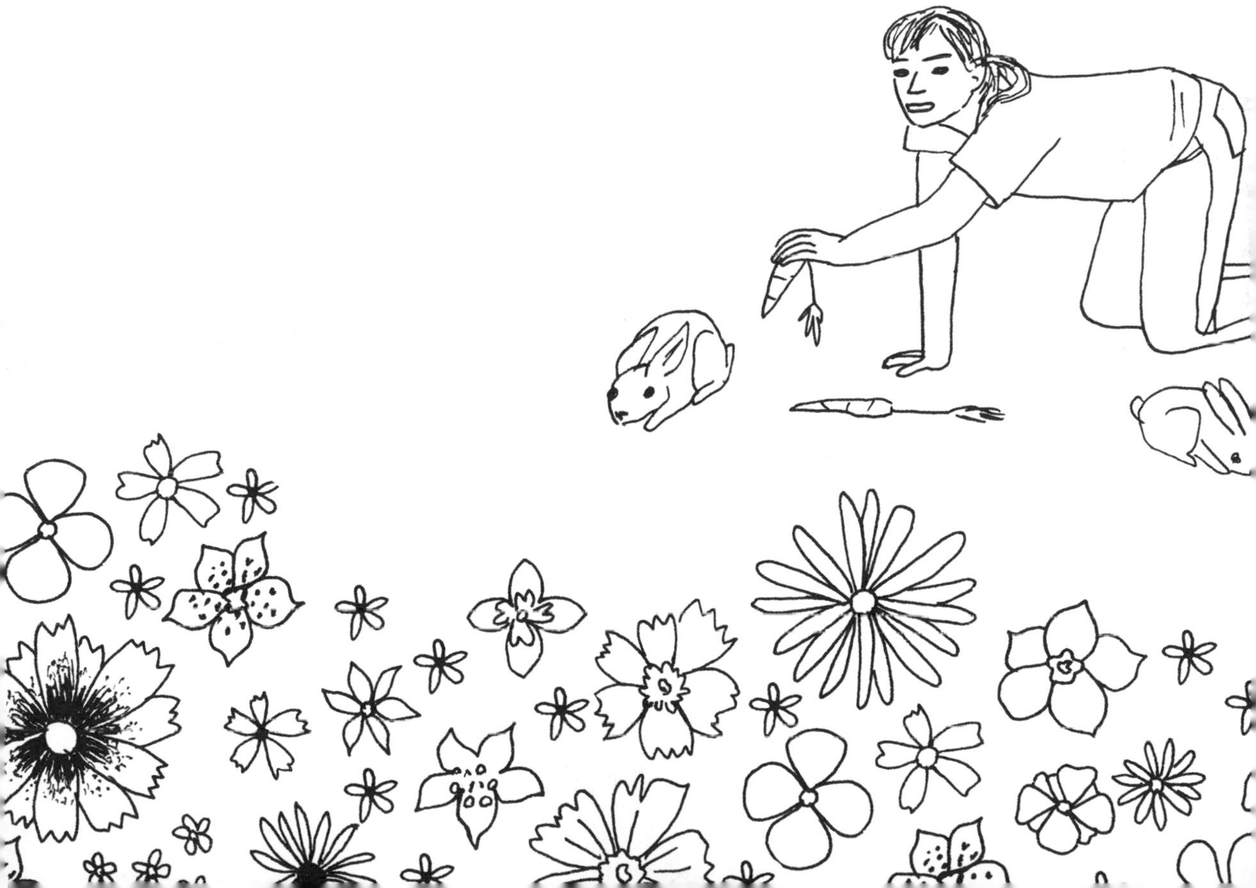

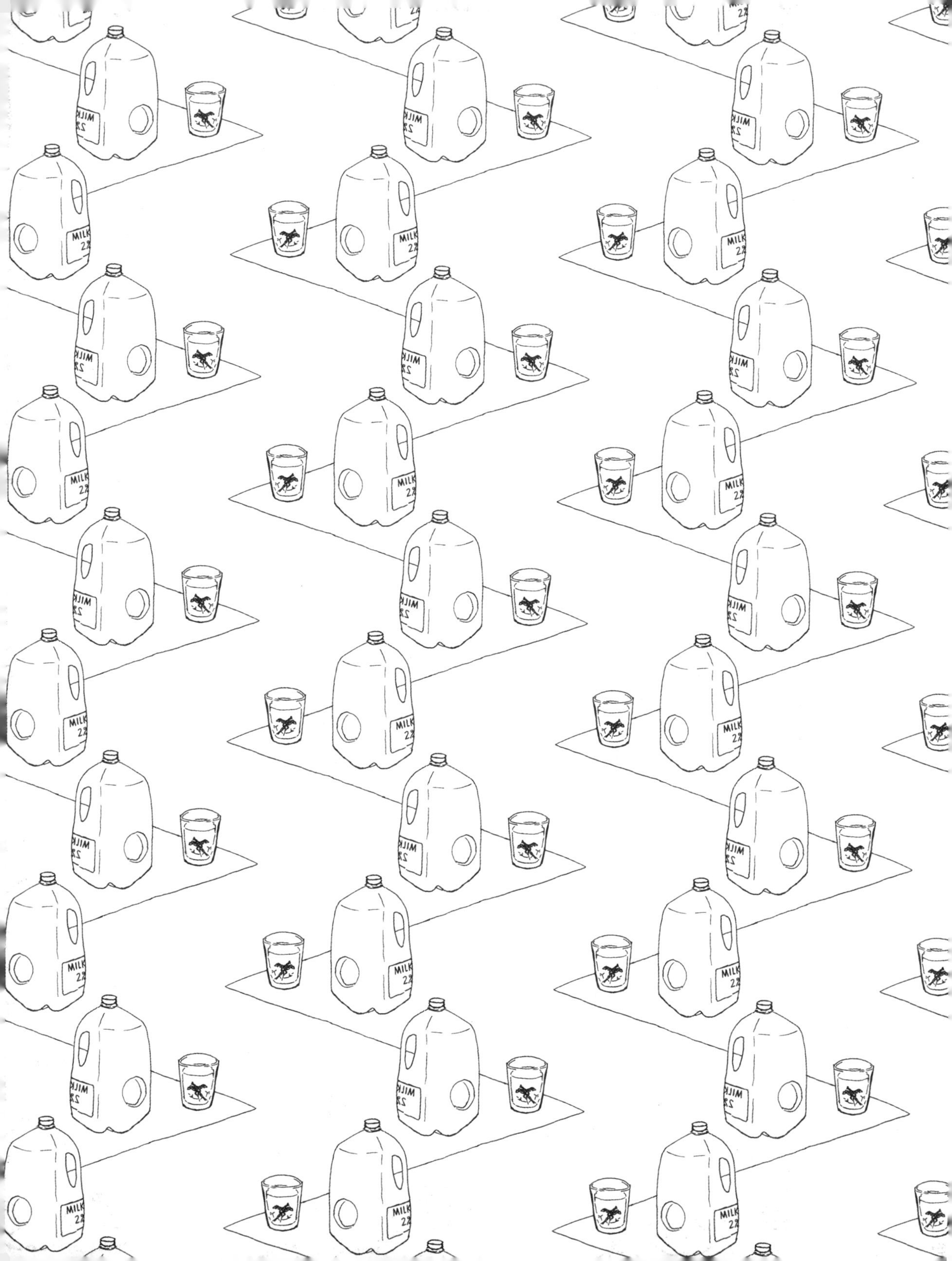
MILK
2%